QUOTATIONS FOR LOVERS

QUOTATIONS

FOR

LOVERS

SELECTED AND EDITED
BY
JORDAN L. LINFIELD
AND
JOSEPH KREVISKY

AN INNOVATION PRESS BOOK

MACMILLAN

First published 1995 by Macmillian Reference Books
A division of Macmillan Publishers Ltd
Cavaye Place London SW10 9PG
and Basingstoke

Associated companies throughout the world

ISBN 0–333–61394–5

A CIP catalogue record for this book is available from the British
Library.

Photoset by Parker Typesetting Service, Leicester
Printed and bound in Great Britain by
Cox and Wyman Ltd, Reading, Berkshire

INTRODUCTION

Love is more than hearts and flowers. Love is more than moon and June. Love is more than forever after.

Love is deception and treason. Love is rapture and laughter. Love is foreplay and afterplay. Love is reaching the stars and feeling post-coital *tristesse*.

In *Quotations for Lovers* we share the most perceptive, witty, astute and caring quotations culled and treasured over years. Many of the entries are amusingly candid and forthright. Some entries are poignantly evocative. But all are truthful. For here is love as women and men truly recall and experience it.

CONTENTS

CONTENTS

CONTENTS

CONTENTS

CONTENTS

CONTENTS

CONTENTS

CONTENTS

CONTENTS

Absence

This is a sad bed
of chosen chastity
because you are miles
& mountains away.
– Erica Jong, 'The Sad Bed'

Morning without you is dwindled dawn.
– Emily Dickinson, *Selected Poems and Letters of Emily
Dickinson*

When you are away, I'm restless, lonely,
Wretched, bored, dejected; only
Here's the rub my darling dear
I feel the same when you are near.
– Samuel Hoffenstein, *Poems in Praise of Practically Nothing*:
'When You're Away'

Your absence has not taught me how to be alone, it merely has
shown that when together we cast a single shadow on this wall.
– Doug Fetherling, 'Your Absence Has Not Taught Me'

Men are merriest when they are from home.
– William Shakespeare, *Henry V*

Wives in their husbands' absences grow subtler
And daughters sometimes run off with the butler.
– George Gordon, Lord Byron, *Don Juan*

With leaden foot time creeps along
    While Delia is away.
– Richard Jago, 'Absence: With Leaden Heart'

Our hours in love have wings; in absence, crutches.
    – Colley Cibber, *Xerxes*

Where you used to be, there's a hole in the world, which I find myself constantly walking around in the day-time, and falling into at night. I miss you like hell.
    – Edna St Vincent Millay, *Letters of Edna St Vincent Millay*

All along, one of my complaints was his absence from home, and even worse, his absence when he *was* home.
    – Sonia Johnson, *From Housewife to Heretic*

The heart may think it knows better: the senses know that absence blots people out.
    – Elizabeth Bowen, *The Death of the Heart*

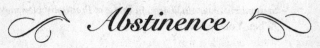

Abstinence

I married the world – the world is my husband. That is why I am so young. No sex. Sex is the most tiring thing in the world.
    – Elsa Maxwell (attributed)

Who will in time present from pleasure refrain, shall, in time to come, the more pleasure obtain.
    – John Heywood, *A Dialogue containing the number in effect of all the Proverbs in the English Tongue*

Praising the lean and sallow abstinence.
    – John Milton, *Comus*

And made almost a sin of abstinence.
> – John Dryden, 'Character of A Good Parson'

'May worry you for a while,' the trustee advised. 'You may have trouble at first. 'Specially if you're used to gettin' yours wet every night. You'll get over it, though,' he said confidently. 'It won't kill you. You'll just think it will.'
> – James Jones, *From Here to Eternity*

I will have nought to do whether with lover or husband . . . albeit he come to me with an erection . . . I will live at home unbulled.
> – Aristophanes, *Lysistrata* (oath taken by women in sex strike against war)

Abstainer: a weak person who yields to the temptation of denying himself a pleasure.
> – Ambrose Bierce, *The Devil's Dictionary*

And he, whom in itching no scratching will forbear,
He must bear the smarting that shall follow there.
> – John Heywood, *A Dialogue containing the number in effect of all the Proverbs in the English Tongue*

No sex is better than bad sex.
> – Germaine Greer (attributed)

Ain't misbehavin'
Savin' all my love for you.
> – Andy Razaf, 'Ain't Misbehavin'' (music by Thomas 'Fats' Waller and Harry Brooks)

Abstinence sows sand all over
The ruddy limbs and flaming hair,
But desire gratified
Plants fruits of life and beauty there.
> – William Blake, *Complete Writings*

Against diseases, here the strongest defence
Is the defensive virtue, abstinence.
– Robert Herrick

Absurdity

Oh, life is a glorious cycle of song,
A medley of extemporanea;
And love is a thing that never can go wrong;
And I am the Queen of Roumania.
– Dorothy Parker, *Enough Rope*

Adolescence

Wanton kittens make sober cats.
– English proverb

Fourteen–year–old, why do you giggle and dote,
Fourteen–year–old, why are you such a goat?
I am fourteen years old and that's the reason,
I giggle and dote in season.
– Stevie Smith, 'The Conversationalist'

Everything you are and do from fifteen to eighteen is what you
are and will do the rest of your life.
– F. Scott Fitzgerald, letter to his daughter, 19 September 1938

So much alarmed that she is alarming.
All Giggle, Blush, half Pertness, and half Pout.
– George Gordon, Lord Byron, *Beppo*

Don't count your boobies until they are hatched.
– James Thurber, *Fables of Our Times*

My salad days,
When I was green in judgment, cold in blood.
– William Shakespeare, *Antony and Cleopatra*

She would eat the cheeseburgers and Dairy Queen sundaes they
bought for her while they fished in her panties for whatever it is
that men fish for in that primitive space.
– Tom Robbins, *Even Cowgirls Get the Blues*

The sexual memory of which I was drenched during that season
in Brooklyn, whenever I forlornly unloosed the flood gates, was
of uneasy darkness, sweat, reproving murmurs, bands and sin-
ews of obdurate elastic, lacerating little hooks and snaps, whis-
pered prohibitions, straining erections, stuck zippers and a
warm miasmal odour of secretions from inflamed and obstructed glands.
– William Styron, *Sophie's Choice*

God, how I envied girls . . . Whatever it was on them, it didn't
dangle between their legs like an elephant trunk. No wonder
boys talked about nothing but sex. That thing was always there.
Every time I went to the john, there it was, twitching around
like a little worm on a fishing hook. When we took baths, it
floated around in the water like a lazy fish and God forbid we
should touch it. It sprang to life like lightning leaping from a
cloud.
– Julius Lester, 'Being a Boy', in *Ms.*, 1973

. . . gentle giglots, maidens blush worthily abud . . .
– Alexander Theroux, *Darconville's Cat*

Nothing to do but wait.
In the stale heat
of the attic, in the rippled

ADOLESCENCE
─────────

5

full-length mirror, she posed
in velvet, in chiffon, in
her mother's useless clothes,
waiting for her breasts
to blossom and fill
the loose bodice of
her grief.
    – Julie Kane, 'Thirteen'

Too chaste an adolescence makes for a dissolute old age.
    – André Gide, *Journals, 1939-1950*

See also: CALF LOVE; PUPPY LOVE; YOUTH.

Adultery

Cease hunting married game: trouble and grief more often come
to you than real enjoyment.
    – Horace

I went into my marriage knowing I would commit adultery at
the earliest chance I had. (It was a goal: committing adultery, in
fact it was one of the reasons for getting married.)
    – Joseph Heller, *Something Happened*

. . . what he felt . . . was a nostalgia for adultery itself – its
adventure, the acrobatics its deception demanded, the tension of
its hidden strings, the new landscapes it makes us master.
    – John Updike, *Couples*

No adultery is bloodless.
    – Natalie Guinzberg, *The City and the House*

Lady Capricorn, he understood, was still keeping open bed.
    – Aldous Huxley, *Antic Hay*

She could commit adultery at one end and weep for her sins at the other, and enjoy both operations at the same time.
   – Joyce Cary, *The Horse's Mouth*

Her exotic daydreams do not prevent her from being small-town bourgeois at heart, clinging to conventional ideas or committing this or that conventional violation of the conventional, adultery being the most conventional way to rise above the conventional.
   – Vladimir Nabokov, *Lectures on Literature*: 'Madame Bovary'

> As I grow older and older,
> And totter toward the tomb,
> I find that I care less and less
> Who goes to bed with whom.
>   – Dorothy L. Sayers, quoted in Janet Hitchman, *Such a Strange Lady*

Adultery is extravagance.
   – Maxine Hong Kingston, *The Woman Warrior*

> When your man comes home late, tells you, you're
>   gettin' old
> When your man comes home late, tells you, you're
>   gettin' old
> That's a true sign he's got someone else bakin' his jelly
>   roll.
>   – Blues song

Adultery may or may not be sinful, but it is never cheap.
   – Raymond Postgate, *Somebody at the Door*

The first breath of adultery is the freest: after it, constraints aping marriage develop.
   – John Updike, *Couples*

Nobody misses a slice off a cut loaf.
   – American proverb

A mug's game. A mug's game is breaking your back at midnight trying to get another man's wife to come.
– Gershon Legman, *Rationale of a Dirty Joke*

From outrage (matrimony) to outrage (adultery) there arose nought but outrage (copulation) yet the matrimonial violator of the matrimonially violated had not been outraged by the adulterous violator of the adulterously violated.
– James Joyce, *Ulysses*

You know, of course, that the Tasmanians, who never committed adultery, are now extinct.
– W. Somerset Maugham

Musical beds is the faculty sport around here.
– Edward Albee, *Who's Afraid of Virginia Woolf?*

> Do not adultery commit
> Advantage rarely comes of it.
> – Arthur Hugh Clough, 'The Last Decalogue'

The bonds of wedlock are so heavy it takes two to carry them – sometimes three.
– Honoré de Balzac, *The Physiology of Marriage*

Now at least I know where he is.
– Queen Alexandra, after the death of King Edward VII, whose infidelities she had accepted with tolerance and understanding

One man's mate is another man's passion.
– Eugene Healy, *Mr Sandman Loses His Life*

She was too fond of her most filthy bargain.
– William Shakespeare, *Othello*

> It is natural
> For a woman to be wild with her husband when he
> Goes in for secret love.
> – Euripides, *Medea* (trans. by Rex Warner)

Such is the way of an adulterous woman; she eateth, and wipeth her mouth, and saith, I have done no wickedness.
> – The Bible: Proverbs

> Little drops of water, little grains of sand
> Every sensible woman got a back-door man.
> – Sara Martin, 'Strange Loving Blues'

Affairs

The happiest moment of any affair takes place after the loved one has learned to accommodate the lover and before the maddening personality of either party has emerged like a jagged rock from the receding tides of lust and curiosity.
> – Quentin Crisp

I can understand companionship. I can understand bought sex in the afternoon. I cannot understand the love affair.
> – Gore Vidal, in *The Sunday Times*, 1973

But an affair wants to spill, to share its glory with the world. No act is so private it does not seek applause.
> – John Updike, *Couples*

> Let's face it, I have been momentary,
> A luxury
> . . .
> I give you back your heart
> I give you permission.
> – Anne Sexton, 'For My Lover, Returning to His Wife'

The maternal instinct leads a woman to prefer a tenth share of a first rate man to the exclusive possession of a third rate one.
– George Bernard Shaw, *Man and Superman*

The number of affairs a man has after his marriage is probably equal to the number he didn't have before it.
. . .
Great love affairs are built on firm foundations which reach all the way down to the tightrope.
– Richard J. Needham, *A Friend in Needham*

When bromides of marriage have started to wear
Contemplate those of the crimson affair:

'I had to see you' and 'Tonight belongs to us.'

'I can't fight you any longer.'

'This thing is bigger than both of us.'

'I don't want just this – I want you.'

'It's not you I'm afraid of, it's myself.'

'You don't want me – you just want sex.'

'We're married in the eyes of heaven.'

'I'm all mixed up.'

'For God sakes be careful or someone will hear you.'
– Peter De Vries, 'Sacred and Profane Love, Or There's Nothing New Under the Moon, Either'

Affection

When I look back on the pain of sex, the love like a wild fox so ready to bite, the antagonism that sits like a twin beside love, and contrast it with affection, so deeply unrepeatable, of two people who have lived a life together (and of whom one must die) it's affection I find richer. It's that I would have again. Not all those doubtful rainbow colours.

> – Enid Bagnold, *Autobiography*

Afterplay

We indulged in some foreplay, some during-play, and sometimes even some afterplay.

> – Isaac Bashevis Singer, *Shosha*

You get a lot of help undressing before sex, but afterwards you have to get dressed again by yourself.

> – John H. Gagnon, *Human Sexualities*

Age and Ageing

> I grow old . . . I grow old
> I shall wear the bottoms of my trousers rolled . . .
> – T.S. Eliot, 'Love Song of J. Alfred Prufrock'

Old meat makes good soup.

> – Italian proverb

Already I am no longer looked at with lechery and love.
My daughters and sons have put me away with marbles
    and dolls,
Are gone from the house
My husband and lovers are pleasant and somewhat
    polite
And night is night.
  – Gwendolyn Brooks, 'A Sunset of the City'

So much has been said and sung of beautiful young girls, why
doesn't somebody wake up to the beauty of old women.
  – Harriet Beecher Stowe, *Uncle Tom's Cabin*

And while she murmurs love, he counts her years.
  – Juvenal, *Sixth Satire* (trans. by William Gifford)

How many loved the moments of glad grace,
And loved your beauty with love false or true,
But one man loved the pilgrim soul in you,
And loved the sorrows of your changing face.
And bending down beside the glowing bars
Murmur, a little sad, 'From us fled Love.
He paced upon the mountains far above,
And hid his face amid a crowd of stars.'
  – W.B. Yeats, *The Countess Cathleen*: 'When You Are Old'

Why, Thais, do you constantly call me old? No one, Thais, is
too old for some things.
  – Martial, *Epigrams* (trans. by Walter C.A. Ker)

You are not permitted to kill a woman who wrongs you, but
nothing forbids you to reflect that she is growing older every
minute. You are avenged fourteen hundred and forty times a
day.
  – Ambrose Bierce, *Epigrams*

But you, may bitter age and time attack you,
    bringing the stealthy wrinkles to your face!
And as the mirror mocks your haggard beauty,
    may white hairs as you pull them, multiply.
– Sextus Aurelius Propertius

Love at the close of our days
is apprehensive and tender.
Slow brighter, brighter farewell rays
of one last love in its evening splendour
. . .
The blood runs thinner, yet the heart
remains as ever deep and tender.
– Fyodor Tyatchev, 'Last Love'

I wept for my youth, sweet passionate
    young thought,
And cozy women dead that at my side
Once lay: I wept with bitter longing,
    not
Remembering how in my youth I cried.
– Stanley Kunitz, 'I Dreamed That I Was Old'

But in my age and in my situation, every erection, penetration,
thrust, and ejaculation, every touch of nipple, stroke of cleft –
there I go, here I come – has the special extra pleasure of its being
very possibly my last.
    – John Barth, *Letters*

There is something sadder than growing old – remaining a child.
    – Cesare Pavese, *The Burning Brand Diaries*

Old age has disgraces of its own: do not add to them the shame
of vice.
    – Cato the Elder, *Apothegms*

. . . she was a smasher, a stunner, a knockout. Where were the varicosities, striations, liver spots? The thickened waist and slacked behind and fallen pectorals? The crow's feet, jowls, and wattles of latter age?
> – John Barth, *Letters*

I have everything now I had twenty years ago – except it's all lower.
> – Gypsy Rose Lee, in *Newsweek*, 16 September 1968

Grow old along with me!
The best is yet to be
The last of life, for which the first was made.
> – Robert Browning, 'Rabbi Ben Ezra'

. . . she thinks me young,
Although she knows my days are past the best.
> – William Shakespeare, 'Sonnet 138'

If the young only knew; if the old only could.
> – French proverb

The young feel tired at the end of an action;
The old at the beginning.
> – T.S. Eliot

Sex with older men? I say grab it. But if your man has had a heart attack don't . . . try to jump start his pacemaker . . . whisper . . . 'This could be your last one, let's make it good.'
> – Phyllis Diller, *The Joys of Aging and How to Avoid Them*

I dread no more the first white in my hair,
Or even age itself, the easy shoe,
The cane, the wrinkled hands, the special chair:
Time, doing this to me, may alter too
My sorrow, into something I can bear.
> – Edna St Vincent Millay, 'Sonnet'

Don't look back. Something may be gaining on you.
– Satchel Paige, the last words in his notebook

. . . I saw my wrinkles in their wrinkles. You know, one looks at herself in the mirror every morning, and she doesn't see the difference, she doesn't realize she is aging. But then she finds a friend who was young with her, and the friend isn't young anymore, and all of a sudden, like a slap on her eyes, she remembers that she, too, isn't young anymore.
– Ingrid Bergman, quoted in Oriana Fallaci, *The Egotists*

See also: DIRTY OLD MEN.

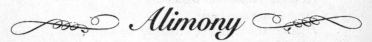

Alimony

Divorce comes from the old Latin word *divorcerum* meaning 'having your genitals torn out through your wallet'. And the judge said, 'All the money and we'll shorten it to alimony.'
– Robin Williams, comedy routine

Marriage is but for a little while. It is alimony that is forever . . .
– Quentin Crisp, *The Naked Civil Servant*

You never realize how short a month is until you pay alimony.
– John Barrymore (attributed)

. . . alimony is one way of compensating women for those financial disabilities aggravated or caused by marriage: unequal educational opportunities; unequal employment opportunities; and an unequal division of family responsibilities, with no compensation for the spouse who works in the house . . .
. . .
. . . women should not be cowed into believing that to ask for alimony is to be unliberated, or that their husbands provide alimony out of the largesse of their noble hearts.
– Susan C. Ross, *The Rights of Women*

The wages of sin is alimony.
> – Carolyn Wells (attributed)

In these days of Women's Lib, there is no reason why a wife, whose marriage has not lasted and who has no child, should have a bread ticket for life.
> – Sir George Baker, in the *Observer*, 3 April 1973

Judges, as a class, display, in the matter of arranging alimony, that reckless generosity that is found only in men who are giving away somebody else's cash.
> – P.G. Wodehouse, *Louder and Funnier*

> He doesn't make much money
> Just five thousand per
> A judge who thinks he's funny
> Says 'You'll pay six to her.'
> – Gus Kahn, 'Makin' Whoopee'

No one is going to take women's liberation seriously until women recognize that they will never be thought of as equals . . . until they eschew alimony.
> – Norman Mailer, in *Love Talk*

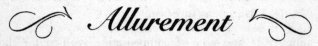

Allurement

Be mysterious.
> – John Bouvier, advice to his daughter Jacqueline Kennedy Onassis.

> Husbands would never go whoring
> They would stay with the ones they adore
> If wives were but half alluring
> After the act as before.
> – *The Greek Anthology*

Anatomy

The excremental is too intimately and inseparably bound up with the sexual: the position of the genitals – *inter urinas at faeces* – remains the decisive and unchangeable factor. One might say here, varying a well-known saying of the great Napoleon, 'Anatomy is destiny.'

> – Sigmund Freud, *On the Universal Tendency to Debasement in the Sphere of Love*

Anatomy is not destiny.

> – Simone de Beauvoir (attributed)

Anger

If you seek Nirvana in the crotch . . . and that's all there is and it disappoints you, you become angry and hostile . . . We are angered because we have asked of sex what it cannot give.

> – Judianne Densen-Gerber, *Walk in My Shoes*

The angry lover tells himself many a lie.

> – Publilius Syrus, *Sententiae*

> When late I attempted your pity to move,
>   Why seemed you so deaf to my prayers?
> Perhaps it was right to dissemble your love.
>   But – why should you kick me downstairs?
> – Isaac Bickerstaffe, 'An Expostulation'

The anger of lovers renews their love.

> – Terence, *The Woman of Andros*

Antipathy

Only a very superficial observer can miss the primitive repulsion and antagonism between the sexes which are as real and more permanent than the attraction.
– Th. Van de Velde, *Ideal Marriage*

Antipathy, dissimilarity of views, hate, contempt can accompany true love.
– August Strindberg, *The Son of a Servant*

Anxiety

There is no such thing as pure pleasure; some anxiety always goes with it.
– Ovid, *Metamorphoses*

Habitually they walk about with tightened buttocks and rigid pelvic musculature. Just as people grind their teeth, tighten their jaws, hunch their shoulders, or curl their toes in an unconscious response to anxiety, these women clamp their vaginas . . . Their vaginal 'clench' is a habitual response to tension.
– Avodah Offit, *The Sexual Self*

See also: PANIC.

Aphrodisiacs

Love charms are temporary things if your mojo ain't total.
– Toni Cade Bambara, *Gorilla My Love*

Like iron or some kind of crowbar standing all the time he must have eaten oysters.
– James Joyce, *Ulysses*

Power is the ultimate aphrodisiac.
– Henry Kissinger, quoted in the *Guardian*, 28 November 1976

The moon is nothing
But a circumambulating aphrodisiac
Divinely subsidized to provoke the world
Into a rising birth rate.
– Christopher Fry, *The Lady's Not for Burning*

Variety is the absolutely foolproof aphrodisiac.
– Author unknown

Bring you magics, spells, and charms
To enflesh my thighs and arms.
Is there no way to beget
In my limbs their former heat?
. . .
Find that medicine, if you can,
For your dry, decrepit man;
Who would fain his strength renew
Were it but to pleasure you.
– Robert Herrick, 'To His Mistress'

Love is its own aphrodisiac and is the main ingredient for lasting sex.
– Mort Katz, *Marriage Survival Kit*

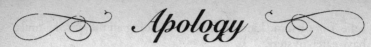

Apology

I accept, regretfully, your vigorous rejection of my proposal, and apologize for any affront it may have given you. I did not mean — but never mind what I did not mean. I accede to the counsel of your countryman Evelyn Waugh: Never apologize; never explain.

      – John Barth, *Letters*

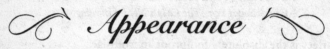

Appearance

Things are seldom what they seem,
Skim milk masquerades as cream.
– W.S. Gilbert, *HMS Pinafore*

Ardent Love

The heart that blazes with the flames of a volcano cannot please the object of its adoration; it commits follies, fails in delicacy, and burns itself away.

      – Stendhal, letter to Métilde Dembowski

If you first don't succeed in love, try a little ardour.

      – Anonymous

The ardour chills us which we do not share.

      – Coventry Patmore

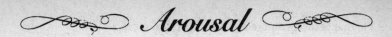

Arousal

Arousal is a miracle . . . Don't try to hide it. [It is] an unsolicited endorsement, a standing ovation, a spontaneous demonstration.
— *Playboy*, December 1981

C'mon, baby, light my fire.
— Jim Morrison, Ray Manzarek, Robby Krieger and John Densmore, 'Light My Fire'

. . . for the vilest things
Become themselves in her, that the holy priests
Bless her when she is riggish.
— William Shakespeare, *Antony and Cleopatra*

There are a number of mechanical devices which increase sexual arousal, particularly in women. Chief among these is the Mercedes-Benz 380SL convertible.
— P.J. O'Rourke, *Modern Manners*

Asking

The lame tongue gets nothing.
— William Camden, *Remains Concerning Britain*

Whether they give or refuse, it delights women to have been asked.
— Ovid, *Ars Amatoria*

By all the soft Pleasures a Virgin can share,
By the critical Minute no Virgin can bear
By the question I burn to ask, but don't dare
I pr'y thee now hear me dear Molly.
— Anonymous, 'The Gallant Schemer's Petition to the Honorable Mrs. F__s' in J.S. Farmer, *Merry Muses*

He that is too proud to ask is too good to receive.
– Thomas Fuller, *Gnomologia: Adagies and Proverbs*

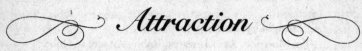

Attraction

What attracts us to a woman rarely binds us to her.
– Churton Collins, *Aphorisms*

I have a big flaw in that I am attracted to thin, tall, good-looking men who have one common denominator. They must be lurking bastards.
– Edna O'Brien, *Some Irish Loving*

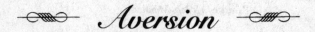

Aversion

'Tis safest in matrimony to begin with a little aversion.
– Richard Brinsley Sheridan, *The Rivals*

Man can start with aversion and end with love, but if he begins with love and comes around to aversion he will never get back to love.
– Honoré de Balzac, *The Physiology of Marriage*

Awakening

Awake, my Fanny, leave all meaner things;
This morn shall prove what rapture swiving brings.
– John Wilkes, *An Essay on Women*

Awe

For he [Henry Miller] captured something in the sexuality of men as it had never been seen before, precisely that it was man's sense of awe before women, his dread of her position one step closer to eternity (for in that step were her powers) which made men detest women, revile them, humiliate them, defecate symbolically upon them, do everything to reduce them so that one might dare to enter them and take pleasure of them.

> – Norman Mailer, *The Prisoner of Sex*

Bachelors

We bachelors grin, but you married men laugh –
till your hearts ache.
> – John Ray, *English Proverbs*

What is it, then, to have, or have no wife
But single thraldom, or double strife?
> – Francis Bacon, *The World*

No lack to lack a wife.
> – John Heywood, *A Dialogue containing the number in effect of all the Proverbs in the English Tongue*

Nowadays all married men live like bachelors, all bachelors live like married men.

> – Oscar Wilde, *The Picture of Dorian Gray*

A bachelor never quite gets over the idea that he is a thing of beauty and a boy forever.

> – Helen Rowland

I'd be equally as willing
For a dentist to be drilling
Than ever let a woman in my life.
– Alan Jay Lerner, *My Fair Lady*

Said a fussy old bachelor named Harridge:
'Connubial life I disparage.
    Every time I get hot
    And poke some girl's spot,
She thinks it is an offer of marriage.'
– Anonymous, quoted in Gershon Legman, *The New Limerick*

A bachelor is a cagey guy
And he has loads of fun.
He sizes all the cuties up
And never Mrs one.
– Anonymous, quoted in B. Cerf, *A Treasury of
  Atrocious Puns*

Down to Gehenna or up to the Throne
He travels the fastest who travels alone.
– Rudyard Kipling, 'The Winners'

I belong to Bridegrooms Anonymous. Whenever I feel like
getting married they send over a lady in a housecoat and hair
curlers to burn my toast for me.
    – Dick Martin, in *Playboy*, 1969

Lord of yourself, uncumber'd with a wife.
    – John Dryden, *Epistles*

BENEDICK: I will live a bachelor.
DON PEDRO: I shall see thee, ere I die, look pale with love.
BENEDICK: With anger, with sickness, or with hunger, my lord,
not with love.
    – William Shakespeare, *Much Ado About Nothing*

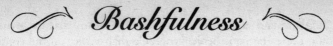

Bashfulness

Love requires Boldness, and scorns Bashfulness.
  – Thomas Fuller, *Gnomologia: Adagies and Proverbs*

Modesty is a Virtue, Bashfulness is a Vice.
  – Benjamin Franklin, *Poor Richard's Almanac*

The bashful always lose.
  – French proverb

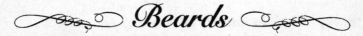

Battle of the Sexes

When Eve ate this particular apple, she became aware of her womanhood, mentally. And mentally she began to experiment with it. She has been experimenting ever since. So has man. To the rage and horror of both of them.
  – D.H. Lawrence, *Fantasia of the Unconscious*

In the sex war, thoughtlessness is the weapon of the male, vindictiveness of the female.
  – Cyril Connolly, *Unquiet Grave*

Beards

Look at this beard and tell me whether
Eunuchs were such or geldings either.
– Samuel Butler, *Hudibras*

He that hath a beard is more than a youth and he that hath no beard is less than a man.
  – William Shakespeare, *Much Ado About Nothing*

In England and America a beard usually means that its owner would rather be considered venerable than virile; on the continent of Europe it often means that its owner makes a special claim to virility.
  – Rebecca West, *The Thinking Reed*

Beautification

That all women of whatever age, rank, profession or degree, whether virgins, maids, or widows [who] shall ... seduce or betray into Matrimony any of His Majesty's subjects by scent, paint, cosmetics ... high-heeled shoes, bolstered hips, shall incur the penalty of law inforce against witchcraft.
  – Act of Parliament (1770), never repealed

To be born a woman is to know –
Although they do not talk of it in school –
That we must labour to be beautiful.
  – W.B. Yeats, 'Adam's Curse'

Beauty

Beauty – a deceitful bait with a deadly hook.
  – John Lyly, *Euphues and His England*

To me, fair friend, you never can be old,
For as you were when first your eye I eyed
Such seems your beauty still.
  – William Shakespeare, 'Sonnet 104'

Beauty is very well at first sight; but who ever looks at it when it has been in the house three days?
> – George Bernard Shaw, *Man and Superman*

There is a garden in her face
> Where roses and white lilies blow.
– Thomas Campion, 'There is a Garden in Her Face'

Love built on beauty, soon as beauty, dies.
– John Donne, *Elegies*: 'The Anagram'

Beauty is but a flower
Which wrinkles will devour.
– Thomas Nashe, 'Summer's Last Will and Testament'

Remember that the most beautiful things in the world are the most useless; peacocks and lilies for instance.
> – John Ruskin, *The Stones of Venice*

What a strange illusion it is to suppose that beauty is goodness.
> – Leo Tolstoy, 'The Kreutzer Sonata'

But the loveliest things of beauty God ever showed to me,
Are her voice, and her hair, and eyes, and the dear red curve of her lips.
– John Masefield, 'Beauty'

Oh no, it wasn't the aeroplanes. It was beauty that killed the beast.
> – James Creeland and Ruth Rose, the final words of the film *King Kong*

A beautiful woman should break her mirror early.
> – Baltasar Gracián

If you get simple beauty and naught else,
You get about the best thing God invents.
– Robert Browning, 'Fra Lippo Lippi'

Beauty is a short-lived reign.
– Socrates (cited by Diogenes Laertius)

There is no excellent beauty that hath not some strangeness in the proportion.
– Francis Bacon, *Essays*: 'On Beauty'

What is lovely never dies,
But passes into other loveliness.
– Thomas Bailey Aldrich, 'A Shadow of the Night'

Beauty unchaste is beauty in disgrace.
– Homer, *The Odyssey* (trans. by Alexander Pope)

What I fancy, I approve,
No dislike there is in love:
Be my mistress short or tall
And distorted there withal:
Be her forehead, and her eyes
Full of incongruities:
Has she thin hair, hath she none
She's to me a paragon.
– Robert Herrick, *Hesperides*

All heiresses are beautiful.
– John Dryden, *King Arthur*

Bait: A preparation which renders the hook more palatable. The best kind is beauty.
– Ambrose Bierce, *The Devil's Dictionary*

Beauty for some provides escape,
Who gain a happiness in eyeing
The gorgeous buttocks of the ape
Or autumn sunsets exquisitely dying.
– Aldous Huxley, 'The Ninth Philosophical Song'

          Well I know
What is this beauty men are babbling of:
I wonder only why they prize it so.
– Edna St Vincent Millay, 'Love is Not Blind, I See With a
   Single Eye'

Beauty draws more than oxen.
    – George Herbert, *Jacula Prudentum*

Beauty soons grows familiar to the lover,
Fades in his eye, and palls upon the sense.
– Joseph Addison, *Cato*

Beauty will not buy beef.
    – Thomas Fuller, *Gnomologia: Adagies and Proverbs*

Beauty is never satisfied
with beauty. Helen
gazing in her glass,
framed by lecherous curtains,
the enchanted bed,
knew herself beautiful. Yet she felt life pass
about her.
– Kathleen Spivack, 'Mythmaking'

Beauty may have fair leaves, yet bitter fruit.
    – Thomas Fuller, *Gnomologia: Adagies and Proverbs*

> Beauty stands
> In the admiration only of weak minds
> Led captive.
> – John Milton, *Paradise Regained*

Wickedness and beauty is the devil's hook baited.
> – Thomas Fuller, *Gnomologia: Adagies and Proverbs*

I'm tired of all this nonsense of beauty being only skin deep. That's deep enough. What do you want – an adorable pancreas?
> – Jean Kerr

> But beauty vanishes; beauty passes;
> However rare – rare it be;
> And when I crumble who will remember
> This lady of the West Country?
> – Walter de la Mare, 'Here Lies a Most Beautiful Lady'

> He who follows Beauty
> Breaks his foolish heart.
> – Bertye Young Williams, 'Song Against Beauty'

Beauty, like male ballet dancers, makes some men afraid.
> – Mordecai Richler, 'Song of a Smaller Hero'

Man soon tires of mere beauty. In fact, the inconstant creature, as soon tires of mere anything.
> – Arnold Haultain, *Hints for Lovers*

> Beauty is a simple passion
> but, oh my friends, in the end
> you will dance the fire dance in iron shoes.
> – Anne Sexton, 'Snow White and the Seven Dwarfs'

> Her hairs are wires of gold,
> her cheeks are made of lilies and roses,

her brows are arches,
her eyes sapphires,
her looks lightning,
her mouth coral,
her teeth pearls,
her paps alabaster,
her body straight,
her belly soft,
and from thence downward to her knees is
all sugar candy.
– Barnabe Rich

No woman can be a beauty without a fortune.
– George Farquhar, *The Beaux' Stratagem*

'Tis not a lip, or eye, we beauty call,
But the joint force and full result of all.
– Alexander Pope, *Essay on Criticism*

Beauty like hers is genius.
– Dante Gabriel Rossetti, 'Genius in Beauty'

Beauty isn't everything! But then what is?
– Sanford Wilson, *The Madness of Lady Bright*

So you can have your beauty
It's skin deep and it only lies.
– Bob Dylan, 'Long Time Gone'

Beauty is ever to the lonely mind
A shadow fleeting; she is never plain
She is a visitor who leaves behind
The gift of grief, the souvenir of pain.
– Robert Nathan, 'Beauty is Ever to the Lonely Mind'

Bed

No, no, I'll never farm your bed
Nor your smock-tenant be.
– Aphra Behn, 'A Song'

. . . a bed fortified with the crazy molecules of a thousand fornications . . .
– Norman Mailer, *The Prisoner of Sex*

Groan, went the bed.
– Thomas Pynchon, *V*

Many a fair nymph has in a cave been spread,
And much good love without a feather bed.
– Juvenal, *Sixth Satire* (trans. by John Dryden)

. . . the bed of conception and birth, of consummation of marriage and breach of marriage, of sleep and of death.
– James Joyce, *Ulysses*

Bored of the foolish things that girls must dream
Because their beds are empty of delight.
– Roy Campbell, 'The Sisters'

Bed is the poor man's opera.
– Italian proverb

. . . this love's hallow'd temple, this soft bed.
– John Donne, 'To His Mistress Going to Bed'

The bed is for lascivious toyings meet,
There use all tricks, and shed shame underneath.
– Ovid, *Elegia XIV* (trans. by Christopher Marlowe)

There goes a saying, and 'twas shrewdly said,
Old fish at table, young flesh in bed
  – Alexander Pope, 'January and May'

It isn't the ecstatic leap across that I deplore, it's the weary
trudge home.
  – Anonymous, a comment on single beds

The grave of lost illusions.
  – Anonymous

> A bed without a woman
> is a thing of wood and springs
>   a pit
> to roll in with the Devil.
>   But let
> her body touch its length and it
>   becomes
> A place of singing wonders, eager
>   springboard
> to heaven and higher.
>   – Ray Souster, 'A Bed Without a Woman'

The place where marriages are decided.
  – Anonymous

> For I've been born and I've been wed –
> All of man's peril comes of bed.
> – C.H. Webb, 'Dum Vivimus Vigilamus'

> We are not sure yet if flesh
> Has merely sprung a trap,
> But, between not knowing and the knowing
> Beds will span the gap.
>   – Joan Finnigan, 'Honeymoon'

<pre>
                        . . . on love
        wet sheets, we play again
        the ancient comedy,
        Your orifice, my oracle.
        – Harry Howith, 'Joanne'
</pre>

. . . there is no sanctuary in one bed from the memory of
another.
> – Cyril Connolly

At night, alone, I marry the bed.
> – Anne Sexton, 'The Ballad of the Lonely Masturbator'

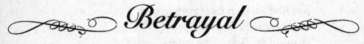 *Betrayal*

My love, I have betrayed you seventy times
In this brief period since our stars met:
. . .
Forgot you, worshipped others, flung a flower
To meaner beauty, proved an infidel.
> – Conrad Aiken, 'Sonnet IV'

I loved you despite your betrayals, how would I have felt had
you been faithful?
> – Jean Racine, *Andromache*

As a rule the person found out in a betrayal of love holds, all the
same, the superior position of the two. It is the betrayed one
who is humiliated.
> – Ada Leverson, *Love's Shadow*

In me you've found the man you care for.
    And, for a while, you'll richly pay me
With kindness, kisses and endearments –
    And then, as usual, you'll betray me.
– Heinrich Heine, 'Ich Liebe Solche Weissen Glieder' (trans.
  by Louis Untermeyer)

She's fickle and false and there we agree;
For I am as false and fickle as she:
We neither believe what either can say;
And neither believing we neither betray.
– John Dryden, *Amphitryon*: 'Hourly I Die'

See also: INFIDELITY; UNFAITHFULNESS.

Bigamy

Two cats and one mouse,
Two wives in one house,
Two dogs and one bone
Never agree in one.
– John Ray, *English Proverbs*

Bigamy is having one wife too many. Monogamy is the same.
– Oscar Wilde

There was a young man named Price
Who remarked, 'They say bigamy's nice.
    Even two are a bore
    I'd prefer three or four,
For the plural of spouse, is spice.
– Anonymous Limerick

There once was an old man of Lyme
Who married three wives at a time.

When asked 'Why a third?'
He replied, 'One's absurd!
And bigamy, Sir, is a crime!'
– William Cosmo Monkhouse, *Nonsense Rhymes*

When two rites make a wrong.
– Anonymous

One wife at a time is enough for most people.
– Mr Justice Smith, in the *Observer*, 13 May 1979

One wife is too much for one husband to hear,
But two at a time there's no mortal can bear.
This way, and that way, and which way I will,
What would comfort the one, t'other wife would take
ill.
– John Gay, *The Beggar's Opera*

 *Birth Control*

Contraceptives should be used on all conceivable occasions.
– Spike Milligan, on *The Last Goon Show of All*, BBC TV

There's a time when you have to explain to your children why they're born, and it's a marvellous thing if you know the reason by then.
– Hazel Scott, in *Ms.*, November 1974

Accidents will occur in the best-regulated families.
– Charles Dickens, *David Copperfield*

See also: CONTRACEPTION.

Blemishes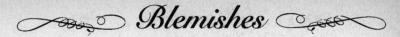

In the eyes of a lover pockmarks are dimples.
– Japanese proverb

. . . the tiniest blemish can twist the roots of the heart.
– M. Levy, *The Moons of Paradise*

See also: IMPERFECTION.

Blindness of Love

Though love is blind, yet 'tis not for want of eyes.
– Thomas Fuller, *English Proverbs*

But love is blind, and lovers cannot see
The petty follies that themselves commit
– William Shakespeare, *The Merchant of Venice*

The swarthy girl is tawny, the scrawny is a gazelle, the dumb is
modest, she that is half-dead with consumption is slender, and
she that is bloated with enormous dugs, is Ceres herself.
– Lucretius, *De Rerum Natura*

Bliss

Pale Bliss
Splitting a bottle of white wine
with a naked woman
in the middle of the day.
– John Updike, 'Tossing and Turning'

Blondes

It was a blonde. A blonde to make a bishop kick a hole in a stained-glass window.
> – Raymond Chandler, *Farewell My Lovely*

Hazel Morse was a large, fair woman of the type that incites some men when they use the word 'blonde' to click their tongues and wag their heads roguishly.
> – Dorothy Parker, *Big Blonde*

She was a blonde – with a brunette past.
> – Gwyn Thomas, on BBC TV, 20 October 1969

It is possible that blondes also prefer gentlemen.
> – Mamie Van Doren (attributed)

That gentlemen prefer blondes is due to the fact that, apparently, pale hair, delicate skin and an infantile expression represent the very apex of frailty which every man longs to violate.
> – Alexander King

A chaste woman ought not to dye her hair yellow.
> – Menander, *Fragments*

Being blonde is definitely a different state of mind ... the artifice of being blonde has some incredible sort of sexual connotation.
> – Madonna, in *Rolling Stone*, 23 March 1989

> a lollipop blonde who leads you on to assault her
> And you've got her skirts around her waist and her
> pants around her feet.
> – A.D. Hope, 'Observation Car'

Gentlemen prefer blondes, but take what they can get.
> – Don Herold (attributed)

Blushes

There's a blush for won't and a blush for shan't
And a blush for having done it;
There's a blush for thought and a blush for naught
And a blush for just begun it.
– John Keats, 'Sharing Eve's Apple'

In a blush, love finds a barrier.
– Virgil, *Ciris*

Blushing is virtue's colour.
– John Ray, *English Proverbs*

Faults done by night will blush by day.
– Robert Herrick, 'The Vision'

Whoever blushes is already guilty, true innocence is ashamed of
nothing.
– Jean-Jacques Rousseau, *Émile*

Girls blush, sometimes, because they are alive,
Half wishing they were dead to save the shame.
The sudden blush devours them, neck and brow;
They have drawn too near the fire of life, like gnats,
And flare up bodily, wings and all. What then?
Who's sorry for a gnat . . . or girl?
– Elizabeth Barrett Browning, *Aurora Leigh*

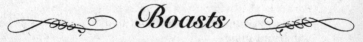

Boasts

The cock-crows of phallic brag . . .
– Gershon Legman, in the introduction to *The Merry Muses of
Caledonia*

The Body

The basic Female Body comes with the following accessories: garter belt, panti-girdle, crinoline, camisole, bustle, brassiere, stomacher, chemise, virgin zone, spike heels, nose ring, veil, kid gloves, fishnet stockings, fichu, bandeau, Merry Widow, weepers, chokers, barrettes, bangles, beads, lorgnette, feather boa, basic black, compact, Lycra stretch one-piece with modesty panel, designer peignoir, flannel nightie, lace teddy, bed, head.

> – Margaret Atwood, *Michigan Quarterly Review*

A woman watches her body uneasily, as though it were an unreliable ally in the battle for love.

> – Leonard Cohen, *The Favorite Game*

For women . . . bras, panties, bathing suits, and other stereotypical gear are visual reminders of a commercial, idealized feminine image that our real and diverse female bodies can't possibly fit. Without these visual references, each individual woman's body demands to be accepted on its own terms. We stop being comparatives. We begin to be unique.

> – Gloria Steinem, 'In Praise of Women's Bodies', in *Ms.*,
>   April 1981

> i like my body when it is with your
> body . . .
> – e.e. cummings

This is a waist the spirit breaks its arm on.

> – Randall Jarrell, *A Girl in a Library*

> What ever happens with us, your body
> will haunt mine –
> – Adrienne Rich, *Twenty One Love Poems*

The fate of man
Turns on the body of woman.
– William Everson, 'The Man-Fate'

The most effective lure that a woman can hold out to a man is the lure that he fatuously conceives to be her beauty. This so-called beauty, of course, is almost always an illusion. The female body, even it its best, is very defective in form; it has harsh curves and very clumsily distributed masses; compared to it the average milk jug or even cuspidor, is a thing of intelligent and gratifying design.
– H.L. Mencken, *A Mencken Chrestomathy*

Bonding

Any woman who wants to see the term 'male bonding' made concrete need only complain of one good 'ole boy to another, and watch the glaze form, instantaneously, over the eyeball of her listener.
– Rosemary Daniell, *Fatal Flowers*

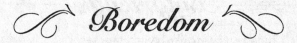

Boredom

. . . entering our lives' third quarter she'd been bored stiff with me and I bored limp with her . . . .
– John Barth, *Letters*

Bore: a man in love with another woman.
– Mary Pettingbone Poole (attributed)

It is impossible to become bored in the presence of a mistress.
— Stendhal

When you are bored with yourself.
Marry and be bored with someone else.
— David Pryce-Jones, *Owls and Satyrs*

In love there are no vacations, no such thing. Love has to be lived fully with its boredom and all that.
— Marguerite Duras

She, while her lover pants upon her breast,
Can mark the figures on an Indian chest.
— Alexander Pope, *Epistle to a Lady*

What shall we do with ourselves this afternoon? And the day after that, and the next thirty years?
— F. Scott Fitzgerald, *The Great Gatsby*

Her boredom took her away. So simple.
She just became bored with me.
— Gavin Ewart, 'Ella Mi Fu Ripita!'

 *Boyfriends*

Bloody men are like bloody buses –
You wait for about a year
And as soon as one approaches your stop
Two or three others appear.
— Wendy Cope, *Serious Concerns*

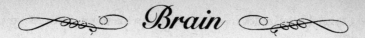

Brain

My brain? It's my second favourite organ.
– Woody Allen and Marshall Brickman, from the film *Sleeper*

We have too much sex on the brain, and too little of it elsewhere.
– Norman Douglas, *An Almanac*

Sex on the brain is the wrong place to have it.
– Malcolm Muggeridge (attributed)

I have a brain and a uterus and I use them both.
– Patricia Schroeder (attributed)

For while we have sex on the mind, we truly have none
    in the body.
– D.H. Lawrence, *Pansies*: 'Leave Sex Alone'

But if God wanted us to think just with our wombs, why did He give us a brain?
– Claire Booth Luce, in *Life* (New York), 18 October 1970

And not a girl goes walking
    Along the Cotswold lanes
But knows men's eyes in April
    Are quicker than their brains.
– John Drinkwater, 'Cotswold Love'

We're equal partners, that is plain;
    Our life cannot grow dull or shoddy.
While I have such a lovely brain
    And you have such a lovely body.
– Louis Untermeyer, 'Equals'

I think I have a dick in my brain. I don't need one between my legs.

> – Madonna, in bell hooks, *Madonnarama*

See also: INTELLIGENCE; THE MIND.

Breach of Promise

> Affection is a noble quality
> It leads to generosity and jollity.
> But it also leads to breach of promise
> If you go around lavishing it on red-hot momise.
> – Ogden Nash, 'Reflection on Caution'

Breakfast

Never make love to a woman before breakfast for two reasons. One, it is tiring. Two, you may meet someone else during the day that you like better.

> – Enrico Caruso (attributed)

The sexual organs are simply the means of exchanging sexual sensations. The real business is transacted at the emotional level. Thus, the foundation of sexual happiness – or misery – is laid not in the bedroom but at the breakfast table.

> – David R. Reuben, in *Reader's Digest*, January 1973

My wife and I tried two or three times in the last forty years to have breakfast together, but it was so disagreeable that we had to stop.

> – Winston Churchill, in *The New York Times*, 4 December 1950

The glances over cocktails
That seemed so sweet;
Don't seem quite so amorous
Over shredded wheat.
– Benny Fields, in *Reader's Digest*, December 1947

One golden rule: Never make love before breakfast.
– C.P. Snow, *Death*

Breathes there a man with soul so dead
Who never to his wife hath said:
Breakfast be damned, come to bed.
– Samuel Hoffenstein

The critical period in matrimony is breakfast-time.
– A.P. Herbert, *Uncommon Law*

The problem with marriage is that it ends every night after making love, and it must be rebuilt every morning before breakfast.
– Gabriel García Márquez, *Love in the Time of Cholera*

Breaking Hearts

When people say 'You're breaking my heart', they do in fact usually mean that you're breaking their genitals.
– Jeffrey Bernard (attributed)

See also: BROKEN HEART; HEARTBREAK.

Break-Up

Since there is no help, come let us kiss and part –
Nay, I have done, you get no more of me;
And I am glad, yea glad with all my heart,
That thus so cleanly I myself can free.
Shake hands for ever, cancel all our vows
And when we meet at anytime again,
Be it not seen in either of our brows
That we one jot of former love retain.
– Michael Drayton, 'Since There is No Help, Come Let Us
  Kiss and Part'

You must live through the time when everything hurts.
– Stephen Spender, 'The Double Shame'

She always believed in the old adage: 'Leave them while you're
looking good.'
– Anita Loos, *Gentlemen Prefer Blondes*

I leave before being left. I decide.
– Brigitte Bardot, in *Newsweek*, 5 March 1973

Cast not out the foul water till you bring in the clean. Part not
with that way of living you had, till you are sure of a better.
– James Kelley, *Complete Collection of Scottish Proverbs*

See also: THE END OF LOVE; PARTING.

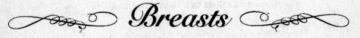

Breasts

. . . her friendly bust
gives promise of pneumatic bliss.
– T.S. Eliot, 'Whispers of Immortality'

How do you like them? Like a pear, a lemon, à la Montgolfier, half an apple, or a canteloupe? Go and choose, don't be embarrassed.
– Colette, *Journey for Myself*

The degree of attention which breasts receive combined with the confusion about what breast fetishists actually want, makes women unduly anxious. They never can be just right; they always are too small, too big, the wrong shape, too flabby.
. . .
A full bosom is actually a millstone around a woman's neck . . . [Breasts] are not parts of a person but lures slung around her neck, to be kneaded and twisted like magic putty, or mumbled and mouthed like lolly ices.
– Germaine Greer, *The Female Eunuch*

Her breasts were milk-proud.
– John Updike, *Couples*

> Breasts and bosoms I have known
> Of varied shapes and sizes
> From poignant disappointments
> To jubilant surprises.
> – Waldo Pierce, in W.R. Espy, *An Almanac of Words at Play*

If you are a girl, worry that your breasts are too round. Worry that your breasts are too pointed . . . If you are a boy, worry that you will get breasts.
– Delia Ephron, *Teenage Romance*

> When I hold you in the night
> Kiss your breast upon the right
> Then you say: 'My love, beware!
> That one is my husband's share.
>
> Take the left one, lover bold;
> That is yours, to have and hold.

Yours is much the better part
For it lies above my heart.
– Deems Taylor, 'Turn to the Left'

'Are you there God? It's me Margaret. I just told my mother I want a bra. Please help me grow God. You know where. I want to be like everyone else.
– Judy Blume, 'Are You There God? It's Me Margaret'

 Bridegrooms

Why have such scores of lovely, gifted girls
    Married impossible men?
Repeat impossible men: not merely rustic
    Foul–tempered or depraved
. . .
Impossible men: idle, illiterate
    Self–pitying, dirty, sly
– Robert Graves, 'A Slice of the Wedding Cake'

Weddings make a lot of people sad,
But if you are the bridegroom it's not so bad.
– Gus Kahn, 'Makin' Whoopee'

See also: HUSBANDS.

Brides

It has been said that a bride's attitude towards her betrothed can be summed up in three words: Aisle, Altar, Hymn.
– Frank Muir and Denis Norden, *Upon My Word*: 'A Jug of Wine'

Bride: A woman with a fine prospect of happiness behind her.
　– Ambrose Bierce, *The Devil's Dictionary*

'Who gives this woman?' Then
　　Whoever does is silly.
She's given herself to countless men.
　　So why not now to Willy?
– Geoffrey R. Riddlehough, 'Give Away'

Bride loved old words, and found her pleasure marred
On the first night, her expectations jarred,
And thirty inches short of being a yard.
– James Vincent Cunningham, 'Five Epigrams'

 # *Broken Heart*

Broken hearts die slowly.
– Thomas Campbell, 'Theodric'

The day breaks not, it is my heart.
– John Donne, 'Break of Day'

Had we never loved sae kindly,
Had we never loved sae blindly,
Never met – or never parted,
We had ne'er been broken-hearted.
– Robert Burns, 'Ae Fond Kiss'

. . . a broken heart is what makes life so wonderful five years later, when you see the guy in the elevator and he is fat and smoking a cigar and saying long-time-no-see. If he had not broken your heart, you couldn't have that glorious feeling of relief!
– Phyllis Battelle, in the *New York Journal*, 1 June 1962

See also: BREAKING HEARTS; HEARTBREAK.

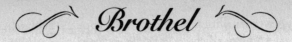

Brothel

Please treat the women as comrades.
> – Notice in Spanish brothels during the Spanish Civil War, 1936–39, quoted in George Orwell, book review in *Time and Tide*, 9 October 1937

No one was ever made wretched in a brothel.
> – Cyril Connolly (attributed)

Prisons are built with stones of law, brothels with bricks of religion.
> – William Blake, *Proverbs of Hell*

Buttocks

Many women loathe their backside, that blind and public mass which belongs to everyone before belonging to them.
> – Jean-Paul Sartre, quoted in R. Melville, *Erotic Art and the West*

. . . the shadow and substance of that warm divide that tends to drive all mankind to mutest adoration.
> – Gilbert Sorrentino, *Mulligan's Stew*

My wife with buttocks of spring.
> – André Breton, 'Freedom of Love'

Think you can run around with a behind like that and get away with it in court? This is a case of intentional assault with a dangerous weapon.
> – Bertolt Brecht, *The Caucasian Chalk Circle*

He kissed the plump mellow smellow melons of her rump, on each plump melonous hemisphere, in their mellow yellow furrow, with obscure prolonged provocative melonsmelonous osculation.
– James Joyce, *Ulysses*

. . . the most beautiful part of her was the long-sloping fall of the haunches from the socket of the back, and the slumberous round stillness of the buttocks. Like hillocks of sand the Arabs say, soft and downward-slipping with a long slope.
– D.H. Lawrence, *Lady Chatterley's Lover*

. . . a thumb-pinch of tush peeking out over each thigh.
– Richard Price, *Ladies Man*

Buxomness

When a woman that's buxom a dotard does wed
'Tis madness to think she'd be tied to his bed.
– Author unknown, 'When a Woman That's Buxom' (1682)

So buxom, blithe and debonair.
– John Milton, *Comus*

Cad

The most disgusting cad in the world is the man who, on the grounds of decorum and morality, avoids the game of love.
– H.L. Mencken, in *Smart Set*, May 1919

Calf Love

Calf love, half love;
Old love, cold love.
– English proverb

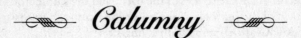

Calumny

Be thou chaste as ice, pure as snow, thou shall not
escape calumny.
– William Shakespeare, *Hamlet*

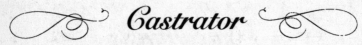

Castrator

She was a free-lance castrator.
– Julius Feiffer, *Harry, the Rat with Women*

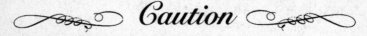

Caution

If not chastely, then at least cautiously.
– Latin proverb

Celibacy

... my celibacy ... more a passive habit than an active
policy ...
– John Barth, *Letters*

Marriage has many pains, but celibacy has no pleasures.
>   – Samuel Johnson, *Rasselas*

I tend to agree that celibacy for a time is worth considering, for sex is dirty if all it means is winning a man, conquering a woman, beating someone out of something, abusing each other's dignity in order to prove that I am a man, I am a woman.
>   – Toni Cade Bambera

As to marriage or celibacy, let man take which course he will, he will be sure to repent.
>   – Socrates

The worst form of self-abuse.
>   – Peter De Vries, in *The New York Times*, 12 June 1983

Marriage may often be a stormy lake, but celibacy is almost always a muddy horsepond.
>   – Thomas Love Peacock, *Melincourt*

> I can live without it all –
> love with its blood pump,
> sex with its messy hungers,
> men with their peacock strutting
> their silly sexual baggage,
> their wet tongues in my ear.
>   – Erica Jong, in S. Berg and S.J. Marks, *About Women*

[Sex is] inconvenient, time-consuming, energy-draining and irrelevant ... Erotic energy is just life-energy and is quickly worked off if you are doing interesting, absorbing things ... [If] genital tensions persist, you can still masturbate. Isn't that a lot easier anyway? This is not a call for celibacy but an acceptance of celibacy as an alternative preferable to the degradation of most male–female sexual relationships.
>   – Dana Densmore, quoted in Linda Grant, *Sexing the Millennium*

[Celibacy] happens to be the most common human sexual adventure.
— Kurt Vonnegut, Jr, *Palm Sunday*

Change in the Beloved

I loved thee once, I'll love no more,
    Thine be the grief and is the blame;
Thou are not what thou wast before –
    What reason should I be the same?
— Sir Robert Aytoun, 'To an Inconstant Mistress'

A Change of Lovers

Love is like linen: often changed, the sweeter.
— Phineas Fletcher, *Sicelides*

Change of Mind

'YES,' I answered you last night,
'No,' this morning, Sir, I say.
Colours seen by candle light
Will not look the same by day.
— Elizabeth Barrett Browning, 'The Lady's "Yes"'

'You gave me the key of your heart, my love;
Then why did you make me knock?'
'Oh that was yesterday, saints above!
And last night – I changed the lock!'
— John Boyle O'Reilly, 'Constancy'

Charm

You know what charm is: a way of getting the answer yes without having asked a clear question.
– Albert Camus, *The Fall*

It's a sort of bloom on a woman. If you have it, you don't need to have anything else; and if you don't have it, it doesn't much matter what else you have.
– J.M. Barrie, *What Every Woman Knows*

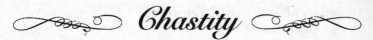

Chastity

Beauty and chastity have always a mortal quarrel between them.
– Spanish proverb

Chastity: The most unnatural of sexual perversions.
– Aldous Huxley

Of all sexual aberrations, chastity is the strangest.
– Anatole France

Bolts and bars will not keep our wives and daughters chaste.
– Molière, *L'École des maris*

Banish all objects of lust, shut up all youth into the severest discipline that can be exercised in any hermitage, ye can not make them chaste, that came not hither so.
– John Milton, *Areopagitica*

If she seems not chaste to me,
What care I how chaste she be?
– Sir Walter Raleigh, 'Shall I Like Hermit Dwell'

'Tis chastity, my brother, chastity:
She that has that, is clad in compleat steel,
And like a quiver'd Nymph with Arrows keen
May trace huge Forests, and unharbour'd Heaths,
Infamous Hills, and sandy perilous wilds,
Where through the sacred rays of Chastity,
No savage, fierce, Bandit, or mountaineer
Will dare to soil her Virgin purity.
  – John Milton, *Comus*

God's rarest blessing.
  – George Meredith

The cement of civilization and progress.
  – Mary Baker Eddy

To love pure and chaste from afar.
  – Joe Darion, 'The Impossible Dream', from the musical *Man of La Mancha* (music by Mitch Leigh)

I had prayed to you for chastity and said, 'Give me chastity and continence but not yet.' For I was afraid that you would answer my prayer at once and cure me too soon of the disease of lust, which I want satisfied, but not quelled.
  – St Augustine, *Confessions*

Chaste as the icicle
That's curdled by the frost from purest snow
And hangs on Dian's temple.
  – William Shakespeare, *Coriolanus*

Chastity is curable, if detected early
  – Graffito

We may come to realize that chastity is no more a virtue than malnutrition.
  – Alex Comfort, in *The New York Times*, 18 February 1968

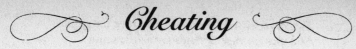

Cheating

When cheated, wife or husband feels the same.
> – Euripides, *Andromache*

See also: DECEIT; LOVER: DECEIVER.

Chivalry

When a man opens the car door for his wife, it's either a new car or a new wife.
> – Prince Philip, Duke of Edinburgh, in *Today*, 2 March 1988

Choice of Lover

Women prefer men who have something tender about them – especially the legal kind.
> – Kay Ingram, in *Reader's Digest*, May 1952

Class Distinctions

When Adam delved and Eve span,
Who was then the gentleman?
> – John Ball, in a speech, 1381

He is a fool who kisseth the maid when he may kiss the mistress.
> – James Howell, *Proverbs*

The sex is turn'd all whore; they love the game:
And mistresses and maids are all the same.
– Juvenal, *Sixth Satire* (trans. by John Dryden)

Night makes no difference between the priest and the clerk;
Joan as my lady is as good i' the dark.
– Robert Herrick, *Hesperides*

Love in a hut, with water and a crust,
Is – Love forgive us! – cinders, ashes, dust;
Love in a palace is perhaps at last
More grievous torment than a hermit's fast.
– John Keats, 'Lamia'

The Closet

Tell your secret to your servant, and you make him your
master.
– Nathaniel Bailey, *Dictionary*

To whom thy secret thou dost tell,
To him thy freedom thou dost sell.
– Benjamin Franklin, *Poor Richard's Almanac*

Clothes

What a man enjoys about a woman's clothes are his fantasies of
how she would look without them.
– Brendon Francis (attributed)

Oh bully barrier between soul and soul,
soul & self,
how it comforts us
to take you down!
How it heartens to strip you off!
    & this is no matter of fashion.
– Erica Jong, 'In Praise of Clothes'

A sweet disorder in dress
Kindles in clothes a wantonness.
– Robert Herrick, *Hesperides*

I bet she snaps a mean garter.
    – Raymond Chandler, *Farewell My Lovely*

. . . the heart throb of garterbelt boils down to nothing but elastic.
    – Seymour Krim, *Views of a Nearsighted Cannoneer*

That girdle will not gird me.
    – Thomas Fuller, *Gnomologia: Adagies and Proverbs*

Your dresses should be tight enough to show you're a woman and loose enough to show you're a lady.
    – Edith Head (attributed)

Ah, when at night my lady sweet
    Loosens the honeyed linen from her thigh,
Girdle and smock and all warm things lie
    Fall'n in a snowdrift round her feet;
. . .
Yea, as I feast upon my lady's clothes,
    I dream I was a bee, and they a rose.
– Richard Le Gallienne, *English Poems*

Away with silks, away with lawn,
I'll have no scenes or curtains drawn:

Give me my mistress as she is,
Dress'd in her nak'd simplicities;
For as my heart, e'en so my eye
Is won by flesh, not drapery.
– Robert Herrick, 'Clothes Do But Cheat and Cozen Us'

A dress has no meaning unless it makes a man want to take it off.
– Françoise Sagan, in the *Observer*, 1969

In olden days a glimpse of stocking
Was looked on as something shocking
Now, heaven knows,
Anything goes.
– Cole Porter, 'Anything Goes'

She wore far too much rouge last night and not quite enough clothes. That is always a sign of despair in a woman.
– Oscar Wilde, *An Ideal Husband*

Seamed stockings aren't subtle but they certainly do the job. You shouldn't wear them when out with someone you're not prepared to sleep with . . . If you really want your escort paralytic with lust, stop frequently to adjust the seams.
– Cynthia Heimel, *Sex Tips for Girls*

. . . the greatest provocations to our lust are from our apparel.
– Robert Burton, *Anatomy of Melancholy*

Women's sexy underwear is a minor but significant growth industry in late twentieth-century Britain in the twilight of capitalism.
– Angela Carter, *Nothing Sacred*

See also: DRESS; LINGERIE.

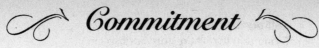

Commitment

Never give all the heart, for love
Will hardly seem worth thinking of
To passionate women if it seems
certain . . .
— W.B. Yeats, 'Never Give All the Heart'

Women would be more charming if one could fall into their
arms without falling into her hands.
— Ambrose Bierce, *Epigrams*

It's gonna be a long drag, but we'll make it.
— Janis Joplin (attributed)

Communication

Mute: marriages
the ten–ton block of ice
obstructing the throat, the heart
the red filler of the liver
the clogged life
. . .
Speak the dream
Follow the red thread
of images
Defrost the glacier
with the live heat
of your breath,
propelled by the heart's explosion.
— Erica Jong, 'Mute Marriages'

Love makes mute of those who habitually speak most fluently.
— Madeleine de Scudéry, *Choix de pensées*: 'De l'amour'

Talking in bed ought to be the easiest
Lying together there goes back so far
An emblem of two people being honest

Yet more and more time passes silently
. . .
It becomes still more difficult to find
Words once true and kind,
Or not untrue and not unkind.
– Philip Larkin, 'Talking in Bed'

A cynical friend of mine tells overeducated couples who are not
getting along to stop communicating and start talking.
. . .
The worst kind of communication is called a continuing
dialogue.
      – Eric Berne, *Games People Play*

Sex is making a fool of yourself, exposing yourself as an asshole.
That is why sex is so intimate. Making mistakes is one of the
most revealing and intimate moments of sexual communication.
      – Jerry Rubin and Mimi Leonard, *The Battle Between the Sheets*

In love there are two things: bodies and words.
      – Joyce Carol Oates

Some nights he said he was tired, and some nights she said she
wanted to read, and other nights no one said anything.
      – Joan Didion, *Play It As It Lays*

If sex were all, then
    every trembling hand
Could make us squeak, like
    dolls, the wished–
for words.
      – Wallace Stevens, 'Le Monocle de mon oncle'

If I speak to thee in Friendship's name
    Thou think'st I speak too coldly;
If I mention Love's devoted flame,
    Thou say'st I speak too boldly.
– Thomas Moore, *National Airs*: 'How Shall I Woo'

          O gentle Romeo
If thou dost love, pronounce it faithfully.
– William Shakespeare, *Romeo and Juliet*

They love indeed who quake to say they love.
– Sir Philip Sidney, 'Sonnet LIV'

If you happen to have experience with Freudian analysis, group psychotherapy, etc. . . . your communications to your mate during marital squabbles will be considerably enhanced. Utilize the special words and phrases you have learned in therapy. Your mate will find these particularly grating . . .
1. 'Will you stop Acting OUT and start RELATING?'
. . .
4. 'Boy do you have a lot of REPRESSED RAGE.'
5. 'You're a classic example of ANAL-RETENTIVE behaviour.'
> – Dan Greenberg and Suzanne O'Malley, *How to Avoid Love and Marriage*

    . . . walking at noon in the ghost town
    surrounded by a silence

    that sounds like the silence of the place
    except that it came with us
    and is familiar
    and everything we are saying until now
    was an effort to blot it out –
    Coming out here we are up against it

Out here I feel more helpless
with you than without you . . .
– Adrienne Rich, 'Trying to Talk to a Man'

Loneliness is never more cruel than when it is felt in close
propinquity with someone who has ceased to communicate.
    – Germaine Greer, *The Female Eunuch*

We love in another's soul
whatever of ourselves
we can deposit in it:
the greater the deposit
the greater the love.
– Irving Layton, 'The Whole Bloody Bird'

My old flame, my wife
. . .
Poor ghost, old love, speak
with your old voice
of flaming insight
that kept us awake all night
In one bed and apart.
– Robert Lowell, 'The Old Flame'

Never seek to tell thy love,
Love that never can be told.
– William Blake, 'Never Seek to Tell Thy Love'

See also: CONVERSATION; SPEECH; TALK.

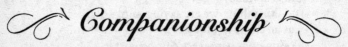 *Companionship*

I need sexual companionship, not just the odd lay.
    – John Barth, *Letters*

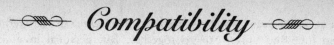

Compatibility

Though few would still subscribe
To the monogamic axiom
That strife below the hip-bones
Need not estrange the heart.
– Robert Graves, 'Call It a Good Marriage'

Considering the two of you
are just alike,
the worst wife and
the worst husband,
I find it quite remarkable
You aren't compatible.
– Martial, *Select Epigrams of Martial* (trans. and adapted by
   Donald C. Goertz)

you fit into me
like a hook in an eye
a fish hook
an open eye
– Margaret Atwood, *Power Politics*

Getting along with men isn't what is important. The vital
knowledge is how to get along with a man, one man.
– Phyllis McGinley

I love her too, but our neuroses don't match.
– Arthur Miller, *The Ride Down Mount Morgan*

It's true love because
If he said quit drinking martinis, but I kept on
drinking them
and next morning I couldn't get out of bed,
He wouldn't tell me he told me.
–Judith Viorst, 'True Love'

Love and sex can go together and sex and unlove can go together and love and unsex can go together. But personal love and personal sex is bad.
— Andy Warhol, *From A to B and Back Again*

Life has taught us that love does not consist in gazing at each other but in looking outward together in the same direction.
— Antoine de Saint- Exupéry, *Wind, Sand, and Stars*

Competency

It is easy to judge from the state of the hay whether the pitchfork is any good.
— Jean de Condé, 'The Beaten Path'

Complaints

Women complain about sex more often than men. Their gripes fall into two major categories: (1) not enough, (2) too much.
— Ann Landers, *Ann Landers Says Truth is Stranger*

Compromise

Dear wife, give in or get out
. . .
So listen my love, here's a compromise:
If your aim is purity, be a pure bore by day;
When I come home at night, I want a rampant whore.
— Martial, *Select Epigrams of Martial* (trans. and adapted by Donald C. Goertz)

If you cannot catch a bird of paradise, better take a wet hen.
– Nikita Khrushchev, in *Time*, 6 January 1958

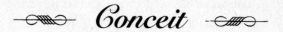 *Conceit*

The height of conceit: A flea floating down the river with a hard-on, whistling for the drawbridge to open.
– Gershon Legman, *The Rationale of the Dirty Joke*

 *Conception*

Behold I was brought forth in iniquity,
And in sin did my mother conceive me.
– The Bible: Psalms

A. wants us to forego all contraception. He wants his seed in me. He wants me pregnant, impregnated, preggers. He wants to get a child on me, to get me with child. He wants us to make a baby: my old egg, his sluggish swimmers. Conceive: he wants me to conceive by him, conceive a new person, our chromosomes together, his genes and mine, the living decipherment of our mingled codes. That's what he thought we ought.
– John Barth, *Letters*

I shall demand perfect men and women out of my love-spendings.
– Walt Whitman, 'A Woman Waits for Me'

. . . but what he did know was if sex had meaning, conception could not be empty of it . . .
. . .

Sex can lead to conception and be as rewarding as cold piss . . .
– Norman Mailer, *The Prisoner of Love*

See also: PREGNANCY.

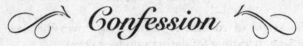

Confession

The things she said to me,
as a man, I won't repeat.
The light of understanding
has made me discreet.
– Federico Garcia Lorca, 'The Faithless Wife'

Never seek to tell thy love
Love that never told can be.
. . .
I told my love, I told my love
I told her all my heart
Trembling, cold, in ghastly fears
Ah! she doth depart.
– William Blake, 'Never Seek to Tell Thy Love'

Strange fits of passion have I known
And I will dare to tell,
But in the lover's ear alone,
What once to me befell.
– William Wordsworth, 'Strange Fits of Passion Have I
  Known'

You find it no great effort to disclose
Your crimes of murder, bigamy and arson
But can you tell them that you pick your nose?
– Norman Cameron, 'Punishment Enough'

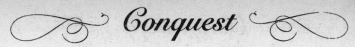

Conquest

Still stoop to conquer: when she thwarts thee, yield;
Do all her bidding, thou shalt win the field;
Thus, when she argues, argue on her side;
What she approves, approve; deny what she denied;
Say and unsay; and as her face appears
Smile on her smiles, and weep on her tears.
– Ovid, *Ars Amatoria*

The way to get on with a girl
Is to drift like a man in a mist,
Happy enough to be caught
Happy to be dismissed.

Glad to be out
of her way,
Glad to rejoin her in bed
Equally grieved or gay
To learn that she's living or dead.
– Author unknown, 'Advice to Lovers' (trans. by Frank
    O'Connor), in Edna O'Brien, *Some Irish Loving*

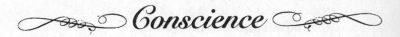

Conscience

A standing prick has no conscience.
    – English proverb, in Eric Partridge, *A Dictionary of
        Catchphrases*

Penis erectus non conscient ius.
    – Gershon Legman, *The Limerick*

Constancy

Let us not undervalue lips or arms
As reassurances of constancy
Or speech as necesssary communication
When troubled hearts go groping
    through the dusk.
– Robert Graves, 'The Starred Coverlet'

Dear were her charms to me,
Dearer her laughter free,
Dearest her constancy –
– Gerald Griffen, 'Eileen Aroon'

Doubt thou the stars are fire;
    Doubt that the sun doth move
Doubt truth to be a liar
    But never doubt I love.
– William Shakespeare, *Hamlet*

As you are woman, so be lovely;
As you are lovely, so be various,
Merciful as constant, constant as various,
So be mine, as I yours forever.
– Robert Graves, 'Pygmalion to Galatea'

Sigh no more ladies, sigh no more,
    Men were deceivers ever,
One foot in the sea and one foot on shore
    To one thing constant never.
– William Shakespeare, *Much Ado About Nothing*

I know not, I ask not, if guilt is in that heart,
But I know that I love thee, whatever thou art.
– Thomas Moore, *Juvenile Poems*: 'Come, Rest in This Bosom'

Since 'tis Nature's law to change,
Constancy alone is strange.
– John Wilmot, Earl of Rochester, 'A Dialogue Between
Strephon and Daphne'

Doth not a man's appetite change? A man loves the meat in his
youth that he cannot endure in his age.
– William Shakespeare, *Much Ado About Nothing*

There is nothing in this world constant, but inconstancy.
– Jonathan Swift, *A Critical Essay on the Faculties of the Mind*

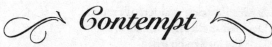

Contempt

Teach not thy lips such scorn; for they were made
For kissing, not for such contempt.
– William Shakespeare, *Richard III*

Continence

Mr Mercaptan went on to preach a brilliant sermon on that
melancholy perversion known as continence.
– Aldous Huxley, *Antic Hay*

Continence is an angelic exercise.
– St Augustine, *On the Good of Marriage*

Continence, under some circumstances, is a duty, but is never a
virtue, it being without any moral quality whatever.
– R.G. White, *Words and Their Uses*

❦ *Contraception* ❦

The best contraceptive is a glass of water: not before, or after,
but instead.
> – Author unknown

Use contraceptives: No deposit – No return.
> – Graffito

When you take your Pill it's like a mine disaster. I think of all the
people lost inside of you.
> – Richard Brautigan, *The Pill Versus the Springhill Mine
> Disaster*

A pretty young maiden of France
Decided she'd take a chance.
    She let herself go
    For an hour or so
And now all her sisters are aunts.
> – Anonymous Limerick, in *More Playboy's Party Jokes*

Where are the children I might have had? . . . Drowned to the
accompaniment of the rattling of a thousand douche bags.
> – Malcolm Lowry, *Under the Volcano*

Mary mother, we believe
That without sin you did conceive,
Teach us we pray thee, us believing
How to sin without conceiving.
> – Anonymous, 'Maiden's Prayer'

I remember when the women in my college dormitory gritted
their teeth and had a plastic article that looked as if it had been
made by Mattell placed inside their bodies. And I remember an
absolutely uproarious all-female brunch where a friend described her first experience with a contraceptive device, which
shot out of a bathroom window into the college quadrangle.

She never retrieved it. I wouldn't have either.
– Anne Quindlen, in *The New York Times*, 17 June 1987

See also: BIRTH CONTROL.

Control

In vayne do the husband set kepers ouer her, for who shall kepe those kepers.
– Plasidas

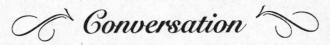

Conversation

. . . apart from theology and sex there is really nothing to talk about.
– Harold J. Laski, *Holmes–Laski Letters*

With thee conversing I forget all time,
All seasons, and their change.
– John Milton, *Paradise Lost*

Ultimately, the bond of all companionship, whether in marriage or friendship, is conversation.
– Oscar Wilde, *De Profundis*

There is no such thing as conversation. There are intersecting monologues, that is all.
– Rebecca West, *There Is No Conversation*

See also: COMMUNICATION; SPEECH; TALK.

Cooking

There is no spectacle on earth more appealing than that of a beautiful woman in the act of cooking dinner for someone she loves.

– Thomas Wolfe, *The Web and the Rock*

Cooling of Love

The feet that run to meet a date
are running slow or running late.
– Gavin Ewart, 'Ending'

Copulation

Birth, and copulation, and death,
That's all the facts when you come to brass tacks;
Birth, and copulation, and death.
– T.S. Eliot, 'Sweeney Agonistes'

Doing, a filthy pleasure is, and short;
and done, we straight repent us of sport:
Let us not rush blindly on unto it,
Like lustful beasts, that only know to do it.
– Petronius, 'Doing a Filthy Pleasure Is, and Short'

The act of sexual union is holy and pure.
– Nahmanides

See also: FORNICATION; LOVEMAKING; SEXUAL INTERCOURSE.

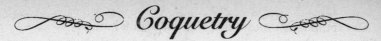

Coquetry

. . . the piquant relish of coquetry, excessively used, does not only inhibit and paralyse. It tastes sour and repellent; arouses distaste and is abjured. Lovers beware!
   – Th. Van de Velde, *Ideal Marriage*

 # Cosmetics

Where the countenance is fair, there need no colours.
   – John Lyly, *Euphues and His England*

Men say y'are fair; and fair ye are 'tis true;
But (Hark!) we praise the Painter now, not you.
   – Robert Herrick, 'Upon a Painted Gentlewoman'

Give me a look, give me a face
That makes simplicity a grace;
Robes loosely flowing, hair as free:
Such sweet neglect more taketh me
Than all the adulteries of art;
They strike my eyes, but not my heart.
   – Ben Jonson, 'Simplex Munditiis'

A girl whose cheeks are covered with paint
Has advantage with me over one whose ain't.
   – Ogden Nash, 'Biological Reflection'

The sexual–industrial complex.
   – Francine du Plessis Gray, describing the cosmetic industry,
      in *The New York Times*, 15 January 1978

Your lover must not find the dressing table covered with lotions. Art conceals its art.
   – Ovid, *Ars Amatoria*

One sprinkles the most sugar where the tart is burnt.
> – Dutch proverb

In the factory we make cosmetics; in the store we sell hope.
> – Charles Revson, quoted in A. Tobias, *Fire and Ice*

Wearing a face that she keeps in a jar by the door.
> – John Lennon and Paul McCartney, 'Eleanor Rigby'

There is no cosmetic for beauty like happiness.
> – Anonymous

All the cosmetic names seem obscenely obvious to me in their promise of sexual bliss. They are all firming or uplifting or invigorating. They make you tingle. Or glow. Or feel young. They were prepared with hormones or placentas or royal jelly. All the juice and joy in the lives of these women were to be supplied by the contents of the jars and bottles. No wonder they would spend twenty dollars for an ounce of face makeup or thirty for a half-ounce of hormone cream. What price bliss? What price sexual ecstasy?
> – Erica Jong, *How To Save Your Own Life*

Cosmetic Surgery

Anyone who gives a surgeon six thousand dollars for 'breast augmentation' should give some thought to investing a little more on brain augmentation.
> – Mike Royko

Couples

Every couple is not a pair.
> – A.B. Cheales, *Proverbial Folklore*

Our bond is not the bond of man and wife.
> – Alfred, Lord Tennyson, *Idylls of the King*

Coupling doesn't always have to do with sex ... Two people holding each other like flying buttresses. Two people depending on each other and babying each other and defending each other against the world outside. Sometimes it was worth all the disadvantages of marriage just to have that: one friend in an indifferent world.
> – Erica Jong, *Fear of Flying*

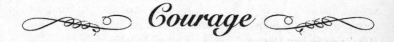

Courage

Faint heart never won fair lady.
> – William Camden, *Remains Concerning Britain*

He that feareth every bush must never go a-birding.
> – English proverb

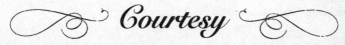

Courtesy

Formal courtesy between husband and wife is even more important than it is between strangers.
> – R.A. Heinlein, *The Notebooks of Lazarus Long*

Courtship

Better to be courted and jilted
Than never be courted at all.
– Thomas Campbell, 'The Jilted Nymph'

. . . women that delight in courting are willing to yield.
– John Lyly, *Euphues and His England*

Courtship to marriage, as a very witty prologue to a very dull play.
– William Congreve, *The Old Bachelor*

She's a woman, therefore may be woo'd
She's a woman, therefore may be won.
– William Shakespeare, *Titus Andronicus*

Then, Julia, let me woo thee
. . .
My soul I'll pour into thee.
– Robert Herrick, 'The Night Piece: To Julia'

Why, having won her, do I woo?
. . .
. . . because in short
She's not and never can be mine.
– Coventry Patmore, 'The Married Lover'

See also: WOOING.

Covetousness

Lechery and covetousness go together.
– English proverb

When all sins grow old, covetousness is young.
  – George Herbert, *Jacula Prudentum*

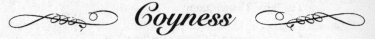

Coyness

Had we but world enough, and time,
This coyness, lady, were no crime.
. . .
But at my back I always hear
Time's wingèd chariot hurrying near.
And yonder all before us lie
Deserts of vast eternity.
  – Andrew Marvell, 'To His Coy Mistress'

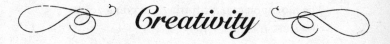

Creativity

With one woman I felt complete . . . I sincerely believed that only the two that make one are a perfect human being. The real problem was a philosophical one. How can one be complete and do something of interest when one has a permanent erection? Unthinkable, because the best part is the erection; as soon as you get rid of it you must get up and work. In order to have peace and erection one must have one right woman only, for life.
  – Jakov Lind, *Numbers: a further biography*

Crossdressing

The woman shall not wear that which pertaineth unto a man, neither shall a man put on a woman's garment; for all that do so are abomination unto the Lord thy God.
　　– The Bible: Deuteronomy

The padded man – that wears the stays.
　　– Alfred, Lord Tennyson, 'The New Timon and the Poets'

Crying

With the persuasive language of a tear.
　　– Charles Churchill, 'The Times'

He said 'I'm leaving mama; and your crying won't
　　make me stay.
The more you cry: the further I'm going away.
　　– Ida Cox, 'Misery Blues'

Cry me a river
Cry me a river
For I cried a river over you.
　　– Arthur Hamilton, 'Cry Me a River'

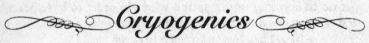

Cryogenics

A widow whose singular vice
Was to keep her late husband on ice.
　　Said, 'It's been hard since I lost him.
　　I'll never defrost him!
Cold comfort, but cheap at the price.'
　　– Anonymous Limerick

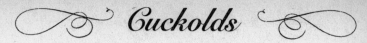

Cuckolds

You can't pluck roses without fear of thorns.
Nor enjoy a fair wife without fear of horns.
– Benjamin Franklin

I pray thee, good Lord, that I may not be married. But if I am to be married, that I may not be a cuckold. But if I am to be a cuckold, that I may not know. But if I am to know, that I may not mind.
– Isak Dinesen, *Seven Gothic Tales*: 'The Poet'

The cuckold is last that knows of it.
– William Camden, *Remains Concerning Britain*

The character of cuckoldry is perpetual; on whom it once fasteneth, it holdeth forever.
– Michel de Montaigne, *Essays III*

He that thinks himself a cuckold carries live coals in his heart.
– Thomas Fuller, *Gnomologia: Adagies and Proverbs*

Cupid

Kick that blind bastard Cupid out the door.
His mother Venus was a common whore.
– Alexander Ratcliff, 'A Satire Against Love'

Curiosity

Remember Lot's wife.
      – The Bible: Luke

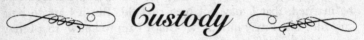

Custody

'Custody' means 'Get even'. The only get even you have . . . is the kids . . . That's the secret revenge. Get the kids!
      – Lenny Bruce, quoted in J. Cohen, *The Essential Lenny Bruce*

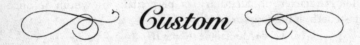

Custom

Marriage should war incessantly against a monster that is the ruin of everything. This is the monster of custom.
      – Honoré de Balzac, *The Physiology of Marriage*

Custom controls the sexual impulse as it controls no other.
      – Margaret Sanger, in *American Mercury*, 1924

Dalliance

Good for thee to have dalliance in a woman's arms.
– Homer, *Iliad*

Sweet dalliance keepeth wrinkles long away;
Repentance follows them that refuse.
– Henry Constable, 'Sonnets to Diana'

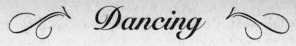

Dancing

Through dancing many maidens have been unmaidened . . .
> – John Northbrooke, *Against Dicing*

Refrain from dancing which was the means that lost John Baptist's head.
> – John Lyly, *Euphues and His England*

Dancing is a perpendicular expression of a horizontal desire.
> – Anonymous

Dancing begets warmth, which is the parent of wantonness. It is, Sir, the great grandfather of cuckoldom.
> – Henry Fielding, *Love in Several Masques*

Dancing is wonderful training for girls, it's the first way you learn to guess what a man is going to do before he does it.
> – Christopher Morley, *Kitty Foyle*

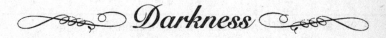

Darkness

In darkness there is no choice.
> – J.C. and A.W. Hare, *Guesses at Truth*

When all candles be out, all cats be grey.
> – John Heywood, *A Dialogue containing the number in effect of all the Proverbs in the English Tongue*

When the candles are out, all women are fair.
> – Plutarch, *Conjugal Precepts*

By candlelight a goat and a lady look alike.
> – French proverb

Regarding what is below the girdle, it is impossible of two women to know an old one from a young one. In the dark all cats are grey.
– Benjamin Franklin, letter, 25 June 1745

The dark night makes every woman beautiful. . . . In the dark all blemishes are hid, every fault overlooked, that hour makes any woman fair . . . Do not let too strong a light come into your bedroom. There are in a Beauty a great many things which are enhanced by being seen only in a half-light.
– Ovid, *Ars Amatoria*

Night hath better sweets to prove
Venus now wakens and wakens love,
Come, let us our rites begin;
'Tis only daylight that makes sin.
– John Milton, 'L'Allegro'

Dating

Don't go with girls you'd be ashamed to marry.
– John Updike, *Couples*

Stop looking at the opposite sex as the enemy . . . Don't tell your life story at a first meeting. Especially avoid talking about your personal problems. Don't describe your long-term marital ambitions on the first date.
– Abby Hirsch

The traditional male–female dynamic is enjoyable. We like doors opened for us and meals paid for on the first date. Otherwise we think he's cheap.
– Christina Hoff Sommers, in *Esquire*, February 1994

It's just time to marry, that's all . . . I'm so tired of dating! I'm so tired of keeping up a good front!
    – Anne Tyler, *Breathing Lessons*

The fellow was supposed to bring me home, lead me safely through the asphalt jungle, protect me from slithering snakes, rapists and the like. But my mother and I knew young men were apt to drink too much, to slosh down so many rye-and-gingers that some hero might well lead me in front of an oncoming bus, smash his daddy's car into Tiffany's window, or less gallantly throw up on my dress. Mad money was for getting home on your own, no matter what form of insanity your date happened to evidence.
    – Anne Roiphe, in Shirley Morahan, *A Woman's Place*

. . . men generally pay all the expenses on a date . . . Either sex may bring a little gift, its value to be determined by the bizarreness of the sexual request to be made later in the evening.
    – P.J. O'Rourke, *Modern Manners*

I feel that the moment a date happens that it is a social encounter. And the question of sex needs to be negotiated from the first moment on.
    – Camille Paglia, *Sex, Art, and American Culture*

⟫⟫— *Daydreaming* —⟪⟪

She was the kind of girl who while being made love to would calmly reflect that tomorrow was the day for cleaning the parlour.
    – Arnold Bennett, 'Things that Have Interested Me In the Tube'

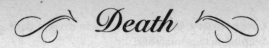

Death

In Heaven
If I cry to you then, will you hear or know?
– A.C. Swinburne 'The Triumph of Time'

Men have died from time to time and worms have eaten them,
but not for love.
– William Shakespeare, *As You Like It*

The difference between sex and death is, with death you can do
it alone and nobody's going to make fun of you.
– Woody Allen, in *The New York Times*, 1 December 1975

May I grow languid in the work of Venus, when I die, may I
perish in the act; and, may a friend, weeping over my body, say
this of me: He died as he lived.
– Ovid, *Ars Amatoria*

He loves too much who dies for love.
– Randle Cotgrave, *Dictionary*

Death is orgasm is rebirth is death is orgasm.
– William Burroughs, *The Ticket that Exploded*

Death is the only pure, beautiful conclusion of a great passion.
– D.H. Lawrence, *Fantasia of the Unconscious*

When I am dead and over me bright April
Shakes out her rain-drenched hair
Though you should lean above me broken-hearted
I shall not care.
– Sara Teasdale, 'I Shall Not Care'

When I am dead, my dearest,
    Sing no sad songs for me;
Plant thou no roses at my head,

Nor shady cypress tree:
Be the green grass above me
    With showers and dewdrops wet;
And if thou wilt, remember,
    And if thou wilt, forget.
– Christina Rossetti, 'When I am Dead'

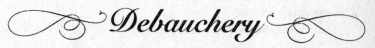

Debauchery

Debauchery and love cannot live together.
    – Jean-Jacques Rousseau, *La Nouvelle Héloïse*

Not joy but joylessness is the mother of debauchery.
    – Friedrich W. Nietzsche, *Human All-Too-Human*

Debauchee: One who so earnestly pursued pleasure that he has had the misfortune to overtake it.
    – Ambrose Bierce, *The Devil's Dictionary*

After a debauch, one feels oneself to be more solitary, more abandoned.
    – Charles Baudelaire, *Intimate Journals*

True debauchery is liberating because it creates no obligations. In it you possess only yourself; hence it remains the favourite pastime of great lovers of their own person.
    – Albert Camus, *The Fall*

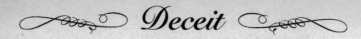

Venus lends deaf ears to love's deceits.
> – Ovid, *Amores*

Men in matters of love have as many ways to deceive as they have words to utter.
> – John Lyly, *Euphues and His England*

Who can deceive a lover?
> – Virgil, *Aeneid*

Deceit is the game of small minds and is therefore the proper pursuit of women.
> – Pierre Corneille, *Nicomède*

It is a double pleasure to deceive the deceiver.
> – Jean de La Fontaine, *Caractères*

He that once deceives is ever suspect.
> – English proverb

A man does not look behind the door unless he has stood there himself.
> – Henri DuBois

> O what a tangled web we weave
> When first we practise to deceive.
> – Sir Walter Scott, *Marmion*

> O what a tangled web we weave
> When first we practise to deceive!
> But when we've practised quite a while
> How vastly we improve our style!
> – J.R. Hope, 'A Word Of Encouragement'

If she be false, O then heaven mocks itself.
I'll not believe it.
– William Shakespeare, *Othello*

It is not difficult to deceive the first time, for the deceived possesses no antibodies, unvaccinated by suspicion, she overlooks latenesses, accepts absurd excuses, permits the flimsiest patching to repair great rents in the quotidian.
– John Updike, *Couples*

Love is only half the illusion; the lover but not his love, is deceived.
– George Santayana, *The Life of Reason*

~⟡ Declarations of Love ⟡~

I get no kick from champagne
Mere alcohol doesn't thrill me at all
So tell me why should it be true
That I get a kick out of you?
– Cole Porter, 'I Get a Kick Out of You', from the musical
Anything Goes

. . . when I look on you a moment, then can I speak no more, but my tongue falls silent, and at once a delicate flame courses beneath my skin, and with my eyes I see nothing, and my ears hum, and a wet sweat bathes me, and a trembling seizes me all over . . .
– Sappho

Night and day, you are the one.
– Cole Porter, 'Night and Day', from the musical *Gay Divorcée*

Come to me
Not as a river willingly downward falls
To be lost in a wide ocean.
But come to me
As flood-time comes to shore-line
Filling empty bays
With a white stillness
Mating earth and sea.
– Anne Wilkinson, 'In June and Gentle Oven'

I want to do with you
What spring does
With the cherry trees.
– Pablo Neruda

. . . I gave you the whole sun and stars to play with. I gave you
eternity in a single moment, strength of the mountains in one
clasp of your arms, and the volume of the seas in one impulse of
your soul . . . I have given you the greatest of all things; and you
ask me to give you little things. I gave you your own soul: you
ask for my body as a plaything. Was it not enough? Was it not
enough?
– George Bernard Shaw, *Getting Married*

You have opened up the prison gates of my womanhood. And
all the passion that was unsatisfied in me for so many years,
leaped into a wild reckless storm boundless as the sea.
– Emma Goldman, Letter to Ben Reitman

Entreat me not to leave thee, and to return from not following
after thee; for whither thou goest, I will go; and whither thou
lodgest, I will lodge; thy people shall be my people, and thy God
my God; where thou diest, will I die, and there will I be buried;
the Lord do so to me, and more also, if aught but death part thee
and me.
– The Bible: The Book of Ruth

terrified again
of not loving
of loving and not you
of being loved and not by you

if you do not love me I shall not be loved
if I do not love you I shall not love
– Samuel Beckett, 'Cascando'

Defects in a Lover

Never look a worm in the apple of your eye.
– Langston Hughes, in *Reader's Digest*, May 1973

. . . a laggard in love.
– Sir Walter Scott, *Marmion*

I'm a one-hour mama, so no one-minute papa
Ain't the kind of man for me.
– Porter Granger, 'One-Hour Mama'

She wanted to be the reason for everything and so was the cause
of nothing.
– Djuna Barnes, *Nightwood*

See also: LOVER: INEPT.

Definitions of Love

It is a fire, it is a coal.
It is a pretty, pretty thing;
It is a prick, it is a sting,

What thing is love for (well I wot) love is a thing
Whose flame creeps in at every hole.
– George Peele, 'The Hunting of Cupid'

Love is an act of endless forgiveness, a tender look which
becomes a habit.
– Peter Ustinov, in *Christian Science Monitor*, 12 September
1958

Love is the wisdom of the fool and the folly of the wise.
– Samuel Johnson, *Johnsonian Miscellanies*

Love is man unfinished.
– Paul Éluard, 'Out of Sight in the Direction of My Body'
(trans. by Samuel Beckett)

Love is not the dying moan of a distant violin; it's the triumphant twang of a bedspring.
– S.J. Perelman (attributed)

Love is the best, most insidious, most effective instrument of
social repression.
– Rainer Werner Fassbinder (attributed)

Love is an attempt to change a piece of the dreamworld into
reality.
– Theodore Reik, *The Psychology of Sex Relations*

Love is a hole in the heart.
– Ben Hecht, *Winkleberg*

Love is the tact of every good,
The only warmth, the only peace.
– Delmore Schwartz, 'For the One Who Would Take Man's
Life in His Hands'

Love is form, and cannot be without
important substance
– Charles Olsen, 'The Maximus Poems'

It was gotten by despair
Upon impossibility.
– Andrew Marvell, 'Definition of Love'

Love is the unconditional acceptance of him and his feelings.
– Marabel Morgan, *The Total Woman*

Love is mutuality of devotion forever subduing the antagonisms
inherent in divided functions.
– Erik Erikson

. . . love is always self-sacrifice, the sacrifice of identity, will and
body integrity, in order to fulfil and redeem the masculinity of
her lover.
– Andrea Dworkin, in a speech, 1975

Love is much nicer to be in than an automobile accident, a tight
girdle, a higher tax bracket or a holding pattern over Phila-
delphia.
– Judith Viorst, in *Redbook* (New York), February 1975

Love is like quicksilver in the hand.
Leave the fingers open and it stays.
Clutch it and it darts away.
– Dorothy Parker

Love is the realization that one woman differs from another.
– M. Levy, *The Moons of Paradise*

Love is the delusion that one woman differs from another.
– H.L. Mencken, *A Mencken Chrestomathy*

Love is not love until love's vulnerable.
— Theodore Roethke, *The Dream*

Love is a mystery which, when solved, evaporates.
— Ned Rorem, *Music From the Inside Out*

Love is sweet, but tastes better with bread.
— Yiddish proverb

Love is the victim's response to the rapist.
— Ti-Grace Atkinson, quoted in the *Sunday Times Magazine*
(London), 14 September 1969

Love is a sickness full of woes
    All remedies refusing.
— Samuel Daniel, 'Love is a Sickness'

Love, it's a bitch.
— Mick Jagger and Keith Richard, 'Bitch'

If love is the answer, could you rephrase the question.
— Lily Tomlin (attributed)

Love is the answer, but while you're waiting for the answer sex
raises some pretty good questions.
— Woody Allen

Love is the most important emotion that people can expect to
feel in U.S. society – it's obligatory for getting married, and lack
of it can legitimate not being married or getting out of a
marriage.
— John Gagnon, *Human Sexualities*

Love doesn't make the world go 'round.
Love is what makes the ride worthwhile.
— Franklin P. Jones (attributed)

Love is a game in which both players cheat.
  – E.W. Howe, *County Town Sayings*

What is love but the payoff for the consent to oppression? What is love but need? What is love but fear? In a just society would we need love?
  – Ti-Grace Atkinson, *Amazon Odyssey*

Love is an irresistible desire to be irresistibly desired.
  – Robert Frost, *Comment*

Love is when two people who care for each other get confused.
  – Bob Schneider (attributed)

  Love is like a faucet, you can turn it off an' on,
  But when you think you've got it, it's done turned off
      and gone.
  – Blues song

Love is, above all, gift of oneself.
  – Jean Anouilh, *Ardèle*

Love is just a four-letter word.
  – Bob Dylan, Title of song

  Love is a universal migraine
  A bright stain on the vision
  Blotting out reason.
  – Robert Graves, 'Symptoms of Love'

Love is so simple.
  – Jacques Prévert (attributed)

Love is two minutes fifty-two seconds of squishing noises. It shows your mind is not clicking.
  – Johnny Rotten (attributed)

Love is a sour delight, a sugar'd grief, a living death, an ever-dying life.
> – Thomas Watson

Love is a fiend, a fire, a hell,
Where pleasure, pain, and repentance dwell.
> – Richard Barnfield

Love is a transitive word.
> – Anonymous

Love, what is it? A cork and a bottle.
> – André Malraux, *Man's Fate*

Love is my religion – I could die for it.
> – John Keats

Love in young men, for the most part, is not love at all but simply sexual desire and its accomplishment is its end.
> – Miguel de Cervantes, *Don Quixote*

Definitions of Sex

Sex is the last refuge of the miserable.
> – Quentin Crisp, *The Naked Civil Servant*

Sex is a short cut to everything.
> – Anna Cummings, *The Love Quest*

Sex is like money; only too much is enough.
> – John Updike, *Couples*

Sex is a conversation carried out by other means.
> – Peter Ustinov, quoted in W. Lewis, *Speaking Frankly*

See also: SEX.

Defloration

Play with me and hurt me not,
Jest with me and shame me not.
– Gabriel Harvey, *Marginalia*

Were not my pipkin crackt before,
I vow I would be his wife.
– *Bagford Ballads*

Love, then unstinted, Love did sip
And cherries plucked fresh from the lip;
On cheeks and roses free he fed;
Lasses like autumn plums did drop.
And lads indifferently did crop
A flower and a maidenhead.
– Richard Lovelace, 'Love Made in the First Age: To Chloris'

See also: VIRGINITY.

Delay

Delay is a great procuress.
– Ovid, *Ars Amatoria*

Desires are nourished by delays.
– John Ray, *English Proverbs*

Sweet reluctant amorous delay.
– John Milton, *Paradise Lost*

Deliberation

When love once pleads admission to our hearts
(In spight of all the virtue we can boast)
The woman that deliberates is lost.
– Joseph Addison, *Cato*

Demi-Vierge

Thais never screws.
Lots of men crave her body,
and lots have tried to get a piece;
but nobody, no one
in the whole city can claim that he
has ever screwed Thais.
Is Thais then Miss Purity?
Not quite, it is just that Thais
believes in oral contraception.
– Martial, *Select Epigrams of Martial* (trans. and adapted by
  Donald C. Goertz)

Denial of Love

Roused by your naked grief and beauty,
For lust he will burn:
'Turn to me sweetheart! Why do you not turn?'
– Robert Graves, 'A Lost Jewel'

You say it is only a trifle
you are asking;
it is true it is only a trifle

you are asking,
then it is only a trifle
I am refusing.
– Martial, *Selected Epigrams of Martial* (trans. and adapted by
    Donald C. Goertz)

I'd rather have my cake burn than you should turn it.
. . . Better to be deny'd than deceived . . .
A civil denial is better than a rude grant.
– Thomas Fuller, *Gnomologia: Adagies and Proverbs*

[Perhaps] a great love is never returned.
– Dag Hammarskjöld, *Markings*

He that asketh faintly beggeth a denial.
– English proverb

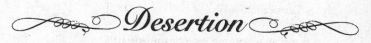

Desertion

[Men] are all but stomachs, and we all but food
They eat us hungrily, and when they are full
They belch us.
– William Shakespeare, *Othello*

I woke up this morning with an awful aching head
My new man had left me; just a room and an empty
    bed.
– Bessie Smith, 'Empty Bed Blues'

Did you ever wake up, just at the break of day
With your arms around the pillow, where your daddy
used to lay.
– Ma Gertrude Rainey, 'Bad Luck Blues'

When you're going to pull out on someone, tell them first.
– John Irving, *The World According to Garp*

 *Desire*

I was tortured by sexual desire and had been for many years.
– W.B. Yeats, *Autobiographies*

To blurt it out in a word – we want laying.
– Aristophanes, *Lysistrata*

The warm beast of desire that lies curled up in our loins and stretches itself with a fierce gentleness.
– Albert Camus, *Notebooks*

I know the nature of women, when you want to, they don't want to; and when you don't want to, they desire exceedingly.
– Terence, *Eunuchus*

> A virgin's longing is a consuming fire,
> A hundred times worse is a man's desire.
– Jean-Baptiste Louis Gresset, *Vert-Vert*

A true saying it is, desire hath no rest.
– Robert Burton, *The Anatomy of Melancholy*

Better go away longing than loathing.
– Thomas Fuller, *Gnomologia: Adagies and Proverbs*

The same desires disturb a gnat and an elephant.
– Michel de Montaigne, *Essays*

If you wish to drown, do not torture yourself with shallow water.
– Bulgarian proverb

> To drink is a small matter,
> To be thirsty is everything.
> – Georges Duhamel, *The Heart's Domain*

Want a thing long enough, and you don't.
> – Chinese proverb

Hungry dogs will eat dirty puddings.
> – Robert Burton, *The Anatomy of Melancholy*

The man's desire is for the woman; but the woman's desire is rarely other than for the desire of the man.
> – Samuel Taylor Coleridge, in *Table Talk*, 23 July 1837

There are two tragedies in life: One is not to get your heart's desire. The other is to get it.
> – George Bernard Shaw, *Man and Superman*

Desire is the very essence of man.
> – Baruch Spinoza, *Ethics*

He who desires, but acts not, breeds pestilence.
> – William Blake, *The Marriage of Heaven and Hell*

'You like doing this? I don't mean simply me. I mean the thing itself?'

'I adore it.'

That is above all what he wanted to hear. Not merely the love of one person, but the animal instinct, the simple undifferentiated desire; that was the force that would tear the Party to pieces.
> – George Orwell, *1984*

> For love, and love alone of all our joys
> By full possession does but fan the fire;
> The more we still enjoy, the more we still desire.
> – Lucretius, *Concerning the Nature of Love* (trans. by John Dryden)

DESIRE

Women wise increase desiring
　　By combining kind delays.
– William Congreve, 'The Reconciliation'

I came upon no wine
So wonderful as thirst.
– Edna St Vincent Millay, 'Feast'

If you drive nature out with a pitchfork, she will soon find a way back.
　　– Horace, *Epistles*

It's ill-becoming for an old broad to sing about how bad she wants it. But occasionally we do.
　　– Lena Horne, in *Time*, 17 October 1988

The shame of ageing is not that desire should fail (who mourns for something he no longer needs?): it is that someone else must be told.
　　– W.H. Auden

'Tis not the meat, but 'tis the appetite
Makes eating a delight.
– Sir John Suckling, 'Of Thee, Kind Boy'

Destiny

Hanging and marriage, you know, go by destiny.
　　– George Farquhar, *The Recruiting Officer*

Detumescence

> But Oh what envy God conspires
> To snatch his Power
> yet leaves him the Desire.
> – John Wilmot, Earl of Rochester 'The Disappointment'

> Too late, too late, you cannot enter now.
> – Alfred, Lord Tennyson, *Idylls of the King*

See also: HAIRTRIGGER TROUBLE.

Devotion

There is nothing in the world like the devotion of a married woman; it is something no married man knows anything about.
> – Oscar Wilde

Diamonds

Kissing your hand may make you feel very, very good but a diamond and sapphire bracelet lasts forever.
> – Anita Loos, *Gentlemen Prefer Blondes*

Diaphragm

. . . nothing can come of us: of me with my grim techniques or you who have sealed your womb with a ring of convulsive rubber.
> – James Dickey, *Poems 1957–1967*: 'Adultery'

A voice from a jar of vaseline: 'This too is love.'
— Gavin Ewart, 'Lifelines'

There was a young couple named Kelly
Who were forced to walk belly to belly.
    Because in their haste,
    They used library paste
For what they thought was vaginal jelly.
— Anonymous English Limerick

Out, vile jelly.
    — William Shakespeare, *King Lear*

See also: BIRTH CONTROL; CONTRACEPTION.

Dieting

. . . unnecessary dieting is because everything from television to fashion ads have made it seem wicked to cast a shadow. This wild, emaciated look appeals to some women, though not many men, who are seldom seen pinning up a *Vogue* illustration in a machine shop.
    — Peg Bracken, *The I Hate to Cook Book*

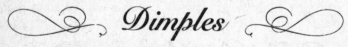

Dimples

Love made those hollows.
    — William Shakespeare, *Venus and Adonis*

A dimple in the chin;
A devil within.
— Irish proverb

Many a man in love with a dimple makes the mistake of marrying the whole girl.
> – Stephen Leacock

Dinner

Better a dinner of herbs where love is, than a stalled ox and
hatred therewith.
> – The Bible: Proverbs

Dirty Old Men

You think it horrible that lust and rage
Should dance attendance upon my old age;
They were not such a plague when I was young,
What else have I to spur me into song?
> – W.B. Yeats, 'The Spur'

I am almost done with harridans, and shall soon become old
enough to fall in love with girls of fourteen.
> – Jonathan Swift, Letter to Alexander Pope at the age of 57

I am rather prone to senile lechery just now – want to touch the
right person in the right place, in order to shake off bodily
loneliness.
> – E.M. Forster, Letter to J.R. Ackerley, 16 October 1961

Even dirty old men need love.
> – Graffito

Discretion

Discreet wives have sometimes neither eyes nor ears.
– Thomas Fuller, *Gnomologia: Adagies and Proverbs*

Disdain

If they be adorned with beauty, they be strait laced and made so
high in the instep, that they disdain them most that desire them.
– John Lyly, *Euphues and His England*

Dismissal

Here is the door, and there is the way, and so . . . farewell.
– John Heywood, *A Dialogue containing the number in effect of all
the Proverbs in the English Tongue*

                        please
close the door
gently as you go.
– Allen Tate, 'Letting Him Go'

Divorce

All women are stimulated by the news that any wife has left any
husband.
– Anthony Powell, *The Acceptance World*

So many persons think that divorce is the panacea for every ill, who find out, when they try it, that the remedy is worse than the disease.
— Dorothy Dix, *Dorothy Dix, Her Book*

What God hath joined together no man shall ever put asunder: God will take care of that.
— George Bernard Shaw, *Getting Married*

Only a marriage with partners strong enough to risk divorce is strong enough to avoid it . . .
— Carolyn Heilbrun, 'Marriage is the Message', in *Ms*., August 1974

Tomorrow to fresh woods and pastures new.
— John Milton, *Lycidas*

The finest shoe often hurts the foot.
— John Clarke, *Paroemiologia Anglo-Latina*

The three 'gets': get a lawyer, get a job, get laid.
— Judith Crist, advice to women contemplating divorce, in *New York*, 8 May 1972

The difference between divorce and legal separation is that legal separation gives a husband time to hide his money.
— Johnny Carson (attributed)

In our family we don't divorce our men – we bury them.
— Ruth Gordon (attributed)

You don't know a woman until you have met her in court.
— Norman Mailer (attributed)

The happiest time of anyone's life is just after the first divorce.
— John Kenneth Galbraith (attributed)

Cast not out the foul water till you bring in the clean.
> – David Fergusson, *Scottish Proverbs*

Divorces are made in heaven.
> – Oscar Wilde, *The Importance of Being Earnest*

Take it if you can take it, and if you can't take it, get out.
> – Erica Jong, *How to Save Your Own Life*

When a marriage goes on the rocks, the rocks are there, right there.
> – Tennessee Williams, *Cat on a Hot Tin Roof*, stage directions: Big Mama points to the bed.

Being divorced is like being hit by a Mack truck – if you survive you start looking very carefully to the right and left.
> – Jean Kerr, *Mary, Mary*

A divorce is like an amputation, you survive, but there is less of you.
> – Margaret Atwood, in *Time*, 1973

Better a tooth out, then always aching.
> – Thomas Fuller, *Gnomologia: Adagies and Proverbs*

You can make divorce as easy as a dog licence, but you can't burn away the sense of shame and waste.
> – A. Alvarez, *Life After Marriage*

There is a rhythm to the ending of a marriage just like the rhythm of a courtship – only backward. You try to start again but get into blaming over and over. Finally you are both worn out, exhausted, hopeless. Then lawyers are called in to pick clean the corpses. The death has occurred much earlier.
> – Erica Jong, *How to Save Your Own Life*

You don't dare entertain
questions like – can I start again?
seek divorce?
– Dannie Abse, *Portrait of a Marriage*

I don't want the cheese; I just want out of the trap.
– Spanish saying

See also: MARRIAGE: END OF.

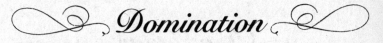 *Domination*

It is a silly flock where the ewe bears the bell.
– David Fergusson, *Scottish Proverbs*

When a man curls his lip, when he uses ridicule, when he grows
angry, you have touched a raw nerve in domination.
– Sheila Rowbotham, *Woman's Consciousness, Man's World*

Who knows not Circe,
The Daughter of the Sun, whose charmed cup
Whoever tasted, lost his upright shape,
And downward fell into a grovelling swine.
– John Milton, *Comus*

Disguise our bondage as we will,
'Tis woman, woman, rules us still.
– Thomas Moore, 'Sov'reign Woman'

Do you come to me to bend me to your will
As conqueror to the vanquished
To make me a bond slave
To bear your children, wearing out my life
In drudgery and silence
No servant will I be.

> If that be what you ask, O lover
>> I refuse you.
> – Christina Walsh, 'A Woman to Her Lover ("Proudly")'

I always run into strong women who are looking for weak men to dominate them.
> – Andy Warhol

See also: POWER.

Don Juans

Unyielding pride, a desire to subjugate others, the provocative lord of battle, the need for ascendancy, these are his predominant features. Sensuality is but a secondary importance compared to these.
> – Hippolyte Taine, quoted in Arno Karlen, *Sexuality and Homosexuality*

If the Don Juans and Don Juanesses only obeyed their desires, they'd have very few affairs. They have to tickle themselves up imaginatively before they can start being casually promiscuous.
> – Aldous Huxley, *Point Counter Point*

Any man that can't find what he is looking for in a thousand women is really looking for a boy.
> – Gershon Legman, *Rationale of the Dirty Joke*

See also: PROMISCUITY.

⇜ *Double Standard* ⇝

The pot calls the pan burnt-arse.
> – John Clarke, *Paroemiologia Anglo-Latina*

When the goose drinks as deep as the gander, pots are soon empty and the cupboard bare.
> – C.H. Spurgeon, *John Ploughman's Pictures*

As well as for the cow calf as for the bull.
> – John Heywood, *A Dialogue containing the number in effect of all the Proverbs in the English Tongue*

Thou rangest like a town bull, why art thou so incensed if she tread awry?
> – Robert Burton, *Anatomy of Melancholy*

> Hogamus higamus,
> Men are polygamous.
> Higamous hogamus,
> Women are monogamous.
> – Anonymous

> Women want monogamy
> Man delights in novelty.
> Love is woman's moon and sun
> Man has other forms of fun.
> Woman lives but in her lord
> Count to ten and man is bored.
> What this the gist and sum of it,
> What earthly good can come of it.
> – Dorothy Parker, 'General Review of the Sex Situation'

We still have these double standards where the emphasis is all on the male's sexual appetites – that it's OK for him to collect as many scalps as he can before he settles down and 'pays the price'. If a woman displays the same attitude, all the epithets that exist

in the English language are laid at her door, and with extra-
ordinary bitterness.
– Glenda Jackson

. . . nothing could be more grotesquely unjust than a code of
morals, reinforced by laws, which relieves men from responsibility for irregular sex acts, and for the same acts drives women
to abortion, infanticide, prostitution, and self-destruction.
– Suzanne LaFollette, *Concerning Women*

Doubt

Mrs Murphy's First Law of When in Doubt: don't.
Mrs Murphy's Second Law of When in Doubt: stop.
Mrs Murphy's Third Law of When in Doubt: go home.
Mrs Murphy's Fourth Law of When in Doubt: fake it.
Mrs Murphy's Fifth Law of When in Doubt: worry.
– Lin Field, *Mrs Murphy's Laws*

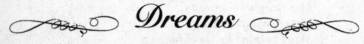

Dreams

A man doesn't dream about a woman because he thinks her
'mysterious'; he decides that she is 'mysterious' to justify his
dreaming about her.
– Henri de Montherlant, 'The Goddess Cypris'

Dreaming is the poor retreat of the lazy, hopeless and imperfect
lover.
– William Congreve, *Love for Love*

I do not understand the capricious lewdness of the sleeping mind.
– John Cheever, *The Journals*

     Come to me in my dreams, and then
By day I shall be well again.
For then the night will be more than
The hopeless longing of day.
– Matthew Arnold, 'Longing'

Forgo your dream, poor fool of love.
– Catullus, *Carmina* (trans. by Sir W. Marris)

Like a dog, he hunts in dreams.
– Alfred, Lord Tennyson, 'Locksley Hall'

(dreaming,
et
    cetera, of
Your smile
eyes knees and of your Etcetera)
– e.e. cummings, 'my sweet old etcetera'

   See also: FANTASY.

Dress

You must have women dressed, if it is only for the pleasure of imagining them as Venuses.
– George Moore

Byron said, her costume began too late and ended too soon.
– William Hazlitt, *Four Generations of a Literary Family*

. . . a freshman section of girls who were almost all dressed *à la négligence* in the present fribble-frabble of fashion, mostly jeans and wee pannikins.
— Alexander Theroux, *Darconville's Cat*

. . . when Dwayne and Trout and I were boys, girls concealed their underpants at all costs and boys tried to see their underpants at all costs.
— Kurt Vonnegut, Jr, *Breakfast of Champions*

You don't have to signal a social conscience by looking like a frump. Lace knickers won't hasten the holocaust, you can ban the bomb in a feather boa just as well as without, and a mild interest in hemlines doesn't necessarily disqualify you from reading *Das Kapital* and agreeing with every word.
— Jill Tweedie

See also: CLOTHES; FETISHES; LINGERIE.

Drinking

Sex and a cocktail: they both lasted about as long, had the same effect, and amounted to about the same thing.
— D.H. Lawrence, *Lady Chatterley's Lover*

There was an old man of Dundee,
Who came home as drunk as could be.
    He wound up the clock
    With the end of his cock
And buggered his wife with the key.
— Norman Douglas, *Some Limericks*

A drunken woman is an open door.
— German proverb

Candy
is dandy
But liquor
is quicker.
– Ogden Nash, 'Reflections on Ice-Breaking'

Litle nips of whisky, little drops of gin
Make a lady wonder where on earth she's bin.
– Anonymous

Drink to me only with thine eyes
        And I will pledge with mine;
Or leave a kiss but in the cup
        And I'll not look for wine.
– Ben Jonson, 'To Celia'

Alcohol is like love. The first kiss is magic, the second is intimate, the third is routine. After that you take the girl's clothes off.
– Raymond Chandler, *The Long Goodbye*

It provokes the desire but takes away the performance. Therefore much drink may be said to be an equivocator: it makes him and it mars him, it sets him on and it takes him off.
– William Shakespeare, *Macbeth*

Absinthe makes the tart grow fonder.
– Hugh Drummond, quoted in S. Hicks, *Vintage Year*

Drugs

. . . that desexing fumigant called grass.
– John Updike, *A Month of Sundays*

Duration of Love

How long shall I love him, I can no more tell,
Than had I a Fever, when I should be well.
– Sir George Etherege, *She Would If She Could*: 'Song'

In time the Rockies may rumble
Gibraltar may tumble
(They're only made of clay)
But our love is here to stay.
– Ira Gershwin, 'Our Love is Here to Stay', from the film
Goldwyn Follies

Duty

Love can not be a duty because it is not subject to the will.
– Bertrand Russell

Ears

Love enters a man through his eyes; a woman through her ears.
– Polish proverb

There is nothing so virtuous as the ear of an abandoned woman.
– Alfred de Musset, *Lorenzacchio*

The ears are chaste,
E'en though the eyes are bold.
– Jean de La Fontaine, *Contes et Nouvelles en Vers*: 'Le tableau'

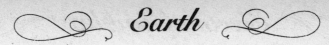

Earth

It's a bawdy planet.
> – William Shakespeare, *The Winter's Tale*

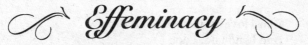

Effeminacy

. . . wanton-loined womanlings.
> – Robert Burton, *Anatomy of Melancholy*

Twiddle-poop: an effeminate looking fellow.
> – Francis Grose, *A Classical Dictionary of the Vulgar Tongue*

> For you muddled with books and pictures and china an'
>   etchings and fans,
> And your room at college was beastly – more like a
>   whore's than a man's.
> – Rudyard Kipling, 'The Mary Gloster'

> Amphibious thing! that acting either part,
> The trifling head, or the corrupted heart;
> Fop at the toilet, flatt'rer at the board,
> Now trips a lady, and now struts a Lord.
> – Alexander Pope, 'Epistle to Dr Arbuthnot'

Eighty Years of Age

My dear, when you are my age you will realize that what you need is the maturer man.
> – Lady Diana Cooper, when her name was coupled with that
> of a man soon to be a hundred years old

Electra Complex

But they pulled me out of the sack
And they stuck me together with glue.
And then I knew what to do
I made a model of you.
A man in black with a Meinkampf look.

And a love of the rack and the screw.
And I said I do, I do.
– Sylvia Plath, 'Daddy'

Elopement

If it were not for the presents, an elopement would be preferable.

– George Ade

Emasculation

It's up to the 'brothers' – they'll have to make up their own minds as to whether they will be divested of just cock privilege or – what the hell, why not say it – divested of cocks.

– Robin Morgan, in *Rat. Subterranean News* (New York)

I'll cut the fellow's knockers off so close that never a hair will stand to tell the tail.

– François Rabelais, *Gargantua and Pantagruel*

There was a young sailor named Bates
Who danced the fandango on skates,

But a fall on his cutlass
    Rendered him nutless
And practically useless on dates.
– Anonymous English Limerick

Embracing

Imparudis'd in one another's arms.
    – John Milton, *Paradise Lost*

Let him rebuke who ne'er has known the pure platonic
    grapple,
Or hugged two girls at once behind a chapel.
– Ezra Pound, 'L'Homme moyen sensuel'

    Embrace me
My sweet embraceable you.
    Embrace me
You irreplaceable you.
– Ira Gershwin, 'Embraceable You', from the musical *Girl Crazy*

Let us embrace, and from this very moment
Vow an eternal misery together.
– Thomas Otway, *The Orphan*

There is no more disturbing experience in the rich gamut of life than when a man discovers, in the midst of an embrace, that he is taking the episode quite calmly . . . His doubts and fears start from this point and there is no end to them. He doesn't know, now, whether it's love or passion. In fact, in the confusion of the moment, he's not quite sure if it isn't something else altogether, like forgery.
    – E.B. White, in *New York Journal – American*, 12 February 1961

who
makes me feel
as empty as the house does
when she's not here
who
else
but
you.
– Adrian Henri, 'Who?'

The End of Love

You like potato and I like po-tah-to,
You like tomato and I like to-mah-to,
Potato, poh-tah-to, tomato to-mah-to
Let's call the whole thing off!
– Ira Gershwin, 'Let's Call the Whole Thing Off'

I loved thee, Attis, once, in days long past.
– Sappho, in Lucas, *Greek Poetry for Everyone*

There lives within the very flame of love
A kind of wick or snuff that will abate it.
– William Shakespeare, *Hamlet*

I no longer love her, that's certain, but how I loved her
My voice tried to find the wind to touch her hearing.
– Pablo Neruda

At the beginning of love and at its end lovers are embarrassed to
be left alone.
– Jean de La Bruyère

At the end, every flower loses its perfume.
> – Italian saying

'Tis hard to drop at once old-standing love.
> – Catullus, *Carmina*

'I don't love you anymore' is the classic exit line in every relationship.
> – John Gagnon, *Human Sexualities*

After all, my erstwhile dear,
My no longer cherished,
Need we say it was not love,
Just because it perished?
> – Edna St Vincent Millay, 'Passer Mortus Est'

           . . . Cupid's curse–
'They that do change old love for new
Pray gods they change for worse.'
> – George Peele, *The Arraignment of Paris*

No argument, no anger, no remorse,
No dividing of blame.
There was poison in the cup – why should we ask
From whose hand it came?
No grief for our dead love . . .
> – Robert Graves, 'Hedges Freaked With Snow'

And if I loved you Wednesday,
     Well, what is that to you?
I do not love you Thursday
     So much is true.
> – Edna St Vincent Millay, 'Thursday'

Yet each man kills the thing he loves,
By each let this be heard.
Some do it with a bitter look,

Some with a flattering word.
The coward does it with a kiss,
The brave man with a sword!
– Oscar Wilde, 'The Ballad of Reading Gaol'

The flowers of our two hearts were bleeding to death
And perhaps we wept without either seeing the tears . . .
– Juan Rámon Jiménez, 'Nudes'

The best and the worst of this is
    That neither is most to blame,
If you've forgotten my kisses
    And I've forgotten your name.
– A.C. Swinburne, 'An Interlude'

I prithee send me back my heart
    Since I cannot have thine;
For if from thine thou wilt not part
    Why then should'st thou have mine?
– Sir John Suckling, 'Song'

The song is ended
But the melody lingers on.
– Irving Berlin, 'The Song is Ended', from the film *The Ziegfeld Follies*

Far away is close at hand
Close joined is far away,
Love shall come at your command
Yet will not stay.
– Robert Graves, *Whipperginny*: 'Song of Contrariety'

The real genius for love lies not in getting into, but getting out of love.
    – George Moore (attributed)

What shall I do
Now my love is gone?

THE END OF LOVE

Toss on an empty
Bed alone?
– Padraig O'Broin, 'Circle'

Love comes into your being like a tidal wave . . . Sometimes it
withdraws like a wave, till there isn't such a thing as a pool left,
and every bit of your heart is as dry as seaweed beyond the
wave's reach.
– Phyllis Bottome

Music I heard with you was more than music
And bread I broke with you was more than bread
Now that I am not with you, all is desolate
All that once was so beautiful is dead.
– Conrad Aiken, 'Bread and Music'

So there are no more words and all is ended
The timbrel is stilled, the clarion laid away
And Love with streaming hair goes unattended
Back to the loneliness of yesterday.
– Joseph Auslander, 'So There Are No More Words'

When love grows diseas'd, the best thing to do is to put it to a
violent death; I can not endure the torture of a lingering and
consumptive passion.
– Sir George Etherege, *The Man of Mode*

The song has ceased; my vision with the song.
– George Meredith, 'Hymn to Colour'

When love turns away, now, I don't follow it. I sit and suffer,
unprotesting, until I feel the tread of another step.
– Sylvia Ashton-Warner, *Teacher*

No, no, not love, not love. Call it by name.
Now that it's over, now that it is gone and can not hear
    us.

THE END OF LOVE
————————

It was an honest thing, Not noble. Yet no shame.
– Edna St. Vincent Millay, *Huntsman, What Quarry?*: 'What
  Savage Blossom'

Ah, when to the heart of man
Was it ever less than treason
To go with the drift of things
To yield with a grace to reason
And bow and accept at the end
Of a love or a season.
– Robert Frost, in *Vogue* (New York), 14 March 1963

The mind has a thousand eyes
    The heart but one
Yet the life of a whole life dies
    When love is done.
– Francis William Bourdillon

Wise after the event, by love withered . . .
– Robert Graves, 'Never Such Love'

Love is all programmed, it's all phasing,
there's a beginning, a middle and an end.
– Gavin Ewart, 'Ella Mi Fu Reparti!'

I had lost the power to love.
    – Henry Miller, *Nexus*

I thought when love for you died, I should die.
It's dead. Alone, strangely, I live on.
– Rupert Brooke

At first you did not love enough
And afterwards you loved too much
And you lacked the confidence to choose
And you have only yourself to blame.
– Stephen Spender, 'The Double Shame'

See also: BREAK-UP; DISMISSAL; PARTING.

THE END OF LOVE

The Enemy

Women are natural guerrillas. Scheming, we nestle in the enemy's bed, avoiding open warfare, watching the options, playing the odds.
— Sally Kempton, in *Esquire* (New York), July 1970

How can you lead us while you still copulate, relate to, traffic with, and are penetrated by the enemy 'the male?'
— Judith Densen-Gerber, *Walking in My Shoes*

If man is my aggressor, my put-down, my oppressor, would somebody tell me why I am sleeping in the enemy camp.
— Bonnie Charles Bluh, *Woman to Woman: European Feminists*

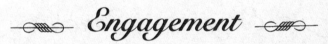

Engagement

We sat in the car park till twenty to one
And now I'm engaged to Miss Joan Hunter Dunn.
— Sir John Betjeman, *New Bats in Old Belfries*: 'A Subaltern's Love-song'

No sooner met but they looked; no sooner looked but they loved; no sooner loved but they sighed; no sooner sighed but they asked one another the reason; no sooner knew the reason but they sought the remedy; and in these degrees have they made a pair of stairs to marriage, which they will climb incontinent, or else be incontinent before marriage.
— William Shakespeare, *As You Like It*

A positive engagement to marry a certain person at a certain time, at all haps and hazards, I have always considered the most ridiculous thing on earth.
— Jane Welsh Carlyle

Equality

. . . we have passed out and beyond the era when the wife was considered sexually as a passive implement, receptacle and incubator and have recognized and accepted her as an active, adult and equivalent sexual being.

> – Th. Van de Velde, *Ideal Marriage*

Man is willing to accept woman as an equal, as a man in skirts, as an angel, as a devil, a baby-face, a machine, an instrument, a bosom, a womb, a pair of legs, an encyclopedia, an ideal, or an obscenity: the only thing he won't accept her as is a human being, a real human being of the female sex.

> – D.H. Lawrence

Erogenous Zones

He moved his lips about her ears and neck as though in thirsting search for an erogenous zone. A waste of time, he knew from experience. Erogenous zones are either everywhere or nowhere.

> – Joseph Heller, *Good as Gold*

. . . strictly speaking, the whole body is an erotogenic zone.

> – Sigmund Freud, *An Outline of Psychoanalysis*

> There was a young student named Jones
> Who'd reduce any maiden to moans.
>   By his wonderful knowledge
>   Acquired in college
> Of the nineteen erogenous zones.
>
> – Anonymous Limerick

Eros

A little more eros and less strife.
  – Norman O. Brown

Eros, the mischief maker.
  – Sigmund Freud, in Rollo May, *Love and Will*

Erotica

. . . women are the only true erotica.
  – John Ciardi, *The Browser's Dictionary*

Eroticism

In this loveless everyday life eroticism is a substitute for love.
  – Henri Lefebvre, *Everyday Life in the Modern World*

Eroticism is like a dance: one always leads the other.
  – Milan Kundera, *Immortality*

Eroticism has its own moral justification because it says that pleasure is enough for me; it is a statement of the individual's sovereignty.
  – Mario Vargas Llosa, in *International Herald Tribune*,
     23 October 1990

Eroticism is a realm stalked by ghosts. It is the place beyond the pale, both cursed and enchanted.
  – Camille Paglia, *Sexual Personae*

Estrangement

My mother and father and I now lived in the intimacy of estrangement that exists between married couples who have nothing left in common but their incompatibility.

– Nadine Gordimer, *The Lying Days*

Sleep on, I sit and watch your tent of Silence
White as a sail upon this sandy sea
And I know the Desert's self is not more boundless
Than is the distance 'twixt yourself and me.

– Laurence Hope, 'Stars of the Desert'

Eternal Love

I shall love you until death do us part and then we shall be together for ever and ever.

– Dylan Thomas, 'Under Milk Wood'

You are woman, so be lovely:
As you are lovely, so be various,
Merciful as constant, constant as various,
So be mine, as I yours for ever.

– Robert Graves, *Poems*: 'Pygmalion to Galetea'

Bind the sea to slumber still,
Bind its odour to the lily,
Bind the aspen ne'er to quiver,
Then bind love to last for ever.

– Thomas Campbell, 'How Delicious is the Winning'

He first deceased; she for a little tried
To live without him; liked it not, and died.

– Sir Henry Wotton, 'Upon the Death of Sir Albert Morton's Wife'

To see her is to love her
　　And love but her ever
For nature made her what she is
　　And never made anither.
– Robert Burns, 'Bonnie Lesley'

And I will love thee still, my dear
　　Till a' the seas gang dry.
– Robert Burns 'A Red, Red Rose'

Grow old along with me!
The best is yet to be.
The last of life, for which the first was made.
– Robert Browning, 'Rabbi Ben Ezra'

I love thee, I love but thee,
With a love that shall not die.
　　Till the sun grows old,
　　And the stars are cold,
And the leaves of the Judgment Book unfold.
– Bayard Taylor, 'Bedouin Song'

Sing the Lover's Litany:
'Love like ours can never die!'
– Rudyard Kipling, 'Lover's Litany'

No, the heart that has truly loved never forgets,
But as truly loves on to the close.
– Thomas Moore, 'Believe Me, If All Those Endearing Young
　　Charms'

It used to be 'Love Me Forever' and now it's 'Help Me Make It
Through the Night'.
　　– Anne Tyler, *Breathing Lesson*

To say that you can love one person all your life is like saying
that one candle will continue to burn as long as you live.
　　– Leo Tolstoy, 'The Kreutzer Sonata'

In a love affair, forever is at least over the weekend.
> – Anonymous

I'll see you again
Whenever spring breaks through again.
> – Noël Coward, *Bitter Sweet*

But to see her was to love her,
Love but her, and love for ever.
> – Robert Burns, 'Ae Fond Kiss'

Two such as you with such a master speed
Cannot be parted nor swept away
From one another once you are agreed
That life is only life forevermore
Together wing to wing and oar to oar.
> – Robert Frost, 'The Master Speed'

Evil

Of two evils choose the prettier.
> – Carolyn Wells (attributed)

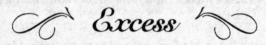

Excess

But love would not be love if it did not slip over into the excessive.
> – Edna O'Brien, *Some Irish Loving*

Even nectar is poison if taken to excess.
> – Hindu proverb

Moderation is a fatal thing: nothing succeeds as excess.
– Oscar Wilde, *A Woman of No Importance*

Excitement

We boil at different degrees.
– Ralph Waldo Emerson, *Society and Solitude: Eloquence*

Man lives by habit indeed, but what he lives for is thrills and excitement.
– William James

Excuses

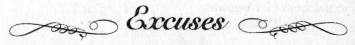

What else could we do, for we were in love?
– Paul Éluard, 'Curfew'

Yes, he said, darling, yes, of course you tried
To come, but you were kept, that's what I thought –
But something in his heart struggled and cried
Mortally, like a bird the cat caught.
– L.A.G. Strong, 'The Appointment'

Exhaustion

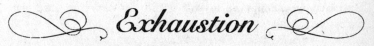

With his pecker hanging down to the floor
And his girl still imploring for more,
He said, 'Eight hours screwing

Has been my undoing –
I simply can't do it any more.'
– Anonymous Limerick

A weary bride – poor little fluff –
Said, 'My thing's all tender and rough
    I realize, Cyril
    You're terribly virile
But fourteen times is enough.'
– Anonymous Limerick

Exhibitionism

This vulgar, filthy country . . . men wagging their things at you from doorways. Disgusting.
    –J.P. Donleavy, *The Ginger Man*

It is always with doors unguarded and open, Lesbia, you offend, nor do you conceal your intrigues; and it is the spectator more than the adulterer that pleases you. No joys are grateful to do if they are hidden.
    – Martial, *Epigrams*

Existentialism

You are who you screw.
– Graffito

Expansion of Consciousness

Find a mate you can groove with. You'll then have an additional brain and sensory organs. The quantity of your experience will be at least doubled and the quality will differ because no two people perceive in exactly the same manner. With a warm, perceptive mate you'll be able to freely give and receive love.
> – Eugene Schoenfeld

Experience

To love women and never enjoy them, is as much to love wine and never taste it.
> – John Lyly, *Euphues and His England*

Drawn wells have the sweetest water.
> – John Clarke, *Paroemiologia Anglo-Latina*

Experimentation

Once, a philosopher; twice, a pervert.
> – Voltaire

Once doesn't count.
> – Lin Field, *Mrs Murphy's Laws*

When Eve ate the particular apple, she became aware of her womanhood, mentally. And mentally she began to experiment with it. She has been experimenting ever since. So has man. To the rage and horror of both of them.
> – D.H. Lawrence, *Fantasia of the Unconscious*

Exploitation

. . . the put-upon women, the delicate prey who woke up in hellish bedrooms to find their sated predators pulling on their pants . . .
> – *Newsweek* (New York), 9 November 1981

> She was one of the early birds,
> And I was one of the worms.
> – T. W. Conner, 'She was Dear Little Dickie-Bird'

See also: PREDATOR: SEXUAL.

Extremes

Be wary of extremes: the green and the over-ripe fruit cause the worst pains.
> – J.H. Rhoades, *Jonathan's Apothegms*

Eyelids

When she raises her eyelids it's as if she were taking off all her clothes.
> – Colette, *Claudine and Annie*

Eyelids: draperies for the conscience.
> – Albert A. Brandt

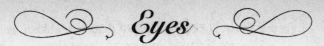

Eyes

Blue eyes say: Love me or I die; black eyes say: love me or I kill thee.
> – Spanish proverb

And in those eyes the love-light lies
And lies – and lies – and lies.
> – Anita Owen, 'Dreamy Eyes'

It needs no dictionary of quotations to remind me that the eyes are the windows of the soul.
> – Max Beerbohm, *Zuleika Dobson*

Turn not Venus into a blinded motion
Eyes are the guides of love.
> – Ezra Pound, 'Quia Pauper Amavi'

. . . the vice of her painted eyes.
> – James Joyce, *Ulysses*

A rolling eye, a roving heart.
> – Thomas Adams, *Sermons*

Choose a wife rather by your ear than your eye.
> – English proverb

Keep the eyes wide open before marriage; and half-shut afterward.
> – Thomas Fuller, *Introductio ad Prudentian*

Love's tongue is in the eyes.
> – Phineas Fletcher, *Piscatory Epilogues*

The eyes are the silent tongues of love.
> – Miguel de Cervantes, *Don Quixote*

Eyes that can feel like a hand, hands that can see like an eye.
—Johann Wolfgang von Goethe, *Roman Elegies*

 *Face*

The glory of the day was in her face,
The beauty of the night was in her eyes.
—James Weldon Johnson, 'The Glory of the Day Was in Her
Face'

Her face was her chaperone.
—Rupert Hughes

As a white candle in a holy place,
So is the beauty of an aged face.
—Joseph Campbell, 'Old Woman'

But tell me yet; this thing, thus daubed and oiled
Thus poulticed, plastered, baked by turns and boiled
Thus with pomatums, ointments, lacquered o'er,
Is it a *face*, Ursidius, or a *sore*?
—Juvenal, *Sixth Satire* (trans. by William Gifford)

My soul abhors the tasteless dry embrace
Of a stale virgin with a winter face.
—Alexander Pope, 'January and May'

My face
that my friends tell me is so full of character;
my face
I have hated for so many years,
my face
I have made an angry contract to live with
Though no one could love it.
—Diane Wakoski, *The Motorcycle Betrayal Poems*: 'I Have to
Learn to Live With My Face'

Nice legs, shame about the boat race.*
  – English catchphrase, *rhyming slang

  A face like yours could
      sell a million floppy
  discs, change hardened admen
      into optimists
  You are as beautiful as low inflation
      as tax evasion
  – Carol Ann Duffy, 'The Businessman's Love Poem'

It has been said that a pretty face is a passport. But it's not, it's a
visa, and it runs out fast.
  – Julie Burchill, 'Kiss and Sell', in the *Mail on Sunday*, 1988

Faithfulness

. . . Young men want to be faithful and are not,
Old men want to be faithless and can not.
  – Oscar Wilde, *The Picture of Dorian Gray*

I have been faithful to thee, Cynara! in my fashion.
  – Ernest Dowson, 'Non Sum Qualis Eram Bonae Sub Regno
      Cynarae'

  If I, by miracle, can be
  This live-long minute true to thee,
  'Tis all that heaven allows.
  – John Wilmot, Earl of Rochester, 'Love and Life'

Those who are faithless know the pleasures of love; it is those
who are faithful who know love's tragedies.
  – Oscar Wilde, *The Picture of Dorian Gray*

The seas shall run dry,
And the rocks melt into sands;
Then shall I love you still, my dear,
When all these things are done.
– Anonymous, 'The Young Man's Farewell to His Love'

 *Faking It*

To know how to live is to know how to simulate.
  – Antoinette Deshoulières, *Le Ruisseau*

Despairing of her own climax, she would give herself in slavish postures as if witnessing . . . the trapped unclotted thump of his ejaculation made it her own.
  – John Updike, *Couples*

Each sister faking orgasm . . . does it to survive.
  – Robin Morgan, *Sisterhood is Powerful*

Help with your own hands, if necessary; have him play with you while he is f . . . . . g you. This is a fairly dumb analogy, but I think declaring to yourself you will have an orgasm is not unlike a politician declaring he will run for office. You have a better chance of getting nominated and elected if you 'declare' – very few politicians get drafted.
  – Helen Gurley Brown

The vast majority of women who pretend vaginal orgasms are faking it to 'get the job'.
  – Ti-Grace Atkinson

The only time a woman has a true orgasm is when she is shopping. Every other time she's faking it. It's common courtesy.
  – Joan Rivers

Women fake orgasm if they really care about the man because they don't want him to feel a sense of failure. I think it's really a kind thing that women do. But they're probably doing themselves an injustice, because probably, if they could get over it, if they didn't fake it, and they learned how to relax, they would probably have their orgasm. Some men aren't good enough to give it to you.

    – Annie Flanders

Falling in Love

Falling in love with love is falling for make-believe.
– Lorenz Hart, Song

Falling in love is something you forget, like pain.
    – Nina Bawden, *The Grain of Truth*

I can't fall in love. That's probably what holds my marriage together.
    – Joseph Heller, *Something Happened*

Do you love me or do you not?
You told me once, but I forgot.
– Anonymous, in W.R.E. (Waldo Espy), *Another Almanac of Words at Play*

In shallow shoals, English soles do it,
Goldfish in the privacy of bowls, do it,
Let's do it, let's fall in love.
– Cole Porter, 'Let's Do It'

One doesn't fall in love; one grows into love, and love grows in him.
    – Karl Menninger

Falling in love consists merely in uncorking the imagination and bottling the common-sense.
– Helen Rowland, *A Guide to Men*

 False Love

> Farewell, false love, the oracle of lies,
> A mortal foe and enemy to rest:
> . . .
> False Love; Desire; Beauty frail adieu
> Dead is the root whence all these fancies grew.
> – Sir Walter Raleigh, 'A Farewell to False Love'

False in one thing, false in everything.
– Legal maxim

> Love in her sunny eyes does basking play;
> Love walks the pleasant mazes of her hair;
> Love does on both her lips forever stray;
> And sows and reaps a thousand kisses there.
> In all her outward parts Love's always seen;
>   But, oh, he never went within.
> – Abraham Cowley, 'The Change'

> False though she be to me and love,
>   I'll ne'er pursue revenge;
> . . .
> And though the present I regret,
>   I'm grateful for the past.
> – William Congreve

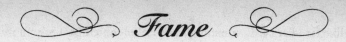

Fame

Fame is a powerful aphrodisiac.
> – Graham Greene, in the *Radio Times*, 10 September 1964

Familiarity

Familiarity breeds contempt.
> – Publilius Syrus, *Sententiae*

Familiarity breeds content.
> – Roy Goliard, *A Scholar's Glossary of Sex*

Familiarity breeds attempt.
> – Anonymous

Familiarity breeds.
> – Leonard Lewis Levinson, *Bartlett's Unfamiliar Quotations*

Though familiarity may not breed contempt, it takes the edge off admiration.
> – William Hazlitt, *Characteristics*

Familiarity doesn't breed contempt. It is contempt.
> – Florence King

Sweets grown common lose their dear delight.
> – William Shakespeare, 'Sonnet 102'

The man who enters his wife's dressing room is either a philosopher or a fool.
> – Honoré de Balzac, *The Physiology of Marriage*

I like familiarity. In me it does not breed contempt. Only more familiarity.
> – Gertude Stein (attributed)

> Be thou familiar, but by no means vulgar.
> – William Shakespeare, *Hamlet*

Familiarity breeds contempt – and children.
> – Mark Twain, *Unpublished Diaries*

Familiarity breeds boldness.
> – Shackerley Marmion, *The Antiquary*

> Familiar acts are beautiful through love.
> – Percy Bysshe Shelley, *Prometheus Unbound*

Fancy

Fancy passes beauty.
> – Alfred Henderson, *Latin Proverbs*

> Ever let the Fancy roam!
> Pleasure never is at home.
> – John Keats, 'Fancy'

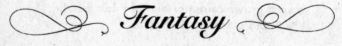

Fantasy

> In maiden meditation, fancy free.
> – William Shakespeare, *A Midsummer Night's Dream*

He said that as a schoolboy sexual thoughts dominated his mind. 'I felt as I grew older this fever would lessen, even leave me. But

it was not the case; it raged on through my twenties, and I thought: Well, surely by the time I am forty, I will receive some release from this torment, this constant search for the perfect love object. But it was not to be; all through the forties it was lurking inside my head. And then I was fifty, and then I was sixty, and nothing changed: sexual images continued to spin around my brain like figures on a carousel. Now here I am in my seventies and I am still a prisoner of my sexual imagination. I'm stuck with it just at an age when I can no longer do anything about it.'
> – E.M. Forster, quoted in Truman Capote, *Music for Chameleons*

Love brought by night a vision to my bed.
> – Meleager of Godora

It is a terrible deception of love that it begins by engaging us in play not with a woman of the external world but with a doll fashioned in our brain – the only woman moreover that we have always at our disposal, the only one we shall ever possess.
> – Marcel Proust, *Remembrance of Things Past: The Guermantes Way*

One's fantasy goes out for a walk and returns with a bride.
> – Bernard Malamud, *Long Work, Short Life*

The Cosmo Girl was the guys' fantasy of the liberated woman, all legs and edible knickers, with her own job and own studio apartment, adept at giving head and getting great breakfast.
> – Linda Grant, *Sexing the Millennium*

I am the master of fantasy.
> – Arthur Rimbaud

See also: DREAMS.

FANTASY

Farewell

Ae fond kiss, and then we sever
Ae farewell, an then forever.
. . .
Fare-thee-well, thou first and fairest!
Fare-thee-well, thou best and dearest!
Thine be ilka joy and treasure
Peace, Enjoyment, Love and Pleasure!
– Robert Burns, 'Ae Fond Kiss'

Farewell! thou art too dear for my possessing.
– William Shakespeare, 'Sonnet 137'

My hands have not touched water since your hands –
No; – nor my lips freed laughter since 'farewell'.
– Hart Crane, 'Carrier Letter'

I will not let thee go.
I hold thee by too many bands:
Thou sayest farewell, and lo!
I have thee by the hands,
And I will not let thee go.
– Robert Bridges, 'I Will Not Let Thee Go'

See also: PARTING.

Fascination

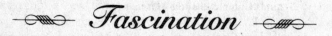

You fascinated me, but I loved you; so it was heaven. This sister
of yours fascinates me; but I hate her; so it is hell.
– George Bernard Shaw, *Heartbreak House*

Fashion

Things are seldom what they seem
Skim milk masquerades as cream.
– W.S. Gilbert, *HMS Pinafore*

Oh, what a tangled web we weave
When bras we put on to deceive.
– Leonard Lewis Levinson, *Bartlett's Unfamiliar Quotations*

The same costume will be
Indecent   10 years before its time
Shameless   5 years before its time
Outré (daring)   1 year before its time
Smart   —
Dowdy   1 year after its time
Hideous   10 years after its time
Ridiculous   20 years after its time
Amusing   30 years after its time
Quaint   50 years after its time
Charming   70 years after its time
Romantic   100 years after its time
Beautiful   150 years after its time.
– James Laver, *Taste and Fashion*

The erogenous zone is always shifting and it is the business of fashion to pursue it, without ever catching it up.
– James Laver (attributed)

The uniform of the eighties career woman was a long, dark jacket, short skirt, dark, sheer stockings, high heels, all worn over a lace teddy with a drenching of Opium just to make sure. A real woman has curves with attitude.
– Linda Grant, *Sexing the Millennium*

 # Fat

Love don't seem dainty on a fat woman.
– Enid Bagnold, *National Velvet*

An elegant degree of plumpness peculiar to the skin of the softer sex.
– Hogarth, *The Analysis of Beauty*

Outside every thin girl there is a fat man trying to get in.
– Katherine Whitehorn, on BBC Radio, 27 July 1982

He likes fat women the way a rat likes pumpkins.
– Rita Mae Brown

    it's a sex object if you are pretty
and no love
or love and no sex if you are fat.
– Nikki Giovanni, 'Woman Poem'

A Venus grown fat.
– Leigh Hunt, *Blue-Stocking Revels*

    Big fat momma with the meat shakin' on her bone,
Each time she wiggles, skinny woman loses her home.
– Blues song

I don't want my girl to be so skinny she can knife me with her knee . . . nor do I want some big two-hundred-pound tomato; meat, not suet, I hold dear.
– Martial, *Epigrams* (trans. by Rolphe Humphries)

He's so fat he hasn't seen his privates in twenty years.
– Carson McCullers, *The Ballad of the Sad Café*

Nobody loves a fat man.
> – Edmund Day, *The Round-Up*

The nearer the bone, the sweeter the meat.
> – English proverb

The flesh is aye fairest that's farthest from the bone.
> – Scottish proverb

To ask women to become unnaturally thin is to ask them to relinquish their sexuality.
> – Naomi Wolf, *The Beauty Myth*

> I'm sorry to say my dear wife is a dreamer,
> And as she dreams she gets paler and leaner.
> 'Then be off to your Dream, with his fly-away hat,
> I'll stay with the girls who are happy and fat.'
> – Stevie Smith, 'Be Off!'

> And a long, tall woman will make a preacher lay his
> Bible down . . .
> But a big, fat mama will make a mule kick his stall
> down.
> – Willie Jackson, Blues song

Father

It is no new observation, I believe, that a lover in most cases has no rival so much to be feared as the father.
> – Charles Lamb, *The Wedding*

Fault

Faults are thick where love is thin.
— John Howell, *Proverbs*

Where love fails we espy all faults.
— John Ray, *English Proverbs*

Fear

To fear love is to fear life, and those who fear life are already three parts dead.
— Bertrand Russell

Fear of sexuality is the new disease . . . the universe of fear in which everyone now lives.
— Susan Sontag, *AIDS and its Metaphors*

Fear of

anything new: kain(o)phobia
bearing a monster: teratophobia
being alone: autophobia; eremiophobia; monophobia
being examined: examination phobia
being looked at: scopophobia
being touched: (h)aphephobia; haptephobia
blood: hematophobia; hemophobia
blushing: ereuthophobia
change: kainophobia; kainotophobia; neophobia
childbirth: maieusiophobia

choking: anginophobia; pnigophobia
daylight: phenogophobia
disease: nosophobia; pathophobia
eating: phagophobia
excrement: coprophobia
female genitals: eurotophobia
girls: parthenophobia
hair: trichopathophobia, trichophobia
jealousy: zelophobia
large objects: meglophobia
light: photophobia
man: androphobia
marriage: gamophobia
naked body: gynophobia
novelty: kainophobia; kaintophobia; neophobia
odour (personal): bromidosophobia
odour(s): olfactophobia; osmophobia; osphresiophobia
pleasure: hedonophobia
rectum: proctophobia
semen: spermatophobia
sex: genophobia
sexual intercourse: coitophobia
sin: harmartophobia
sinning: peccatiphobia
syphilis: syphilophobia
venereal disease: cypridophobia, cypriphobia
women: gynophobia, horror feminae
– Adapted from Robert Jean Campbell, *Psychiatric Dictionary*

Femme Fatale

She [the actress Elizabeth Taylor] wields the sexual power that
feminism cannot explain and has tried to destroy. Through stars
like Taylor, we sense the world-disordering impact of women

like Delilah, Salome, and Helen of Troy. Feminists have tried to dismiss the femme fatale as a misogynist libel, a hoary cliché. But the femme fatale expresses woman's ancient and eternal control of the sexual realm. The spectre of the femme fatale stalks all men's relations with women.

> – Camille Paglia, *Sex, Art, and American Culture*

 *Fetishes*

> How beautiful are thy feet with shoes,
> O prince's daughter.
> – The Bible: Song of Songs

The abnormal heel.

> – Charlotte Perkins Gilman, *Herland*

We, being modern and liberated and fully cognizant of women's sexual, intellectual, emotional, and economic oppression, can never for a moment cease our vigilance against the imperialistic male supremacist. We must never relax our guard against his chauvinistic sexual fantasies.

So don't even for an instant consider keeping the following hidden in the back of your closet: a see-through nurse's uniform . . . a cheerleader's costume . . . a little black French maid's outfit.

And if you do, don't tell anyone.

> – Cynthia Heimel, *Sex Tips for Girls*

Let him be inflamed by the love of your dress.

> – Ovid, *Ars Amatoria*

> Though you know the dress full well,
> What know you of the wearer?
> – Sadi Gulistan, 'Apologue 5'

I for one venerate a petticoat.
– George Gordon, Lord Byron, *Don Juan*

Chains of iron or of silk – both are chains.
– Friedrich von Schiller, *The Fiesio*

Like every young man grown up in England, he was conditioned to get a hardon in the presence of certain fetishes, and then conditioned to feel shame about his new reflexes.
– Thomas Pynchon, *Gravity's Rainbow*

It would not grieve him to be hanged, if he might be strangled in her garters.
– Robert Burton, *The Anatomy of Melancholy*

There is no unhappier creature on earth than a fetishist who yearns for a woman's shoe and has to embrace the whole woman.
– Karl Kraus, *Aphorisms and More Aphorisms*

Prof. Higgins was right – men wish that woman's sexuality was like theirs, which it isn't. Male sexuality is far brisker and more automatic. Your clothes, breasts, odour, etc. aren't what he loves instead of you – simply the things he needs in order to set sex in motion to express love. Women find this hard to understand.
– Alex Comfort, *The Joy of Sex*

See also: CLOTHES; DRESS; LINGERIE.

Fickleness

A fickle thing and changeful is a woman always.
– Virgil, *Aeneid*

# *Fidelity*

Fire heat shall lose, and frosts of flame be born;
Air, made to shine, as black as hell shall prove;
Earth, heaven, fire, air, the world transformed shall
    view,
Ere I prove false to faith, or strange to you.
– John Dowland, 'Dear If You Change'

I love I love whose lips I love
but conscience she has none
nor can I rest upon her breast
for faith's to her unknown.
– Conrad Aiken, 'The Accomplices'

When my love swears that she is made of truth
I do believe her, though I know she lies.
– William Shakespeare, 'Sonnet 138'

Lovers' vows do not reach the ears of the gods.
– Callimachus, *Epigrams*

It is as absurd to say that a man can't love one woman all the
time as it is to say that a violinist needs several violins to play the
same piece of music.
– Honoré de Balzac

Fidelity: A virtue peculiar to those who are about to be betrayed.
– Ambrose Bierce, *The Devil's Dictionary*

Your idea of fidelity is not having more than one man in bed at
the same time. You're a whore, baby, just a whore and I don't
take whores in taxis.
– Frederic Raphael, from the film *Darling*

Look you, Amanda, you may build Castles in the Air, and
fume, and fret, and grow thin and lean, and pale and ugly, if you

please. But I tell you, no man worth having is true to his wife, or can be true to his wife, or ever was, or ever will be so.
— Sir John Vanbrugh, *The Relapse, or Virtue in Danger*

Love interferes with fidelities.
— Sylvia Ashton-Warner, *Teacher*

When a man declares, 'I am sure of my wife,' it means he is sure of his wife. But when a woman declares, 'I am sure of my husband,' it means that she is sure of herself.
— Francis de Croisset, in *Reader's Digest*, January 1943

> We only part to meet again.
> Change, as ye list, ye winds: my heart shall be
> The faithful compass that still points to thee.
> — John Gay, 'Sweet William's Farewell to Black-Eyed Susan'

What a fuss people make about fidelity! Why, even in love it is purely a question of physiology. It has nothing to do with your own will. Young men want to be faithful, and are not; old men want to be faithless, but cannot; that is all one can say.
— Oscar Wilde, *The Picture of Dorian Gray*

> Who, who will be the next man to entrust his girl to a
>   friend?
> Love interferes with fidelities.
> — Ezra Pound, 'Homage to Sextus Propertius'

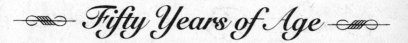

Fifty Years of Age

> They don't tell;
> They don't yell;
> They don't swell;
> And they're grateful as hell.
> — Author unknown, 'Ode to Women Over Fifty'

Love is lame at fifty years.

> – Thomas Hardy, 'The Revisitation'

From 35 to 45 women are old, and at 45 the devil takes over, and they're beautiful, splendid, maternal, proud. The acidities are gone and in their place reigns calm. They are worth going out to find, and because of them some men never grow old. When I see them my mouth waters.

> – Jean-Baptiste Troisgros, in *The New York Times*, 24 October 1974

After 50 his performance is of poor quality, the intervals between are wide, and its satisfactions of no great value to either party; whereas his great-grandmother is as good as new. There is nothing the matter with her plant. Her candlestick is as firm as ever, whereas his candle is increasingly softened and weakened by the weather of age, as the years go by, until it can no longer stand, and is mournfully laid to rest in the hope of blessed resurrection which is never to come.

> – Mark Twain

He was fifty. It's the age when clergymen first begin to be preoccupied with the underclothing of little schoolgirls in trains, the age when eminent archaeologists start to take a really passionate interest in the Scout movement.

> – Aldous Huxley, *Brief Candles*

Figure

She wore a short skirt and a tight sweater and her figure described a set of parabolas that could cause cardiac arrest in a yak.

> – Woody Allen, *Getting Even*

See also: THE BODY.

FIGURE

154

First Love

All men can't be first.
> – Thomas Fuller, *Gnomologia: Adagies And Proverbs*

One always returns to one's first love.
> – Charles Étienne, *La Joconde*

Men always want to be a woman's first love. That is their clumsy vanity. We women have a more subtle instinct about things. What we like is to be a man's last romance.
> – Oscar Wilde, *A Woman of No Importance*

Those whom we first love we seldom marry.
> – O. Henry, 'No Story'

The magic of first love is our ignorance that it can ever end.
> – Benjamin Disraeli, *Henrietta Temple*

First love is only a little foolishness and a lot of curiosity.
> – George Bernard Shaw, *John Bull's Other Island*

We always believe our first love to be our last, and our last love our first.
> – George John Whyte-Melville, *Katerfelto*

Love (understood as the desire of good for another) is in fact so unnatural a phenomenon that it can scarcely repeat itself, the soul being unable to become virgin again and not having energy enough to cast itself out again into the ocean of another's soul.
> – James Joyce, *Exiles*

O my first love, You are in my life forever.
> – Hugh MacDiarmid, 'Of My First Love'

First Night

The fate of the house hangs on the first night.
– Honoré de Balzac, *The Physiology of Marriage*

First Sight

She lovede Right fro first sighte.
– Geoffrey Chaucer, *Troilus and Criseyde*

Who ever lov'd that lov'd not at first sight?
– Christopher Marlowe, *Hero and Leander*

I took one look at you
That's all I meant to do
And my heart stood still.
– Lorenz Hart and Richard Rodgers, 'My Heart Stood Still'

Love not at the first look.
– John Clarke, *Paroemiologia Anglo-Latina*

Sudden love is latest cured.
– Jean de La Bruyère, *Les Caractères*

The only true love is love at first sight; second sight dispels it.
– Israel Zangwill

The moment my eyes fell on him, I was content.
– Edith Wharton

First Time

. . . your groin and buttocks and thighs ache like hell and you're all wet and bloody and it wasn't like a Hollywood movie at all but Jesus, at least you're not a virgin anymore but is this what it is all about?

And meanwhile he's asking you, 'Did you come?'
> – Robin Morgan, *Sisterhood is Powerful*

I was too polite to ask.
> – Gore Vidal, when asked whether his first sexual encounter had been hetero- or homosexual

Flattery

He who can not learn to love must flatter.
> – Johann Wolfgang von Goethe

If you want to lick the old woman's pot, scratch her back.
> – Jamaican proverb

Flirtation

She who trifles with all
Is less likely to fall
Than she who but trifles with one.
> – John Gay, 'The Coquet Mother and the Coquet Daughter'

For whom does the blind man's wife paint herself?
> – English proverb

One must cease letting oneself be eaten when one tastes best; that is known to those who want to be loved long.

> – Friedrich Nietzsche, *Thus Spake Zarathustra* (trans. by Walter Kaufman)

Why does a man take it for granted that a girl who flirts with him wants him to kiss her – when, nine times out of ten, she only wants him to want to kiss her.

> – Helen Rowland, *A Guide to Men*

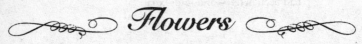

Flowers

Why is it no one ever sent me yet
One perfect limousine, do you suppose?
Ah no, it's always just my luck to get
One perfect rose.
> – Dorothy Parker, 'One Perfect Rose'

. . . the genital
organs of plants.
> – Lenore Kandel, 'Bus Ride'

A fox is a wolf who sends flowers.
> – Ruth Weston, quoted in the *New York Post*, 8 November 1955

Folly

My only books
Were woman's looks
And folly's all they've taught me.
> – Thomas Moore, *Juvenile Poems*: 'The Time I've Lost'

If thou remember'st not the slightest folly
That ever love did make thee run into,
Thou has not lov'd.
– William Shakespeare, *As You Like It*

Food

Dagwood complex: food satisfaction to replace unsatisfactory or
non–existent sex.
– Gershon Legman, *Rationale of the Dirty Joke*

Fool

To be intimate with a foolish man is like going to bed with a razor.
– Benjamin Franklin

Nickumpoop or nincumpoop. A foolish fellow; also one who
never saw his wife's ★★★★.
– Francis Grose, *A Classical Dictionary of the Vulgar Tongue*

One fool at least in every marriage.
– Henry Fielding, *Amelia*

I am two fools, I know,
For loving, and saying so
In whining poetry.
– John Donne, 'The Triple Fool'

Take my word for it, the silliest woman can manage a clever man,
but it takes a very clever woman to manage a fool.
– Rudyard Kipling, *Plain Tales from the Hills*: 'Three and – an
Extra'

Never let loving make a fool of you.
– Sextus Aurelius Propertius

Tho' marriage makes man and wife one flesh, it leaves 'em still
two fools.
– William Congreve, *The Double Dealer*

Forbidden Fruit

Adam was but human – this explains it all. He did not want the
apple for the apple's sake, he wanted it only because it was
forbidden.
– Mark Twain, *The Tragedy of Pudd'nhead Wilson*

Foreplay

may i feel said he
(i'll squeal said she
just once said he)
it's fun said she
. . .
(let's go said he
not too far said she
what's too far said he
where you are said she)
– e.e. cummings, 'may i feel said he'

License my roving hands, and let them go
Before, behind, between, above, below.
– John Donne, 'To His Mistress Going to Bed'

Ye praise the wine before ye taste the grape.
> – John Heywood, *A Dialogue containing the number in effect of all the Proverbs in the English Tongue*

> I will go down to her, I and no other,
> Close with her, kiss her and mix her with me.
> – A.C. Swinburne, 'The Triumph of Time'

> i like, slowly stroking the shocking fuzz
> of your electric fur, and what-is-it comes
> over parting flesh . . .
> – e.e. cummings, 'i like my body when it is with your body'

> Let us together closely lie and kiss
> There is no labour, nor no shame in this;
> This hath pleased, doth please, and long will please;
>> never
> Can this decay, but is beginning ever.
> – Petronius Arbiter (trans. by John Dryden)

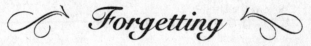

Forgetting

No never forget! . . . Never forget any moment; they are too few.
> – Elizabeth Bowen, *The House in Paris*

Love is so short, forgetting so long.
> – Pablo Neruda

> My once dear love; hapless that I no more
> Must call thee so; the rich affection's store
> That fed our hopes, lies now exhaust and spent.
> Like sums of treasure unto bancrupts lent.
>> We that did nothing study but the way

To love each other, with which thought the day
Rose with delight to us, and with them set,
Must learn the hateful art, how to forget.
– Henry King, 'The Surrender'

The only thing that can cure love is the glass of forgetfulness.
– Graffito

As one nail by strength drives out another,
So the remembrance of my former love
Is by the newer object quite forgotten.
– William Shakespeare, *Two Gentlemen of Verona*

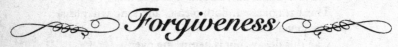

Forgiveness

We pardon to the extent that we love.
– François, duc de La Rochefoucauld, *Sentences et maximes*

She hugg'd the offender, and forgave th'offence,
Sex to the last.
– John Dryden, 'Cymon and Iphigenia'

Once a woman has forgiven her man, she must not reheat his sins for breakfast.
– Marlene Dietrich, *Marlene Dietrich's ABC*

If you really worship women they'll forgive you anything, even if your balls are falling off.
– Lawrence Durrell (attributed)

Love is no pardoner.
– Louis Simpson, 'The Man Who Married Magdalane'

Fornication

Fornication is a filthy business,
The briefest form of lechery,
And the most boring, once you're satisfied,
So let's not rush blindly upon it
Like cows in a rut.
That's the way passion wilts
And the fire goes out.
– Petronius Arbiter

Doing a filthy pleasure is, and short,
And done, we straight repent us of the sport.
– Ben Jonson

See also: COPULATION; LOVEMAKING; SEXUAL
INTERCOURSE.

Forty Years of Age

At the age of forty she is very far from being cold and insensible;
her fire may be covered with ashes, but it is not extinguished.
– Mary Wortley Montagu, letter to Lady —, 13 January 1716

A fool at forty is a fool indeed.
– Edward Young, *Love of Fame*

Fat, fair and forty.
– Sir Walter Scott, *St Ronan's Well*, in reply to a question as to
what a wife should be.

This is it, you know, baby. This is the one that does it. You have
said farewell to the thirties for the tenth and last time. Now face it,
baby. Now take it smack in the teeth, baby. Quote baby unquote.
– Dorothy Parker, *The Middle or Blue Period*

My notion of a wife of forty is that a man should be able to change her, like a bank note, for two twenties.
– Douglas Jerrold (attributed)

Women are most fascinating between the age of thirty-five and forty after they have won a few races and know how to pace themselves. Since few ever pass forty, maximum fascination can continue indefinitely.
– Christian Dior

Pushing forty? She's clinging on to it for dear life.
– Ivy Compton-Burnett (attributed)

When forty winters shall besiege thy brow,
And dig deep trenches in thy beauty's field,
– William Shakespeare, 'Sonnet 2'

I'm forty-nine but I could be twenty-five except for my face and legs.
– Nadine Gordimer, *Not for Publication and Other Stories*

Four-Letter Words

Oh perish the use of the four-letter words
Whose meanings are never obscure;
The Angles and Saxons, those bawdy old birds,
Were vulgar, obscene and impure.
But cherish the use of the weaseling phrase
That never says quite what you mean.
You had better be known for your hypocrite ways
Than vulgar, impure and obscene.
Let your morals be loose as an alderman's vest
If your language is always obscure.

Today not the act, but the word is the test
Of vulgar, obscene and impure.
  – Anonymous, in Ashley Montagu, *The Anatomy of Swearing*

Immodest words admit no defence,
For want of decency is want of sense.
  – Wentworth Dillon, Earl of Roscommon 'Essay on
    Translated Verse'

Not the lover but his language wins the lady.
    – Japanese proverb

I was beyond simple desire, borne away rather by a near swoon of lust. Couldn't she know what she did to me with this concubine speech, with these foul, priceless words which assail like sharp spears the bastion of my own Christian gentility with its aching repressions and restraints.
    – William Styron, *Sophie's Choice*

I know that the wiser sort of men will consider, and I wish that the ignorant sort would learn, how it is not the baseness or homeliness either of words or matters, that makes them foul or obscene, but their base minds, filthy conceits, or lewd intents that handle them.
    – John Harington, *The Metamorphosis of Ajax*

. . . we can write the four commonest sexual obscenities backward or sideways as cuff, swerk, kirp, and tunc without misleading or offending anyone.
    – Eric Berne, *Games People Play*

Bad language or abuse
I never, never use,
Whatever the emergency;
Though 'Bother it' I may
Occasionally say
I never swear a big, big D.
  – W.S. Gilbert, *HMS Pinafore*

FOUR-LETTER WORDS

Expletive deleted.
> – The Watergate tapes of Richard M. Nixon

Nudge, nudge, wink, wink. Know what I mean? Say no more.
> – *Monty Python's Flying Circus*, BBC TV

. . . of all the worn, smudged, dog-eared words in our vocabulary 'love' is surely the grubbiest, smelliest, slimiest . . .
> – Aldous Huxley, *Tomorrow and Tomorrow and Tomorrow*

Sex is a three-letter word which sometimes needs some old-fashioned four-letter words to convey its full meaning; words like help, give, care, love.
> – Sam Levenson, *Sex and the Single Child*

> We knew, my generation
> Those words and plenty more.
> But liked the implication
> They shocked us to the core
> One offers no excuses
> Hypocrisy is done
> Forgive me if I mention
> We found it rather fun.
> – Dorothy Drain, 'Remember When Damn was Spelled d..m?'

You don't know what love means. To you it's just another four-letter word.
> – Tennessee Williams, *Cat on a Hot Tin Roof*

It is good to find modest words to express immodest things.
> – Author unknown

See also: OBSCENITY.

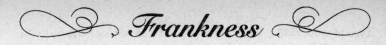

Frankness

A sound marriage is not based on complete frankness; it is based on sensible reticence.
> – Morris L. Ernst

Often the difference between a successful marriage and a mediocre one consists of leaving about three or four things a day unsaid.
> – Harlan Miller

See also: COMMUNICATION; SPEECH; TALK

Freedom

Him that I love, I wish to be free –
even from me.
> – Anne Morrow Lindbergh, *The Unicorn and Other Poems*

If you want something very very badly,
let it go free. If it comes back to you
it's yours forever. If it doesn't, it was
never yours to begin with.
> – Jesse Lair, 'I Ain't Much Baby, But I'm All I Got'

Free Love

Free love is sometimes love but never freedom.
> – Elizabeth Bibisco, *Haven*

The big difference between sex for money and sex for free is that sex for money costs a lot less.
> – Brendon Francis

Free love is seldom free. Teens pay for it in worry – the fear that they will be caught, or that their partner may tire of them. It's hurried and furtive and not much fun.
– Helen Bottel, in *Family Circle* (New York), November 1969

I have said it again and again: 'Everyone who preached free love in the Sixties is responsible for AIDS.' And we must accept moral responsibility for it. The idea that it is an accident, a historical accident, a microbe that sort of fell from the heaven – absurd. We must face what we did.
– Camille Paglia, *Sex, Art, and American Culture*

You pay a great deal too dear for what is given freely.
– William Shakespeare, *The Winter's Tale*

Frequency

Staled by frequence, shrunk by usage into
commonplace!
– Alfred, Lord Tennyson, 'Locksley Hall Sixty Years After'

A maid oft seen, and a gown oft worn
Are disesteemed and held in scorn.
– H.G. Bohn, *A Handbook of Proverbs*

Friendship

Friendship often ends in love, but love in friendship – never.
– C.C. Colton, *Lacon*

Love and friendship exclude one another.
> – Jean de La Bruyère, *Les Caractères*

> Love is only chatter,
> Friends are all that matter.
> – Gellett Burgess, *Willy and the Lady*

A friend married is a friend lost.
> – Henrik Ibsen, *Love's Comedy*

> But for lust we could be friends
>   On each other's necks could weep:
> In each other's arms could sleep
>   In the calm of the cradle lend.
> – Ruth Pitter, 'But for Lust'

No man can be friends with a woman he finds attractive. He always wants to have sex with her. Sex is always out there. Friendship is ultimately doomed and that's the end of the story.
> – Nora Ephron, from the film *When Harry Met Sally*

When all is said and done, friendship is the only trustworthy fabric of the affections. So-called love is a delirious inhuman state of mind: when hot it substitutes indulgence for fair play; when cold it is cruel, but friendship is warmth in cold, firm ground in bog.
> – Miles Franklin, *My Career Goes Bung*

> Love is like the wild rose-briar;
> Friendship like the holly tree.
> The holly is dark when the rose-briar blooms,
> But which will bloom most constantly?
> – Emily Brontë, 'Love and Friendship'

Friendship versus Love

Friendship is a disinterested commerce between equals; love an abject intercourse between tyrants and slaves.
> – Oliver Goldsmith, *The Good-Natur'd Man*

Friendship is constant in all other things
Except in the office and affairs of love.
> – William Shakespeare, *Much Ado About Nothing*

Frigidity

My love is like to ice, and I to fire:
How comes it then that this her cold so great
Is not dissolved through my hot desire,
But harder grows the more I entreat?
> – Edmund Spenser, 'My Love is Like to Ice'

A watched pot never boils.
> – English proverb

A 'cold' passionless woman is a woman who has not yet met the man she is bound to love.
> – Stendhal, quoted in Th. Van de Velde, *Ideal Marriage*

In the coldest flint there is hot fire.
> – John Ray, *English Proverbs*

Men always fall for frigid women because they put on the best show.
> – Fanny Brice (attributed)

There was a young maiden of Ealing
Who professed to lack sexual feeling,
    But a cynic named Boris
    Just touched her clitoris
And she had to be scraped off the ceiling.
   – Anonymous Limerick

The girl who can't dance says the band can't play.
   – Yiddish proverb

There are no frigid women, only clumsy men.
   – Old maxim

There are both frigid women and clumsy men, and they are usually married to each other.
   – Joseph LoPiccolo, *Handbook of Sex Therapy*

Sexually frigid is intellectually rigid.
   – Eric Berne, *Games People Play*

Show me a frigid woman and, nine times out of ten, I'll show you a little man.
   – Julie Burchill, in *Arena* (London)

She looked like butter wouldn't melt in her mouth – or anywhere else.
   – Elsa Lanchester (attributed)

When a country wench cannot get her butter to come, she says the witch is in her churn.
   – John Seldon, *Table-Talk: Peace* (1654)

See also: ORGASM.

Frivolity

The ability to make love frivolously is the chief characteristic which distinguishes human beings from beasts.
> – Heywood Broun, quoted in Robert E. Drennan, *The Algonquin Wits*

Frustration

Frustration of sexual wishes is the exact reverse of seduction. The sabotaging partner is highly sensitive to what the other desires and withholds this, usually with the excuse that the craved activity is too anxiety provoking, disgusting, taxing, or immoral.
> – Helen Singer Kaplan, *The New Sex Therapy*

The basic formula of all sin is: frustrated or neglected love.
> – Franz Werfel, *Between Heaven and Earth*

He who desires but acts not, breeds pestilence.
> – William Blake, *Proverbs of Hell*

Gambling

Sex and gambling don't go together either. If men win they have erections. If they win big, they come. And if they lose, it makes them impotent.
> – Natalie Gittelson, *The Erotic Life of the American Wife*

Gifts

Ever since Eve gave Adam the apple, there has been a misunderstanding between the sexes about gifts.
> – Nan Robertson, in *The New York Times*, 28 November 1957

Win her with gifts, if she respect not words,
Dumb jewels often in their silent kind
More than quick words do move a woman's mind.
> – William Shakespeare, *Two Gentlemen of Verona*

She that takes gifts herself she sells.
> – David Fergusson, *Scottish Proverbs*

She must refuse all presents offer'd her by men; for now-a-days nothing is given for nothing.
> – Molière, *Ozell*

Frivolous minds are won by trifles.
> – Ovid, *Ars Amatoria*

Giving presents to a woman to secure her love, is as vain as endeavouring to fill a sieve with water.
> – Edward Ward, *Female Policy*

No: I don't want no gold and no diamonds. I'm a good girl I am.
> – George Bernard Shaw, *Pygmalion*

Don't give to lovers – you will replace irreplaceable presents.
> – Logan Pearsall Smith

Faint heart ne'er won fur, lady.
> – Anonymous

Diamonds are a girl's best friend.
> – Leo Robin, title of a song from the musical *Gentlemen Prefer Blondes*.

> I could never curl my lip
> To a dazzlin' diamond clip
> Though the clip meant 'let 'er
>   rip,' I'd not say nay.
> – Cole Porter, 'Always True to You in My Fashion'

See also: DIAMONDS; JEWELLERY.

Gigolos

Stallion: a man kept by an old lady for secret services.
> – Francis Grose, *A Classical Dictionary of the Vulgar*

> The hungry pauper Gellius
> married a rich, old lady
>   he got fat and
>   she got screwed.
> – Martial, *Select Epigrams of Martial* (trans. and adapted by Donald C. Goertz

Girlfriends

I don't know of any young man, black or white, who doesn't have a girl friend besides his wife. Some have three or four sneaking around.
> – Muhammad Ali, in the *Observer*, 28 November 1975

It hurts me to say it, but I'd have given ten conversations with Einstein for a first meeting with a pretty chorus girl.

— Albert Camus, *The Fall*

If anyone wants to trade a couple of centrally located, well-cushioned show-girls for an eroded slope ninety minutes from Broadway, I'll be on the corner tomorrow at eleven with my tongue hanging out.

— S.J. Perelman, *Acres and Pains*

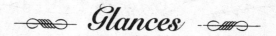

Glances

Love stories have so overworked the power of love's gaze, that finally people agreed to discount it. We hardly dare, nowadays, to admit that two human beings loved one another because they looked at one another. Yet – love dawns thus, and only thus. The rest – comes afterwards. Nothing is more true, more real, than the primeval magnetic disturbances that two souls may communicate to one another, through the tiny sparks of a moment's glance.

— Victor Hugo, quoted in Th. Van de Velde, *Ideal Marriage*

Gobbledegook

Amorance, or being in love, is a cognitive affective state characterized by intrusive and obsessive fantasizing concerning reciprocity of amorant feelings by the object of the amorance.

— American delegate to the Conference of Love and Attraction, quoted in the *Observer*, 11 November 1977

Goodbye

Everytime we say goodbye
I die a little.
– Cole Porter, 'Everytime We Say Goodbye', from the
  musical *Seven Lively Arts*

See also: PARTING.

Gossip

Men have always detested women's gossip because they suspect
the truth: their measurements are being taken and compared.
– Erica Jong, *Fear of Flying*

Whoever gossips to you will gossip of you.
– Spanish proverb

Aspersion is the babbler's trade
To listen is to lend him aid.
– William Cowper, 'Friendship'

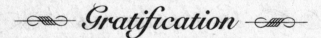

Gratification

The desire accomplished is sweet to the soul.
– The Bible: Proverbs

Here is a perfect poem: to awaken a longing, to nourish it, to
develop it, to stimulate it, and to gratify it.
– Honoré de Balzac

Greying

You mock me for my greying hair, but you don't consider that
my nature is like the leeks, which we find white on top when its
tail is green, straight and vigorous.
> – François Rabelais, *Gargantua and Pantagruel*

Grumbling

Grumbling is the death of love.
> – Marlene Dietrich, *Marlene Dietrich's ABC*

Guilt

What is our innocence
What is our guilt? All are
naked, none is safe.
> – Marianne Moore, 'What Are Years?'

There's nothing bolder than a woman caught;
Guilt gives 'em courage to maintain their fault.
> – Juvenal, *Sixth Satire* (trans. by John Dryden)

When lovely lady stoops to folly,
    And finds too late that men betray,
What charm can soothe her melancholy,
    What art can wash her guilt away?
The only art her guilt to cover,
    To hide her shame from every eye,
To give repentance to her lover,
    And wring his bosom is – to die.
> – Oliver Goldsmith, song from *The Vicar of Wakefield*

When lovely woman stoops to folly and
Paces about her room again, alone
She smooths her hair with automatic hand,
And puts a record on the gramophone.
– T.S. Eliot, 'The Waste Land'

The most depressing thing, you know, the most depressing thing is that I used to feel a certain amount of post-coital tristesse. Well guilt. But these days I can't be bothered to feel shifty when I get home. Extra-marital sex is as over-rated as pre-marital sex. And marital sex, come to think of it.
– Simon Gray, on *Two Sundays*, BBC TV, 1975

 *Habit*

Marriage must continually vanquish a monster that devours everything: the monster of habit.
– Honoré de Balzac, quoted in Th. Van de Velde, *Ideal Marriage*

Habit causes love . . . love depends on habit quite as much as the wild ways of passion.
– Lucretius, *De Rerum Natura* (trans. by Rolfe Humphries)

I've grown accustomed to the trace
of something in the air
Accustomed to her face.
– Alan Jay Lerner, *My Fair Lady*

Habit has a kind of poetry.
– Simone de Beauvoir, *The Coming of Age*

Habit is a great deadener.
– Samuel Beckett, *Waiting for Godot*

[Habit] is the chloroform of love.
– Geneviève Antoine-Dariaux, 'The Men in Your Life'

Hair

Fair tresses man's imperial race ensnare,
And beauty draws us with a single hair.
– Alexander Pope, *The Rape of the Lock*

One strand of pubic hair can be stronger than the Atlantic cable.
– Gene Fowler (attributed)

Ladies with curly hair
Have time to spare.
– Phyllis McGinley

Hairtrigger Trouble

. . . like so many modern men, he was finished before he had
begun.
– D.H. Lawrence, *Lady Chatterley's Lover*

Sad conquest: when it is the victor's fate
To die at the entrance of the opening gate.
– John Wilmot, Earl of Rochester, 'The Imperfect Enjoyment'

. . . he thought about everything except this, thought, counted,
thought of nothing, so that this would not end, tried to fill his

mind with seas, sands, winds, fruits, houses, fishes and sowings, so that it might not end . . .
– Carlos Fuentes

Alas, Julian's chimes rang before the appointed hour.
– Tom Robbins, *Even Cowgirls Get the Blues*

Nothing is more vulgar than haste.
– Ralph Waldo Emerson, *The Conduct of Life*

What is soon done, soon perishes.
– Latin proverb

. . . it was thirty seconds of action, and an hour of apology.
– Mordecai Richler, *Joshua Then and Now*

Haste makes waste.
– John Heywood, *Proverbs*

Haste makes waste, and waste makes want, and want makes strife between the goodman and his wife.
– John Ray, *English Proverbs*

A common suggestion [how to retard premature ejaculation] is to fantasize repugnant images or concepts. For example, an AMA official with this problem might think about various forms of national insurance.
– Eugene Schoenfeld

Dr. Brothers advised the viewer to tell her husband to concentrate on his income tax in order to forestall his orgasm. The long form, presumably.
– Paul Krasner, in *The Realist* (New York), 1958

> My sex life is pretty humdrum
> When I'm ready and want George to plumb.
> He says, 'Wait a minute –

HAIRTRIGGER TROUBLE

I've hardly got in it.'
Then before I begin it, he's done.
– Anonymous American Limerick

The action which we should have jointly done,
Each had unluckily performed alone;
. . .
Our flames are punish'd by their own excess,
We'd more pleasure had our loves been less.
She blush'd and frown'd, perceiving we had done
The sport she thought we scarce had yet begun.
. . .
Phyllis, let this comfort ease your care,
You'd been more happy had you been less fair.
– Sir George Etherege, *The Imperfect Enjoyment*

See also: HASTE.

Hand

But when the wearied band
Swoons to a waltz, I take her hand,
And there we sit in peaceful calm,
Quietly sweating palm to palm.
– Aldous Huxley, 'Frascati'

Our hands have met but not our hearts;
Our hands will never meet again.
– Thomas Hood, 'To a False Friend'

I scarcely seem to be able to keep my hands off you.
– Ovid, *Metamorphoses*

Paws off, Pompey!
– Frederick Marryat, *Jacob Faithful*

He belongs to the Wandering Hand Society.
> – Raymond Chandler, *Farewell My Lovely*

Happiness

Happiness is having a scratch for every itch.
> – Ogden Nash

Happy is he who sees thee,
Happier he who hears thee,
A demigod he who kisses thee,
A god he who possesses thee.
> – *The Greek Anthology*

Happiness is having your girlfriend's lipstick the same colour as your wife's.
> – Anonymous

Haste

Hasty love is soon hot and soon cold.
> – Anonymous, *Wit and Science*

Good and quickly seldom meet.
> – George Herbert, *Jacula Prudentum*

Marry in haste and repent in leisure.
> – John Ray, *English Proverbs*

Hate and Love

The greatest hate springs from the greatest love.
> – Thomas Fuller, *Gnomologia: Adagies and Proverbs*

Underneath love there always lies in wait hatred.
> – Th. Van de Velde, *Ideal Marriage*

The sex life of a spider is very interesting.
He screws her.
She bites his head off.
> – Women's Liberation Poster

I love her and she loves me, and we hate each other with a wild hatred born of love.
> – August Strindberg

Women have very little idea how much men hate them.
> – Germaine Greer, *The Female Eunuch*

Love must be learned, and learned again and again. Hate needs no instruction, but waits only to be provoked.
> – Katherine Anne Porter, *The Days Before*

To love you was pleasant enough
And, oh! 'tis delicious to hate you!
> – Thomas Moore, *Juvenile Poems*: 'To — When I Lov'd You'

My only love sprung from my only hate!
> – William Shakespeare, *Romeo and Juliet*

I hate, I love – the cause thereof
Belike you ask of me;
I do not now, but feel 'tis so,
And I'm in agony.
> – Catullus, *Carmina* (trans. by Sir W. Marris)

Though me she hate, I cannot choose but to love her.
– Walter Davison, 'Ode'

No doubt in time I'd learn
To hate you like the rest
I once loved.
– W.D. Snodgrass, 'No Use'

Love is dialectic, man, back and forth, hate and sweet.
– Norman Mailer, *Why Are We in Vietnam*

If we judge love by the majority of its results, it rather resembles
hatred than friendship.
– François, duc de La Rochefoucauld, *Réflexions ou sentences et
maximes morales*

There never was a great love that was not followed by a great
hatred.
– Irish proverb

I am in someone
who hates me.
. . .
It burns the thing
inside it. And that thing
screams.
– Imanu Amiri Baraka, 'An Agony, As Now'

We've practised loving long enough
Let's come at last to hate.
– Georg Herwegh, 'Lied vom Hasse'

Hatred of Men

He'll swim a river of snot, wade nostril deep through a mile of vomit, if he thinks there'll be a friendly pussy awaiting him. He'll screw a woman he despises, any snaggle-tooth hag, and further, pay for the opportunity. And he'll also screw babies and corpses.

– Valerie Solanas, *S.C.U.M. Manifesto*

The difference between a man and a turd is that after you've laid a turd you don't have to hug it.

– Julian Barnes, *Staring at the Sun*

Hatred of Women

it's a point of honour
with them to treat their wives
like whores, they talk about bedding
them as they talk
about going to the privy.

– Alden Nowton, 'Cousins'

. . . the beliefs that women are stupid, petty, manipulative, dishonest, silly, gossipy, irrational, incompetent, undependable, narcissistic, castrating, dirty, over-emotional, unable to make altruistic or moral judgments, oversexed, undersexed . . . culminate in attitudes that demean our bodies, our abilities, our characters, and our efforts, and imply that we must be controlled, dominated, subdued, abused and used, not only for male benefit but for our own.

– Sheila Ruth, 'A Feminist Analysis of the New Right', in *Women's Studies International Forum*

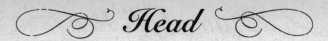

Head

The head is always the dupe of the heart.
> – François, duc de La Rochefoucauld, *Réflexions ou sentences et maximes morales*

. . . Henry Miller's observation somewhere that sex is all in the head, i.e. dumb girls, dumb screwing.
> – William Styron, *Sophie's Choice*

See also: THE MIND.

Heart

The heart of a maiden is a dark forest.
> – Russian proverb

> I understand the ties that are between us too well to talk
>   about the heart –
>   that pump!
> It lies between the brain box and the penis.
>   and when these masters stir that slave will jump.
> – James Simmons, 'The Summing Up'

What they call 'heart' is located far lower than the fourth waistcoat button.
> – Georg Christopher Lichtenberg (attributed)

> Never give all the heart, for love
> . . .
> O never give the heart outright,
> – W.B. Yeats, 'Never Give All the Heart'

> When Adam found his rib was gone
> He cursed and sighed and cried and swore

And looked with cold resentment on
The creature God had used it for.
. . .
Though shoulder, bosom, lip and knee
Are praised in every kind of art,
Here is love's true anatomy:
His rib is gone, he'll have her heart.
– John Hollander, 'The Lady's Maid's Song'

When I was one and twenty
I heard a wise man say,
'Give crowns and pounds and guineas
But not your heart away;'
. . .
And I am two and twenty
And oh, 'tis true 'tis true.
– A.E. Housman, 'When I was One and Twenty'

From whence do glance love's piercing darts,
That make such holes into our hearts.
– George Peele, 'The Hunting of Cupid's Song'

What comes from the heart, goes to the heart.
– Samuel Taylor Coleridge

Never love with all your heart,
It only ends in aching.
– Countee Cullen

The heart is a lonely hunter
– Carson McCullers, title of novel

My heart is a lonely hunter that hunts on a lonely hill.
– William Sharp, 'The Lonely Hunter'

My heart belongs to Daddy
'Cause my daddy, he treats it so well.
– Cole Porter, 'My Heart Belongs to Daddy', from the
   musical *Leave It to Me*

The heart has its reasons, which reason does not know.
– Pascal, *Pensées*

A pity beyond all telling
Is hid in the heart of love.
– W.B. Yeats, *The Countess Cathleen*: 'The Pity of Love'

I thought no more was needed
Youth to prolong
Than dumbbell and foil
To keep the body young.
Oh, who could have foretold
That the heart grows old?
– W.B. Yeats, 'Song'

Flaubert says that the heart is like a palm tree – 'it grows as soon
as it is stripped' – I disagree. The heart is constantly gouged until
in the end it is a ghost of a heart.
– Edna O'Brien, quoted in D. Halpern, *Our Private Lives*

Nobody has ever measured, not even poets, how much the heart
can hold.
– Zelda Fitzgerald

There are strings in the human heart that had better not be
vibrated.
– Charles Dickens, *Barnaby Rudge*

No use telling us love's
No use. Parched, cracked, the heart
Drains that love it loves
And still thirsts.
– W.D. Snodgrass, 'No Use'

Woman, though so kind she seems, will take your heart
        and tantalize it,
Were it made of Portland stone, she'd manage to
        McAdamize it.
        Dairy-maid or duchess,
        Keep it from her clutches
If you ever wish to know a quiet moment more.
– James Robinson Planché, 'Love, You've Been a Villain'

Heartbreak

Lie still, lie still, my breaking heart
My silent heart, lie still and break.
– Christina Rossetti, 'Mirage'

Beauty more than bitterness
Makes the heart break.
– Sara Teasdale, 'Capri'

Don't waste time trying to break a man's heart; be satisfied if
you can manage to chip it in a brand new place.
– Helen Rowland, *A Guide to Men*

I was cryin'
Cause you broke my heart in two
. . .
So I was cryin'
On account of
You.
– Langston Hughes, 'Late Last Night'

See also: BROKEN HEART.

Heaven and Hell

Hell, madame, is to love no longer.
– Georges Bernanos, *The Diary of a Country Priest*

Parting is all we know of heaven,
And all we need of hell.
– Emily Dickinson, 'Life'

Heav'n has no rage like love to hatred turn'd
Nor hell a fury like a woman scorned.
– William Congreve, *The Mourning Bride*

O what a heaven is love!
O what a hell!
– Thomas Dekker, *The Honest Whore*

Henpecked Husbands

They are sorry houses, where hens crow, and the cock holds his peace.
– John Florio, *Firste Frutes*

The missus is master. Petticoat government.
– James Joyce, *Ulysses*

But – Oh! ye lords of ladies intellectual
Inform us truly, have they not henpeck'd you all?
– George Gordon, Lord Byron, *Don Juan*

Cursed be the man, the poorest wretch in life,
The crouching vassal to the tyrant wife,
Who has no will but by her permission.
. . .
Who dreads a curtain lecture worse than hell.
– Robert Burns, 'The Henpecked Husband'

Hesitation

She who hesitates is lost.
> – Anonymous

He who hesitates is bossed.
> – Sonia Chapman (attributed)

Heterosexuality

Breathes there a man with hide so tough
Who says two sexes aren't enough.
> – Samuel Hoffenstein, 'The Sexes'

Hiding Love

To hide a passion is inconceivable: not because the human subject is too weak, but because passion is in its essence made to be seen: I want you to know that I am hiding something from you, that is the active paradox I must resolve; I want you to know that I don't want to show my feelings: that is the message I address to the other.
> – Roland Barthes, *A Lover's Discourse*

Hips

. . . the language of hips.
> – Juan Goytisolo, *Makbara*

(hips pumping pleasure into hips)
  – e.e. cummings, 'Sonnets – Actualities X'

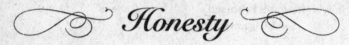

Honesty

No more masks! No more mythologies.
  – Muriel Rukeyser, in F. Howe and E. Bass, *No More Masks!*

> She tore off mask after mask –
> Wonder Woman
> Noble Martyr
> Big Mama
> Con Woman
> Tough Broad
> Sexy Kitten
> Cold Bitch
> Daddy's Girl
> Frightened Child
> Whiny Brat
> and on and on . . .
>   – Nancy Green, 'Masks and Mirrors', in *True to Life Adventure
>   Stories*

There was altogether too much candour in married life; it was an indelicate modern idea, and frequently led to upsets in the household, if not divorce.
  – Muriel Spark, *Memento Mori*

Honesty is praised and starves.
  – Juvenal, *Satires*

Honeymoon

Honeymoon: applied to those married persons that love well at first, and decline in affection afterward; it is honey now, but it will change as the moon.

– Thomas Blount, *Glossographia*

When a couple are newly married, the first month is honey-moon, or smick smack; the second is hither and thither; the third is thwick thwack; the fourth, the devil take them that brought thee and I together.

– John Ray, *English Proverbs*

> Said a newly-wed maiden of Ealing,
> 'A honeymoon seems so appealing
>   But for nearly two weeks
>   I've heard only bed squeaks,
> And seen nothing but cracks in the ceiling.'

– Anonymous English Limerick

Niagara Falls is only the second biggest disappointment of the standard honeymoon.

– Oscar Wilde

> Of all the things that change
> The one that shows most fickle and strange
> And takes the most eccentric range
> Is the moon, so called of honey.

– Thomas Hood, *Miss Kilmansegg*

> The indifferent clerk he knowing what was going to
>   happen
> The lobby zombies they knowing what
> The whistling elevator man he knowing
> The winking bellboy knowing
> Everybody knowing! I'd almost be inclined not to do
>   anything!

– Gregory Corso, 'Marriage'

The honeymoon wasn't such a ghastly experience really; it was afterwards that was really awful.
. . .
Honeymooning is a very overrated occupation.
> – Noel Coward, *Private Lives*

The terrible question which confronts all brides is whether to pin up their curls and cream their faces before going to bed.
> – Virginia Graham, *Everything's Too Something*

The honeymoon is over when he phones that he'll be late for supper – and she has already left a note that it's in the refrigerator.
> – Bill Lawrence, in *Reader's Digest*, January 1955

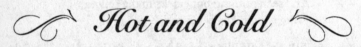

Hot and Cold

Over hot, over cold.
> – David Fergusson, *Scottish Proverbs*

Hote loue is soon colde.
> – R. Whitford, *Werke for Householders*

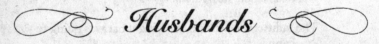

Husbands

He tells you when you've got on too much lipstick,
And helps you with your girdle when your hips stick.
> – Ogden Nash, *Verses*: 'The Perfect Husband'

Marriage is not harmed by seducers but by cowardly husbands.
> – Søren Kierkegaard, *Either/Or*

Changing husbands is only changing troubles.
> – Kathleen Norris, *Handful of Living*

Chumps make the best husbands. When you marry, Sally, grab a chump. Tap his forehead first, and if it rings solid, don't hesitate. All the unhappy marriages come from the husbands having brains. What good are brains to a man? They only unsettle him.
> – P.G. Wodehouse, *The Adventures of Sally*

> The men that women marry
> And why they marry them, will always be
> A marvel and a mystery to the world.
> – Henry Wadsworth Longfellow, 'Michael Angelo'

A husband is what is left of a lover after the nerve has been extracted.
> – Helen Rowland, *The Rubaiyat of a Bachelor*

The calmest husbands make the stormiest wives.
> – Thomas Dekker, *The Honest Whore*

Who needs a husband. To hump and jump and bump and pump.
> – John Gregory Dunne, *Dutch Shea, Jr*

> If ever two were one, then surely we,
> If ever man were lov'd by wife, then thee.
> . . .
> Thy love is such I can no way repay,
> The heavens reward thee manifold I pray.
> – Anne Bradstreet, 'To My Dear and Loving Husband'

There is so little difference between husbands you might as well keep the first.
> – Adela Rogers St John (attributed)

HUSBANDS

Husbands are like fires. They go out if unattended.
> – Zsa Zsa Gabor, in *Newsweek,* 1960

To a fond spouse a wife shows no mercy.
> – Juvenal, *Sixth Satire* (trans. by William Gifford)

There is only one real tragedy in a woman's life. The fact that the past is always her lover, and the future invariably her husband.
> – Oscar Wilde, *An Ideal Husband*

There you are you see, quite simple. If you cannot have your dear husband for a comfort and a delight, for a breadwinner and a crosspatch, for a sofa, chair, or hot-water bottle, one can use him as a Cross to be borne.
> – Stevie Smith, *Novel on Yellow Paper*

The most popular labour-saving device is still a husband with money.
> – Joey Adams, *Cindy and I*

> Why have scores of such lovely, gifted girls
>   Married impossible men?
> . . .
> Repeat 'impossible men'; not merely rustic,
> Foul-tempered or depraved
> . . .
> Impossible men: idle, illiterate
> Self-pitying, dirty, sly,
> . . .
> Has God's supply of tolerable husbands
> Fallen, in fact ,so low?
> – Robert Graves, 'A Slice of Wedding Cake'

The son of a bitch is acting even when he takes his pyjamas off.
> – Carole Lombard, speaking of her husband William Powell

The trouble with some women is they get excited about nothing
– and then marry him.
> – Cher (attributed)

To catch a husband is an art, to keep him a job.
> – Simone de Beauvoir (attributed)

I think everybody really will concede that on this, of all days, I
should begin my speech with the words 'My husband and I'.
> – Elizabeth II, in the *Observer* (London), on her 25th wedding
> anniversary

> Mender of toys, leader of boys,
> Changer of fuses, kisser of bruises,
> Bless him, dear Lord.
> Mover of couches, soother of ouches,
> Pounder of nails, teller of tales
> Reward him, O Lord.
> Hanger of screens, counsellor of teens,
> Fixer of bikes, chastiser of tykes,
> Help him, O Lord.
> Raker of leaves, cleaner of eaves,
> Dryer of dishes, fulfiller of wishes . . .
> Bless him, O Lord.
> – Jo Ann Heidbreder

> . . . I grant the husband in the home
> Disrupts its neat machinery.
> His shaving brush, his sorry comb,
> Mar tidy bathroom scenery.
> . . .
> What gadget's useful as a spouse?
> Considering that a minute,
> Confess that every proper house
> Should have a husband in it.
> – Phyllis McGinley, 'Apology for Husbands (in answer to a
> friend's observation that they're more bother than they're
> worth)'

The lover in the husband may be lost.
– Lord Lyttelton, quoted in S. Friedman, *Secret Loves*

See also: BRIDEGROOMS.

Husbands and Wives

I know not which lives more unnatural lives,
Obeying husbands, or commanding wives.
– Benjamin Franklin, *Poor Richard's Almanac*

Tho' marriage makes man and wife one flesh, it leaves 'em still two fools.
– William Congreve, *The Double Dealer*

You can bear your own faults, and why not a fault in your wife?
– Benjamin Franklin

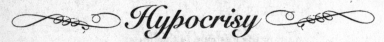

Hypocrisy

Hypocrisy is a sort of homage that vice pays virtue.
– Thomas Fuller, *Gnomologia: Adagies and Proverbs*

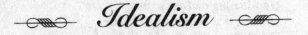

Idealism

A man struggles for an ideal, a principle, and always his cock gets in the way.
– Meyer Levin, *Gore and Igor*

Imagination

My imaginations are as foul
As Vulcan's stithy.
– William Shakespeare, *Hamlet*

A lady's imagination is very rapid; it jumps from admiration to love, from love to matrimony in a moment.
– Jane Austen, *Pride and Prejudice*

Think of your mistress.
– Honoré de Balzac, *The Physiology of Marriage*, advice to bored husbands

Does the imagination dwell most
Upon a woman won or lost.
– W.B. Yeats, 'The Tower'

The finest bosom in nature is not so fine as what imagination forms.
– Dr Gregory, *A Father's Legacy to His Daughters*

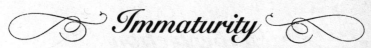

Immaturity

why this baby, this boy, this baby-man
he's just a mass of contradictions
claims reason for himself
institutionalizes his hatred
gives her his seat on the bus
wages war in Indochina
and nods off in front of the TV
and dreams of mommy
and dreams of power
This baby will not grow up

he thinks he can do what he wants
he has fastened his mouth on my life.
– Sondra Segal, 'The Baby–Man', in *Heresies 1981*

Immodesty

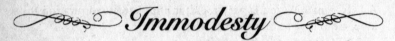

Immodest creature, you do not want a woman who will accept your faults, you want one who pretends that you are faultless – one that will caress the hand that strikes her and kiss the lips that lie to her.

> – George Sand, *Intimate Journals*

Impatience

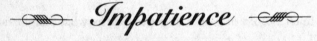

He who is not impatient is not in love.

> – Italian proverb

Imperfection

The lover who has not felt the hot tears rise at the sight of some slight, infinitely poignant imperfection in the body of the beloved, has never loved.

> – M. Levy, *The Moons of Paradise*

See also: BLEMISHES.

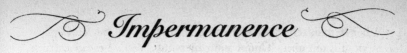

Impermanence

Impermanence – all is impermanence.
The cock rises to fall again.
– Erica Jong, 'To the Goddess'

Impotence

Gather ye rosebuds while ye may
    Old time is still a-flying;
And the penis which is stiff today
    Tomorrow will be dying.
– Anonymous, 'Chanson Antique'

I have seen it happen, often, to men who could not friggle when they wanted, because they hadn't wanted when they could.
– François Rabelais, *Gangantua and Pantagruel*

May your fire never go out.
– Traditional Irish toast

Impotent with her, he is a standing bone with me.
– John Barth, *Letters*

Domine Do Little: An impotent old fellow.
– Francis Grose, *A Classical Dictionary of the Vulgar Tongue*

When all else fails, pray.
– Tim and Beverly La Haye, *The Act of Marriage*

Use it or lose it.
– Popular saying

When a man tells you he's run out of steam in the sex depart-
ment, I'll tell him, 'Count your blessings; you've escaped from
the clutches of a cruel tyrant. Enjoy!'
– Richard J. Needham

While a person does not give up on sex, sex does not give up on
a person.
– Gabriel García Márquez (attributed)

> She does her softest Joys dispense,
> Off'ring her virgin Innocence
> A victim to Love's Sacred Flame;
> While the o'er Ravished Shepard lies
> Unable to perform the Sacrifice.
> – Aphra Behn, 'The Disappointment'

> Ev'n her fair hand, which might bid heat return
> To frozen Age, and make cold Hermits burn,
> Appl'd to my dead Cinder, warms no more
> Than Fire to Ashes cou'd past flames restore.
> . . .
> Trembling, confus'd, despairing, limber, dry
> A wishing, weak, unmoving lump I lie
> . . .
> This dart of Love . . .
> . . .
> Which Nature still directed with such Art,
> That it through ev'ry Port, reached ev'ry Heart,
> Stiffly resolv'd, 'twould carelessly invade,
> Woman or man nor ought its fury staid;
> Where e'er it pierc'd, entrance it found or made –
> Now languid lies, in this unhappy hour,
> Shrunk up, and Sapless, like a wither'd Flow'r.
> – John Wilmot, Earl of Rochester, 'The Imperfect Enjoyment'

> You've been a good ole wagon daddy, but you done
> broke down.
> – Bessie Smith, 'You've Been a Good Ole Wagon'

IMPOTENCE

He curs'd his Birth, his Fate, his Stars;
But more the Shepardess's charms,
Whose soft bewitching influence
Had damned him to the Hell of Impotence.
– John Wilmot, Earl of Rochester, 'The Disappointment'

To succeed with the opposite sex, tell her you're impotent. She can't wait to disprove it.
– Cary Grant (attributed), at age 72

John Anderson, my Jo, John
    When first when ye began,
Ye had as good a tail-tree
    As any ither man;
But now it's waxen wan, John
    And aft requires my helping hand
– Robert Burns, 'John Anderson, My Jo'

There is nothing certain in man's life but this:
That he must lose it.
– Owen Meredith, *Clytemnestra*

This is the monstrosity in love lady – that the will is infinite and the execution confined, that the desire is boundless, and the act a slave to limit.
– William Shakespeare, *Troilus and Cressida*

The pitcher that goes too often to the well is broken and lost.
– English proverb

When the snows cover the mountains, there can be scant heat in the valleys of the codpiece.
– François Rabelais, *Gargantua and Pantagruel*

It is vain to water the plant
When the root is dead.
– Robert Greene, *Morando*

Women, fire in their crotch, won't burn out, begin by fighting off pricks, end by going wild hunting for one that still works.
— John Updike, *Rabbit Redux*

═══ *Impregnation* ═══

You cleft me with your beauty's pulse, and now
Your pulse has taken body.
— Genevieve Taggard, 'With Child'

I plant so lovingly now.
— Walt Whitman, 'A Woman Waits for Me'

He said it was artificial respiration, but now I find I am to have his child.
— Anthony Burgess, *Inside Mr Enderby*

I pour the stuff to start sons and daughters fit for these
     States,
   I press slow rude muscle,
I brace myself effectually, I listen to no entreaties,
I dare not withdraw until I deposit what
     has so long accumulated within me.
— Walt Whitman, *Leaves of Grass*

A surly and pessimistic Druid,
A defeatist, if only he knew it,
    Said, 'The world's on the skids,
    And I think having kids
Is a waste of good seminal fluid.'
— Anonymous Limerick

Incest

The trouble with incest is that it gets you involved with relatives.
> – George S. Kaufman (attributed)

Men often marry their mothers.
> – Edna Ferber, *Saratoga Trunk*

Incompatibility

The notion that a true and loving . . . wife inspires a man to high endeavour is largely illusory. Every sane woman knows instinctively, as a matter of fact, that the highest aspirations of her husband are fundamentally inimical to her, and that the realization is apt to cost her her possession of him.
> – H.L. Mencken, *Prejudices*

A little imcompatibility is the spice of life, particularly if he has income and she is pattable.
> – Ogden Nash, *Versus*, 'I do, I will, I have'

Dear wife, give in or get out
. . .
I like my loving in the light; for you
the darkest night is still too bright.
Beneath your girdles and gowns you hide
yourself, while for me
naked is barely nude enough.
> – Martial, *Select Epigrams of Martial* (trans. and adapted by
> Donald C. Goertz)

What a woman wants, you are out of.
> – O. Henry, 'Cupid à la Carte'

Poor ghost, old love, speak
with your old voice
of flaming insight
that kept us awake all night
In one bed and apart.
– Robert Lowell, 'The Old Flame'

The distance is wide that sheets will not decide.
– John Ray, *English Proverbs*

The two extremes appear as man and wife,
Coupled together for the sake of strife.
– Charles Churchill, 'The Rosciad'

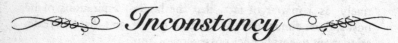

Inconstancy

She is constant only in her inconstancy.
– Ovid, *Tristia*

Love lodged in a woman's breast
Is but a guest.
– Sir Henry Wotton, *A Woman's Heart*

A fickle and changeful thing is a woman ever.
– Virgil, *Aeneid*

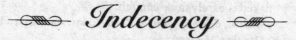

Indecency

The most virtuous woman is often indecent without knowing it.
– Honoré de Balzac, *The Physiology of Marriage*

Indecency and fun are old cronies.
— S.S. Cox, *Why We Laugh*

The older one grows, the more one likes indecency.
— Virginia Woolf (attributed)

Is nakedness indecent? No, not inherently. It is your thought, your sophistication, your fear, your respectability, that is indecent. There come moods when these clothes of ours are not only irksome to wear, but are themselves indecent.
— Walt Whitman, *Specimen Days and Collect*

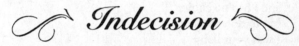

Indecision

While we ponder when to begin it becomes too late.
— Quintilian, *De Institutione Oratoria*

Indifference

The tragedy of love is indifference.
— W. Somerset Maugham, *The Trembling of a Leaf*

Indiscretion

Women in love pardon great indiscretions more easily than little infidelities.
— François, duc de La Rochefoucauld, *Réflexions ou sentences et maximes morales*

A lover without indiscretion is no lover at all.
– Thomas Hardy, *The Hand of Ethelberta*

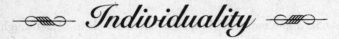

Individuality

> I said
> your words
> till my throat
> closed up
> and I had
> no voice
> and I had no choice
> but to do your song
> I was your baby
> I was you too long.
> – Dory Previn, 'I Was You'

You love me so much, you want to put me in your pocket. And I should die there smothered.
– D.H. Lawrence, *Sons and Lovers*

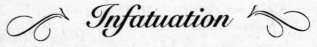

Infatuation

Infatuation is like paralysis, it is often all on one side.
– Helen Rowland

Infatuation is when you think he's as sexy as Robert Redford, as smart as Henry Kissinger, as noble as Ralph Nader, as funny as Woody Allen, and as athletic as Jimmy Connors. Love is when you realize he's as sexy as Woody Allen, as smart as Jimmy

Connors, as funny as Ralph Nader, as athletic as Henry Kissinger and nothing like Robert Redford – but you'll take him anyway.

– Judith Viorst, in *Redbook* (New York), 1975

I know I am but summer to your heart,
And not the full four seasons of the year.

– Edna St Vincent Millay, 'I Know That I Am But Summer to
Your Heart'

Infidelity

Frankie and Johnny were lovers, oh Lordy, how they
could love,
Swore to be true to each other, true as the stars above;
He was her man, and he done her wrong.

– Anonymous, 'Frankie and Johnny'

Between a man and a woman a husband's infidelity is nothing. A man imposes no bastards on his wife.

– Samuel Johnson, quoted in James Boswell, *The Life of
Samuel Johnson*

When Eve saw her reflection in a pool, she sought Adam and accused him of infidelity.

– Ambrose Bierce, *The Devil's Dictionary*

There are women whose infidelities are the only link thay have with their husbands.

– Sacha Guitry (attributed)

It is the fear of middle-age in the young, of old-age in the middle-aged, which is the prime cause of infidelity, that infallible rejuvenator.

– Cyril Connolly (attributed)

Love grows bitter with treason.
– A.C. Swinburne

See also: BETRAYAL; UNFAITHFULNESS.

Innocence

A gaudy dress and gentle air
   May slightly touch the heart,
But it's innocence and modesty
   That polishes the dart.
– Robert Burns, 'She Walks in Beauty'

There is no aphrodisiac like innocence.
   – Jean Baudrillard, *Cool Memories*

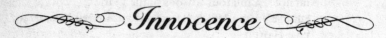

Insatiability

. . . it seems to make no difference how much the poor bastard actually gets, for he is dreaming about tomorrow's pussy even while pumping away at today's.
   – Philip Roth, *Portnoy's Complaint*

Verily, I can no more do without a woman than a blind man without his staff; my gimlet must drill or I could not live.
   – François Rabelais, *Gargantua and Pantagruel*

I cry we have sex in the head in the pants in the street waking sleeping reading writing thinking dying – and I have seen me and seen you wince and jerk with the heat of it beat of it meat of it and I swear there is no relief in sight.
   – Seymour Krim, *Views of a Nearsighted Cannoneer*

You always have a ready mouth for a ripe cherry.
. . .
The sea complains for want of water.
   – Thomas Fuller, *Gnomologia: Adagies and Proverbs*

Like a lady can't go through a plate glass window and go to bed with you five seconds later. But every guy in the audience is the same – you can idolize your wife, just be crazy about her, be on the way home from work, have a head-on collision with a Greyhound bus, in a disaster area. Forty people lying dead on the highway – not even in the hospital, in the ambulance the guy makes a play for the nurse.
   – Lenny Bruce, quoted in J. Cohen, *The Essential Lenny Bruce*

Insensitivity

My nakedness the mask itself
covers the spirit completely.
I grow large and plastic
I am the enormous doll
and you dive into me
and hold on to the limbs,
wriggling like a fish
and expire on my dry beach
and never know I am there.
– Elizabeth Fenton, 'Masks'

It's what you do, unthinking,
That makes the quick tear start;
The tear may be forgotten –
But the hurt stays in the heart.
– Ella Higgenson, 'Wearing out Love'

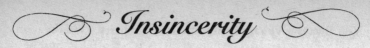

Insincerity

Marriage always demands the greatest understanding of the art of insincerity possible between two human beings.

    – Vicki Baum, *And Life Goes On*

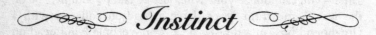

Instinct

Nine-tenths of that which is attributed to sexuality is the work of our magnificent ability to imagine, which is no longer an instinct, but exactly the opposite: a creation.

    – José Ortega y Gasset

Intelligence

After a girl has got a good figure and wavy hair and a smooth complexion and attractive teeth it will be time enough to worry about brains.

    – Anonymous, *Reflexions of a Bachelor*

       See also: BRAIN, THE MIND.

Interchangeability of Lovers

'Tis sweet to think, that, where'er we rove
We are sure to find something blissful and dear,
And that, when we're far from the lips we love,
We've but to make love to the lips we are near.

    – Thomas Moore, *Juvenile Poems*: ''Tis Sweet to Think'

When I'm not near the girl I love, I love the girl I'm near
Every femme that flutters by me is a flame that must be
    fanned.
When I can't fondle the hand I'm fond of
I fondle the hand at hand.
   – E.Y. Harburg, song from the musical *Finian's Rainbow*,
    (music by Burton Lane)

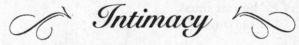

Intimacy

The eyes start love: intimacy perfects it.
   – Publilius Syrus, *Sententiae*

Intimacy is a difficult art.
   – Virginia Woolf, *The Second Common Reader*: 'Geraldine and
    Jane'

Sweet, casual intimacy, the soft-fleshed loveliness indisputably
possessed.
   – Carson McCullers, *The Ballad of the Sad Café*

Jealousy

There's more self-love than love in jealousy.
   – François, duc de La Rochefoucauld, *Réflexions ou sentences et
    maximes morales*

Jealousy, the great exaggerator.
   – Friedrich von Schiller (attributed)

Jealousy is the great preservative of family life and marital faith-
fulness . . . Jealousy is the inseparable companion of love and its
intensity is the pure gauge of love's strength.
> – William McDougal, in A. Ellis and A. Abarbanel,
> *Encyclopedia of Sexual Behavior*

> O! beware, my lord, of jealousy.
> It is the green eye'd monster which doth mock
> The meat it feeds on.
> – William Shakespeare, *Othello*

Jealousy and love are sisters.
> – Russian proverb

Love that survives jealousy is like a pretty face after small pox; a
bit pockmarked forever.
> – Paul Bourget, *La Physiologie de l'amour moderne*

> Thou tyrant, tyrant jealousy,
> Thou tyrant of the mind.
> – John Dryden, 'Song of Jealousy, Love Triumphant'

> Nor Jealousy
> was understood, the injured lover's hell.
> – John Milton, *Paradise Lost*

A woman's natural jealousy is not a man's loving another, but
his forsaking her.
> – James Hinton, *Life in Nature*

A lewd bachelor makes a jealous husband.
> – H.G. Bohn, *Handbook of Proverbs*

Jealousy has always been the whetstone of love and some would
say that without it love does not have its inner shiver.
> – Edna O'Brien, *Some Irish Loving*

Jealousy is the greatest of all sufferings, and the one that arouses the least pity in persons who cause it.
> – François, duc de La Rochefoucauld, *Réflexions ou sentences et maximes morales*

He who loves without jealousy does not truly love.
> – The Zohar

Inquisitiveness as seldom cures jealousy, as drinking in a fever quenches the thirst.
> – William Wycherley, *Love in a Wood*

A jealous man always finds more than he is looking for.
> – Madeleine de Scudéry, *Choix de pensées*: 'De la Jalousie'

Her jealousy never slept.
> – Mary Shelley, *The Mortal Immortal*

Man is jealous because of his *amour propre*; woman is jealous because of her lack of it.
> – Germaine Greer, *The Female Eunuch*

And why should I be cold, my lad,
    And why should you repine,
Because I love a dark head
    That never shall be mine?
> – Edna St Vincent Millay, 'Sonnet'

Jealousy is the most dreadfully involuntary of all sins.
> – Iris Murdoch, *The Black Prince*

. . . it's matrimonial suicide to be jealous when you have a really good reason.
> – Clare Booth Luce, *The Women*

The 'Green-Eyed Monster' causes much woe, but the absence of this ugly serpent argues the presence of a corpse whose name is Eros.

    – Minna Antrim, *Naked Truths and Veiled Allusions*

Jealousy, that dragon which slays love under the pretence of keeping it alive.

    – Havelock Ellis, *On Life and Sex*

The fundamental torment of adult jealousy is not the sense of betrayal but uncertainty. The jealous are driven by the need, above all, to know.

    – A. Alvarez, *Life After Marriage*

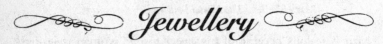

Jewellery

Dumb jewels, in their silent kind
More than quick words, do move a woman's mind.
    – William Shakespeare, *Two Gentlemen of Verona*

Orators of love.
    – Samuel Daniel, 'The Complaint of Rosamund'

See also: DIAMONDS; GIFTS.

Jilting

Heiresses are never jilted.
    – George Meredith

Jobs

I have found it impossible to carry the heavy burden of responsibility and to discharge my duties of King as I would wish to do without the help and support of the woman I love.
— Edward VIII, abdication speech

Jokes

The smutty joke is like a denudation of a person of the opposite sex toward whom the joke is directed. Through the utterance of obscene words, the person attacked is forced to picture the parts of the body in question, or the sexual act . . .
— Sigmund Freud, *Wit and its Relation to the Unconscious*

Joy

My candle burns at both ends;
    It will not last the night;
But, ah, my foes, and oh, my friends –
It gives a lovely light.
— Edna St Vincent Millay, *A Few Figs from Thistles*: 'First Fig'

Kinds of Love

Inebriations of love, shadows of love, fantasies of love, but never yet the one true love.
— Edna O'Brien, *Some Irish Loving*

There is only one kind of love, but there are a thousand different imitations of it.
> – François, duc de La Rochefoucauld, *Réflexions ou sentences et maximes morales*

Perfect love means to love one through whom one becomes unhappy.
> – Søren Kierkegaard

> How do I love thee? Let me count the ways.
> . . .
> I love thee to the level of everyday's
> Most quiet need, by sun and candlelight.
> I love thee freely, as men strive for Right;
> I love thee purely, as they turn from Praise.
> I love thee with the passion put to use
> In my old griefs, and with my childhood faith.
> > – Elizabeth Barrett Browning, 'How do I Love Thee?'

Immature love says: 'I love you because I need you.'
Mature love says: 'I need you because I love you.'
> – Erich Fromm, *The Art of Loving*

Nuptial love maketh mankind;
Friendly love perfecteth it;
But wanton love corrupteth and embaseth it.
> – Francis Bacon, *Essay Ten*: 'On Love'

Young love is a flame, often very hot and fierce but still only light and flickering. The love of the older and disciplined heart is as coals deep-burning, unquenchable.
> – Henry Ward Beecher

Kiss and Tell

'Tis no sin love's fruits to steal,
But the sweet thefts to reveal;
To be taken, to be seen,
These have crimes accounted been.
– Ben Jonson, *Volpone*

'Gin a body, kiss a body, need the world ken.
– Robert Burns, 'Comin' Thro' the Rye'

You must not kiss and tell.
– William Congreve, *Love for Love*

Like all skirt-chasers, he had to report on his successes.
– Isaac Bashevis Singer, *Shosha*

Some men kiss and do not tell, some kiss and tell; but George
Moore told and did not kiss.
– Susan Mitchell, quoted in Oliver St John Gogarty, *As I Was
Going Down Sackville Street*

Kisses

Kisses may not spread germs, but they certainly lower
resistance.
– Louise Erickson, in *Reader's Digest*, May 1949

Let him kiss me with the kisses of his mouth:
For thy love is better than wine.
– The Bible: The Song of Songs

Why this delay? Why waste the time in kissing?
What is the very meaning of a kiss?

Think of the best, the ultimate joy we are missing!
  Hasten the moment of our mutual bliss.
. . .
So come to bed; there's time for dawdling after.
– Petronius, 'A Plea for Haste' (trans. by Louis Untermeyer)

Give me a kiss, and to that kiss a score;
Then to that twenty, add a hundred more;
A thousand to that hundred; so kiss on,
To make that thousand up a million;
Treble that million, and when that is done,
Let's kiss afresh, as when we first begun.
– Robert Herrick, 'To Anthea'

A kiss, when all is said, what is it?
An oath that's given closer than before;
A promise more precise; the sealing of
Confessions that till then were barely breathed;
A rosy dot placed on the i in loving;
A secret that is confined to a mouth
And not to ears.
– Edmond Rostand, *Cyrano de Bergerac*

But you would have felt my soul in a kiss,
  And known that once if I loved you well;
And I would have given my soul for this
  To burn for ever in burning hell.
– A.C. Swinburne, 'Les Noyades'

It takes a lot of practice for a girl to kiss like a beginner.
– Anonymous, in the *Ladies Home Journal* (New York)

A delectable gal from Augusta
vowed that no one ever had bussed her.
  But an expert from France
  took a bilingual chance
and the mixture of tongues quite nonplussed her.
– Conrad Aiken, *A Seizure of Limericks*

He kissed me and now I am somebody else.
> – Gabriela Mistral, 'He Kissed Me'

Where do the noses go?
> – Ernest Hemingway, *For Whom the Bell Tolls* (Ingrid
> Bergman to Gary Cooper in the movie of the novel)

. . . kissing puberty-stricken boys until their groins turned blue
and ached.
> – Gilbert Sorrentino, *Mulligan's Stew*

> I twist your arm,
> You twist my leg.
> I make you cry,
> You make me beg.
> I dry your eyes
> You dry my nose,
> And that's the way
> The kissing goes.
> – William Wood, 'A Deux'

> I fear thy kisses, gentle maiden,
>> Thou need not fear mine,
> My spirit is too deeply laden
>> Ever to burden thine.
> – Percy Bysshe Shelley, 'To —, I Fear Thy Kisses'

Never let a fool kiss you or a kiss fool you.
> – Joey Adams (attributed)

> Strephon kissed in the spring,
>> Robin in the fall,
> But Colin only looked at me
>> And never kissed at all.

> Strephon's kiss was lost in jest,
>> Robin's lost in play,

But the kiss in Colin's eyes
    Haunts me night and day.
– Sara Teasdale, 'The Look'

When a rogue kisses you, count your teeth.
    – Yiddish proverb

. . . there is nothing like a kiss long and hot down to your soul almost paralyses you . . .
    – James Joyce, *Ulysses*

Kissing is man's greatest invention. All animals copulate, but only humans kiss.
    – Tom Robbins, *Even Cowgirls Get the Blues*

To lip a wanton is to secure a couch.
    – William Shakespeare, *Othello*

What is this thing called a kiss? French, tongue, soul, chaste, motherly, fatherly, brotherly, sisterly, ass, genital, Judas, trembling, rough, hesitant, sweet, soft, wet, dying, fevered, good-night, farewell, burning, and chocolate.
    – Gilbert Sorrentino, *Mulligan's Stew*

A kiss can be a comma, a question mark or an exclamation mark. That's a basic spelling that every woman should know.
    – Mistinguette (attributed)

Reap many kisses and little love.
    – Robert Greene, *Orpharion*

The first kiss is stolen by the man;
The last is begged by the woman.
    – H.L. Mencken, *A Mencken Chrestomathy*

The kiss originated when the first male reptile licked the first female reptile, implying in a subtle, complimentary way that she

was as succulent as the small reptile he had for dinner the night before.
    – F. Scott Fitzgerald, *The Crack-Up*

Oh, what lies there are in kisses.
    – Heinrich Heine, 'In den Küssen welche Lüge'

    I wonder who's kissing her now.
    – Frank Adams and Will M. Hough, title of song

Blondes have the hottest kisses. Red-heads are fair to middling torrid, and brunettes are the frigidest of all. It's something to do with hormones, no doubt.
    – Ronald Reagan (attributed)

    A fine romance with no kisses,
    A fine romance, my friend, this is.
    We should be like a couple of hot tomatoes,
    But you're as cold as yesterday's mashed potatoes.
    – Dorothy Fields, 'A Fine Romance' (music by Jerome Kern)

    Rose kissed me today.
        Will she kiss me tomorrow?
    Let it be as it may,
        Rose kissed me today.
    – Austin Dobson, 'A Kiss'

You have to kiss an awful lot of frogs before you find a prince.
    – Graffito

i like kissing this and that of you,
    – e.e. cummings, 'i like my body when it is with your body'

The storm, the storm of a kiss.
    – Theodore Roethke, 'Her Words'

Knees

Her rich attire creeps rustling to her knees.
– John Keats, 'The Eve of St Agnes'

The human knee is a joint and not an entertainment.
– Percy Hammond, in F. Sullivan, *Our Times*

Up to the knee is free.
– German proverb

. . . knees modestly kissing.
– James Joyce, *Ulysses*

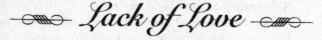

Lack of Love

I saw that lack of love contaminates.
You know I know you know I know you know.
– Thom Gunn, 'Carnal Knowledge'

Without love our life is . . . a ship without a rudder . . . like a
body without a soul.
– Sholem Aleichem

Life after life after life goes by
without poetry
without seemliness
without love . . .
– Denise Levertov, *The Sorrow Dance*: 'The Mutes'

Lack of Sex

Yes, I haven't had enough sex.
> – Sir John Betjeman, on BBC TV, February 1983, when asked
> if he had any regrets about his life

I ain't had no lovin'
Since April, January, June, or July.
> – Jack Norworth, 'Shine On, Harvest Moon' (music by Nora
> Bayes-Norworth)

My wife doesn't. Understand me?
> – Anonymous

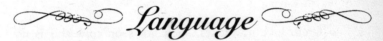

Language

I had a feeling that Pandora's box contained the mysteries of woman's sensuality, so different from man's, and for which man's language was inadequate. The language of sex is yet to be invented. The language of the senses is yet to be explored.
> – Anaïs Nin, *Diary*

Lasses

Glasses and lasses are brittle ware.
> – James Kelly, *Complete Collection of Scottish Proverbs*

Lasting Love

Of all my loves the last, for hereafter I shall glow with passion for no other woman.
　　　– Horace, *Odes*

> Eternity is passion, girl or boy
> Cry on the onset of their sexual joy
> 'For ever and for ever'
> – W.B. Yeats, 'Whence Had They Come?'

> For the sword outwears its sheath,
> And the soul outwears the breast,
> And the heart must pause to breathe,
> And love itself have rest.
> – George Gordon, Lord Byron, 'So, We'll Go No More
> 　A-Roving'

. . . so fareth love nowadays, soon hot soon cold: this is no stability. But the old love was not so.
　　　– Sir Thomas Malory, *Le Morte D'Arthur*

Great passions, my dear, don't exist: they're liars' fantasies. What do exist are little loves that may last for a short or longer while.
　　　– Anna Magnani, quoted in Oriana Fallaci, *The Egotists*

> Parrots, tortoises and redwoods
> Live longer than men do,
> Men longer than dogs do,
> Dogs a longer life than love does.
> – Edna St Vincent Millay, 'Pretty Love I Must Outlive You'

Love is free: to promise for ever to love the same woman is no less absurd than to promise to believe the same creed; such a vow in both cases excludes us from all inquiry.
　　　– Percy Bysshe Shelley, *Prometheus Unbound*

See also: ETERNAL LOVE.

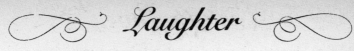

Laughter

A maid that laughs is half taken.
> – John Ray, *English Proverbs*

Sexiness wears thin after a while and beauty fades, but to be married to a man who makes you laugh every day, ah, now that's a treat.
> – Joanne Woodward (attributed)

Some women blush when they are kissed; some call the police; some swear; some bite. But the worst are those that laugh.
> – Anonymous

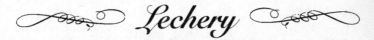

Lechery

An itching, tainted intellectual pride
Goads the salt lecher till he has to know
Whether all women's eyes grow bright and wide
All wives and whores and virgins shudder so.

Hunters of women burn to show their skill,
Yet when the panting quarry has been caught
Mere force of habit drives them to the kill;
The soft flesh is less savoury than their sport.
> – John Press, 'Womanizers'

Reefer was a wenchman.
> – James Joyce, *Finnegan's Wake*

He's had more dolly than you've had cream cakes.
> – Harold Pinter, *The Homecoming*

Legs

. . . soft–limbs new–bathed and fair with olive oil.
– Hesiod, in Lucas, *Greek Poetry for Everyone*

Fain would I kiss my Julia's dainty Leg
Which is as white and hairless as an egg.
– Robert Herrick, *Hesperides*: 'On Julia's Legs'

. . . a fattish leg leaks obscenely from the dress.
– e.e. cummings, 'Sonnets – Realities XIV'

(set on big legs nice to pinch
assiduously which just graze each other)
– e.e. cummings, 'Sonnets – Realities XVI'

Lewdness

Lewdness grows by degrees, from a wart to a wen.
– Oswald Dykes, *English Proverbs*

. . . irreproachable ladies firmly lewd
– e.e. cummings, 'Sonnets – Realities X'

Libido

Libido is a term used in the theory of instincts for describing the
dynamic manifestation of sexuality.
– Sigmund Freud

There was a young man of Toledo
Who travelled around incognito.
    The reason he did
    Was to bolster his id
While appeasing his savage libido.
– Anonymous Limerick

Lies

When the heart is full of lust the mouth's full of leasings.*
  – James Kelly, *Complete Collection of Scottish Proverbs*
    [*leasings=lies]

Fool, not to know that love endures no tie
And Jove but laughs at lovers' perjury.
– John Dryden, *Palamon and Arcite*

    At lovers' perjuries
They say, Jove laughs.
– William Shakespeare, *Romeo and Juliet*

Everybody lies about sex.
  – R.A. Heinlein, *The Notebooks of Lazurus Long*

I don't approve of guys using false pretences on dolls, except, of
course, when nothing else will do.
  – Damon Runyon, *Take It Easy*

By the time you swear you're his,
Shivering and sighing,
And he vows his passion is
Infinite, undying –
Lady, make a note of this:
One of you is lying.
– Dorothy Parker, 'Unfortunate Coincidence'

When my love swears that she is made of truth,
I do believe her, though I know she lies,
That she might think me some untutor'd youth,
Unlearned in the world's false subtleties.
– William Shakespeare, 'Sonnet 138'

Every man should love his wife.
But a promise can't make you love.
It only makes you lie.
–J.L. Williams, 'Why Marry?'

The cruellest lies are often told in silence.
– Robert Louis Stevenson, *Virginibus Puerisque*

Actions lie louder than words.
– Carolyn Wells (attributed)

Telling lies is a fault in a boy, an art in a lover, an accomplishment in a bachelor, and second-nature in a married man.
– Helen Rowland, *A Guide to Men*

Life

Life is a sexually transmitted disease.
– Graffito

Oh, love is real enough. You'll find it some day, but it has one arch-enemy – and that is life.
–Jean Anouilh, *Ardèle*

Light

Venus is spoilt by serving her in darkness;
Surely you know, sight is the path of love.
– Sextus Aurelius Propertius

Grey daylight, loathed of lovers . . .
– Meleager of Gadora, in Lucas, *Greek Poetry for Everyone*

Daylight love . . . 'tis the best.
– John Updike, *Rabbit Redux*

Liking and Loving

I never liked the men I loved, and never loved the men I liked.
– Fanny Brice, in Norman Katkov, *The Fabulous Fanny*

We must love one another, yes, yes, that's all true enough, but nothing says we have to like each other.
– Peter De Vries, *The Glory of the Hummingbird*

Lingerie

Brevity: the soul of lingerie.
– Dorothy Parker, quoted in A. Woollcott, *While Rome Burns*

A century ago women wore unmentionables; today they wear nothing to speak of.
– Anonymous

. . . let eyesight see that the film of breast-sheath and panty-crotch are mere cloth of this world and not the webbing of paradise.
– Seymour Krim, *Views of a Nearsighted Cannoneer*

A lady is one who never shows her underwear unintentionally.
– Lillian Day, *Kiss and Tell*

A century and a half ago there were no knickers and girls read the Bible, now they wear impenetrable body stockings and read *Portnoy's Complaint*.
– Kenneth Tynan

I consider it is better to be trussed up than flopping about, but I suppose it depends on the individual.
– John Cavanagh, a comment on no-bra fashions

See also: CLOTHES; DRESS; FETISHES.

Lips

Free of her lips, free of her hips.
– English proverb

Her lips suck forth my soul.
– Christopher Marlowe, *Dr Faustus*

Kissable lips and flirtable eyes still foul the good and fool the wise.
– J.B. Opdyke, *Amor Vitaque*

> Sweet lips . . .
> Men touch them, and change in a trice
> The lilies and languors of virtue
> For the roses and rapture of vice.
> – A.C. Swinburne, 'Dolores'

. . . her odalisk lips lusciously smeared with the salve of swine fat and rosewater.
> – James Joyce, *Ulysses*

Her lips are lilies, flowing with liquid myrrh.
> – The Bible: Song Of Songs

> Red hair she had and golden skin,
> Her sulky lips were shaped for sin.
> – Sir John Betjeman, *A Few Late Chrysanthemums*: 'The Licorice Fields at Pontefract'

> But the loveliest things of beauty God ever has showed to me,
> Are her voice, and her hair, and eyes, and the dear red curve of her lips.
> – John Masefield, 'Beauty'

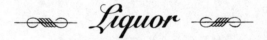

Liquor

Enjoyed it? One more drink and I'd have been under the host.
> – Dorothy Parker, quoted in R.E. Drennon, *Wit's End*

> Candy
> Is dandy
> But liquor
> Is quicker.
> – Ogden Nash, 'Reflection on Ice-Breaking'

> Many a miss would not be a missus
> If liquor did not add a spark to her kisses.
> – E.L.C., 'Listen', in *Life*, March 1933

Literature

Literature is mostly about having sex and not much about having children; life is the other way around.
— David Lodge, *The British Museum is Falling Down*

Little

Little pot, soon hot.
— John Heywood, *A Dialogue containing the number in effect of all the Proverbs in the English Tongue*

Little dogs have long tails.
— James Kelly, *Complete Collection of Scottish Proverbs*

Little strokes fell great oaks.
— John Ray, *English Proverbs*

Living Together

Do you think your mother and I should have liv'd comfortably so long together, if ever we had been married?
— John Gay, *The Beggar's Opera*

There would be no society if living together depended upon understanding each other.
— Eric Hoffer, *Reflections on the Human Condition*

In the old days, one married a wife; now one forms a company with a female partner, or moves in to live with a friend. Then one seduces the partner, or defiles the friend.
— August Strindberg, *The Father*

Come live with me and be my love.
And we will all the pleasures prove. . .
– Christopher Marlowe, 'The Passionate Shepherd to His
   Love'

Come, live with me and be my love
And we shall all the pleasures prove
Of peace and plenty, bed and board
That chance employment may afford.
– C. Day Lewis, 'Two Songs'

Come live with me and be my love
In statutory Christian sin.
And we shall all the pleasures prove
Of two-room flats and moral gin.
– Samuel Hoffenstein, 'Invocation'

Horses (thou sayest) and asses men may try,
And ring suspected vessels ere they buy;
But wives, a random choice, untried that take,
They dream in courtship, but in wedlock wake.
– Geoffrey Chaucer, *The Wife of Bath's Tale* (trans. by
   Alexander Pope)

Lolitas

Lolita, light of my life, fire of my loins, my sin, my soul.
   – Vladimir Nabokov, *Lolita*

Loneliness

Be good and you will be lonesome.
— Mark Twain, *Following the Equator*

If you are afraid of loneliness, do not marry.
— Anton Chekhov

Sadly, there are whole segments of the population that believe the answer to existential loneliness is the next passing crotch.
— Judianne Densen-Gerber, *Walk in My Shoes*

God created man, and finding him not sufficiently alone, gave him a female companion to make him feel his solitude more keenly.
— Paul Valéry, *Mauvais Pensées et autres*

I have not known no loneliness like this
Locked in your arms and bent beneath your kiss.
— Babette Deutsch, *Banners*: 'Solitude'

The desert of loneliness and recrimination that men call love.
— Samuel Beckett, quoted in the *New York Review of Books*, 1971

Forever at her side, yet always alone.
— Felix Arvers, *Mes Heures perdues*

Two fears alternate in marriage, the one of loneliness and the other of bondage. The dread of loneliness is greater than the fear of bondage so we get married.
— Cyril Connolly, *The Unquiet Grave*

But when he's gone
Me and them lonesome blues collide
The bed's too big
The frying pan is too wide.
— Joni Mitchell, 'My Old Man'

Get off me baby, get off and leave me alone
I'm lonely when you're gone but I'm lonelier when
     you're home . . .
– Holly Near, 'Get Off Me Baby'

What makes loneliness an anguish
Is not that I have no one to share my burden
But this: I have only my own burden to bear.
– Dag Hammarskjöld, *Markings*

Longing

Will these wild oats never be sown?
    – Thomas Heywood, *The Wise Woman of Hogsden*

I have heard the mermaids singing, each to each.
I do not that think they will sing to me.
    – T.S. Eliot, 'The Love Song of J. Alfred Prufrock'

                  Oh lovelorn heart, give o'er –
Cease thy vain dreams of beauty's warmth – forget
    The face thou longest for.
    – Meleager, 'Lost Desire'

Somewhere there was a gentle man with a cock that wore a
jaunty grin and stayed long enough for you to get to know him.
    – Jill Robinson, *Bed/Time/Story*

I'm a young woman, and I ain't done running around.
    – Bessie Smith, 'Young Woman Blues'

Everywhere pass, with lips for me unmoved
The lovely ladies that I might have loved
That never now will love me, late or soon.
   . . .

O loves forbidden, I'll go home and start
My pipe and light my fire and break my heart
And read a book on sexual morality.
– Gerald Gould, 'From Monogamy'

Why am I crying after love?
– Sara Teasdale, 'Spring Night'

When you really want to love you will find it waiting for you.
– Oscar Wilde, *De Profundis*

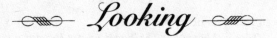 *Looking*

Loving comes from looking.
– John Clarke, *Paroemiologia Anglo-Latina*

Wine comes in at the mouth
And love comes in at the eye;
That's all we know for truth
Before we grow old and die.
I lift my glass to my mouth
I look at you, and I sigh.
– W.B. Yeats, 'A Drinking Song'

He gave her a look you could have poured on a waffle.
– Ring Lardner

. . . her very looks a cunt.
– John Wilmot, Earl of Rochester, 'The Imperfect Enjoyment'

May not a woman look, but she must love?
– Robert Greene, 'Metamorphosis'

I looked and I loved.
– Edward Gibbon, *Memoirs*

See also: VOYEURS.

Loss of Love

'Tis not love's going hurts my days,
But that it went in little ways.
– Edna St Vincent Millay, 'The Spring and the Fall'

I hold it true, what e'er befall;
    I feel it, when I sorrow most ;
    'Tis better to have loved and lost
Than never to have loved at all.
– Alfred, Lord Tennyson, *In Memoriam*

And if I never fall in love again,
That's soon enough for me.
I'm going to lock my heart and throw away the key.
– Jimmy Eaton and Terry Shand, 'I'm Going to Lock My
  Heart'

How can I go on living, now that we're apart?
  – George Brown (Billy Hill), 'Have You Ever Been Lonely'

Murmur, a little sadly, how love fled.
– W.B. Yeats, 'When You Are Old'

    The man is quickened so with grief,
He wanders god-like or like thief
Inside and out, below, above,
Without relief seeking lost love.
– Robert Graves, 'Lost Love'

The kiss of virgins, first-fruits of the bed,
Soft speech, smooth touch, the lips, the maidenhead:
These, and a thousand sweets, could never be
So near, or dear, as thou wast once to me.
– Robert Herrick, 'His Farewell to Sack'

Love

Here is a perfect poem:
to awaken a longing,
to nourish it,
to develop it,
to increase it,
to stimulate it,
to gratify it.
– Honoré de Balzac, quoted in Th. Van de Velde, *Ideal
    Marriage*

Love, oh love, oh careless love.
– Blues song

Love doesn't just sit there, like a stone, it has to be made, like
bread, re-made all the time, made new.
– Ursula Le Guin, *The Lathe of Heaven*

I know of only one duty, and that is to love.
– Albert Camus, *The Notebooks*

I love you no matter what you do, but do you have to do so
much of it?
– Jean Illsley Clarke, *Self-Esteem: A Family Affair*

If you be loved, be worthy of love.
– Ovid

Love seeketh not itself to please
Nor for itself hath any care,
But for another gives its ease
And builds a Heaven in Hell's despair.
– William Blake, *Songs of Experience*: 'The Clod and the
Pebble'

I would have made love to a goat, to know what love is.
– Samuel Beckett, *Molloy*

People need a little loving, and God, sometimes it's sad all the
shit they have to go through to find some.
– Richard Brautigan, *The Betrayed Kingdom*

Love can deny naught to love.
– Codex Amoris, in Th. Van de Velde, *Ideal Marriage*

If thou be loved – love!
– Seneca, *Epiistolae*

Follow love and it will flee,
Flee love and it will follow thee.
– John Ray, *English Proverbs*

If of herself she will not love.
Nothing can make her.
– Sir John Suckling, 'Song'

You can't make a person love another person. You can only
pray for it.
– John Barth, *Letters*

What is precious is never to forget
The essential delight of the blood drawn from ageless
springs
. . .

Never to deny its pleasure in the morning light
Nor its grave evening demand for love.
– Stephen Spender, 'I Think Continuously of Those Who
  Were Truly Great'

Give all to love
Obey thy heart
Friends, kindred, days
Estate, good fame
Plans, credit, and the muse
Nothing refuse.
– Ralph Waldo Emerson, 'Give All to Love'

You can give without loving, but you cannot love without giving.
– Ami Carmichael

Oh love will make a dog howl in tune.
– Francis Beaumont and John Fletcher, *The Queen of Corinth*

Love is indescribable and unconditional. I could tell you a thousand things that it is not, but not one that it is.
– Duke Ellington, *Music is My Mistress*

All you need is love
Love is all you need.
– John Lennon, 'All You Need Is Love'

It's love's illusions I recall
I really don't know love at all.
– Joni Mitchell, 'Both Sides, Now'

A woman of 47 who has been married 27 years and has six children knows what love really is and once described it for me like this: 'Love is what you have been through with somebody.'
– James Thurber, in *Life*, 14 March 1960

To some people
Love is given
To others
Only heaven.
– Langston Hughes, 'Luck'

Love consists of this, that two solitudes protect and touch and
greet each other.
> – Rainer Maria Rilke, *Letters to a Young Poet* (trans. by M.D.
> Herter Norton

Like love we don't know where or why
Like love we can't compel or fly
Like love we often weep
Like love we seldom keep.
– W.H. Auden, 'Law Like Love'

All women think they merit to be lov'd.
> – Ovid, *Ars Amatoria* (trans. by John Dryden)

I'll be damned if I'll love just to love – there's got to be more to it
than that.
> – Julius J. Epstein, Philip G. Epstein and Howard Koch, from
> the film *Casablanca*, spoken by Humphrey Bogart

No, there's nothing half so sweet in life
As love's young dream.
– Thomas Moore, *Juvenile Poems*: 'Love's Young Dream'

Amo, amas, I love a lass,
As a cedar tall and slender,
Sweet cowslip's grace
Is her nom'native case
And she's of the feminine gender.
– John O'Keefe, *Agreeable Surprise*: 'Amo, Amas'

CLEOPATRA: If it be love indeed, tell me how much.
ANTONY: There's beggary in the love that can be reckoned.
CLEOPATRA: I'll set a bourn how far to be belov'd.
ANTONY: Then must thou needs find new heaven, new earth.
> – William Shakespeare, *Antony and Cleopatra*

Love has as few problems as a motorcar. The only problems are the driver, the passengers, and the road.
> – Franz Kafka (attributed)

Love is always revolutionary.
> – Andrei Voznesensky (attributed)

Ah – love – the walks over soft grass, the smiles over candlelight, the arguments over just about everything else.
> – Max Headroom

. . . and love is only and always about the lover and never the beloved.
> – Nikki Giovanni, 'They Clapped'

Love wakes men, once a lifetime each.
> – Coventry Patmore, 'The Revelation'

Love: Change of

My love is like foliage in the woods. Time will change it as winter changes trees.
> – Emily Brontë, *Wuthering Heights*, describing Cathy's love
> for Heathcliff

Love: Con

Love says, mine. Love says, I could eat you up. Love says, stay as you are, be my private thing, don't you dare have ideas I don't share. Love has just got to gobble the other, bones and all, crunch. I don't want to do that. I am sure I don't want it done to me.
> – Marge Piercy, *Braid and Lies*

And all the little emptiness of love.
> – Rupert Brooke, *New Numbers*: 'Peace'

Love is monotonous, incessant, boring; no one can stand for anyone's repeating the most ingenious statement so many times and yet the lover demands unending reiteration that his beloved adores him. And vice versa: when someone is not in love, love bestowed upon him oppresses him and drives him mad by its utter plodding quality.
> – José Ortega y Gasset

To be wise, and love,
Exceeds man's might.
> – William Shakespeare, *Troilus and Cressida*

Love is a game – yes?
I think it is a drowning.
> – Amy Lowell, 'What O'Clock'

Love, love, love – all the wretched cant of it, masking egotism, lust, masochism, fantasy under a mythology of sentimental postures, a welter of self-induced miseries and joys, blinding and masking the essential personalities in frozen gestures of courtship, in the kissing and the dating and the desire, the compliments and quarrels which vivify its barrenness.
> – Germaine Greer, *The Female Eunuch*

Love is a shadow
How can you lie and cry after it.
– Sylvia Plath, 'Elm'

Oh love you've been a villain since the days of Troy
    and Helen,
When you caused the fall of Paris and of very many
    more.
– James Planché, 'Love You've Been a Villain'

Love, oh love, oh loveless love
Has set our hearts on goalless goals
From silkless silk and milkless milk
We've grown used to soulless souls.
– Billie Holliday, 'Loveless Love'

Love: Course of

I suppose one thing led to another.
    – Prince Philip, Duke of Edinburgh, on his engagement to
    Princess Elizabeth

Love: Differences between Men and Women

To women, love is an occupation; to men; it is a preoccupation.
    – Lionel Strachey (attributed)

Woman wants monogamy;
Man delights in novelty.
Love is a woman's moon and sun;
Man has other forms of fun.

Woman lives but in her lord;
Count to ten and man is bored.
With this the gist and sum of it,
What earthly good can come of it?
– Dorothy Parker, *Not So Deep at the Well*: 'General Review of
  the Sex Situation'

The word love has by no means the same sense for both sexes,
and this is one cause of the serious misunderstandings between
them.
   – Simone de Beauvoir

Man dreams of fame while woman wakes to love.
– Alfred, Lord Tennyson, *Idylls of the King*

Man's love is of man's life a thing apart
'Tis woman's whole existence.
– George Gordon, Lord Byron, *Don Juan*

Man's love is of man's life a thing apart;
    Girls aren't like that.
– Kingsley Amis, 'A Bookshop Idyll'

Man begins by making love and ends by loving a woman;
woman begins by loving a man and ends by loving love.
   – Rémy de Gourmont

In her first passion woman loves her lover,
In all others all she loves is love,
Which grows a habit she can ne'er get over
And fits her loosely – like an easy glove.
– George Gordon, Lord Byron, *Don Juan*

For a woman loves forever, but a man loves for a
    day . . .
But it is the woman, ever the woman, who pays.
– W.D. Cobb. 'It's the Woman Who Pays'

LOVE: DIFFERENCES BETWEEN MEN AND WOMEN

Love: Madness of

. . . you must know how madly in love with you I am; why I can neither piddle or cack for love of you.
> – François Rabelais, *Gargantua and Pantagruel*

My love's a noble madness.
> – John Dryden, *All for Love*

Love: Nature of

Soon hot, soon cold
> – English proverb

Hot love is soon cold.
> – John Heywood, *A Dialogue containing the number in effect of all the Proverbs in the English Tongue*

Love will creep where it cannot go.
> – English proverb

Love will find a way.
> – English proverb

Love begets love.
> – Latin proverb

In love, everything is true, everything is false; and it is the one subject on which one cannot express an absurdity.
> – Nicolas Chamfort, *Maximes et pensées*

Love is an affectation of a mind that has nothing better to engage it.
> – Theophrastus

Love is a capricious creature which desires everything and can be contented with almost nothing.
– Madeleine de Scudéry, *Choix de pensées*: 'De l'Amour'

Teenagers don't know what love is. They have mixed-up ideas. They go for a drive, and the boy runs out of gas, and they smooch a litle and the girl says she loves him. That isn't love. Love is when you are married twenty-five years, smooching in your living room, and he runs out of gas and she says she still loves him. That's love.
– Norm Crosby, comedy routine

A woman can be proud and stiff
When on love intent;
But Love has pitched his mansion in
The place of excrement;
For nothing can be sole or whole
That has not been rent.
– W.B. Yeats, *Words For Music Perhaps*, 'Crazy Jane Talks With the Bishop'

In real love you want the other person's good. In romantic love you want the other person.
– Margaret Anderson, *The Fiery Fountains*

Love: New

A new love drives out the old.
– French proverb

'Tis good to be off wi' the old love
Before you are on wi' the new.
– Richard Edwards, *Damon and Pythias*

And I shall find some girl perhaps
And a better one than you
With eyes as wise, but kinder
And lips so soft, but true
And I dare say she will do.
– Rupert Brooke, 'The Chilterns'

Love: Power of

Naughty Love, to what dost thou not compel our mortal hearts?
– Robert Burton, *Anatomy of Melancholy*

Love: Pro

The one thing that I know about love for sure is that it is the only game in town and that you must keep going back to bat again and again and again. I have no respect for anyone who says they've given up, or that they're not looking or that they're tired. That is to abrogate one's responsibility as a human being.
– Harlan Ellison, in John Winokur, *A Curmudgeon's Garden of Love*

Love: Pure

If pure love exists, free from the dross of our other passions, it lies hidden in the depths of our hearts and unknown to ourselves.
– François, duc de La Rochefoucauld, *Réflexions ou sentences et maximes morales*

Love: Quality of

He loves but little who
Can say and count in words, how much he loves.
– Dante Alighieri, *Vita Nuova*

Yes, this was love, the ridiculous bouncing of the buttocks and
the wilting of the poor, insignificant moist little penis.
– D.H. Lawrence, *Lady Chatterley's Lover*

No one ever loved anyone the way everyone wants to be loved.
– Mignon McLaughlin (attributed)

Love: Reasons for

I love not for those eyes, nor hair,
Nor cheeks, nor lips, nor teeth so rare,
Nor for thy speech, thy neck, nor breast,
Nor for thy belly, nor the rest;
   Nor for thy hand, nor foot so small:
   But would'st thou know, dear sweet? – for All.
– Thomas Carew, 'Love's Compliment'

If thou must love me, let it be for naught
Except for love sake's only.
– Elizabeth Barrett Browning, 'If Thou Must Love Me'

Love: Renunciation of

Don't send me off, now that your thirst
Is quenched and all seem so stale to you.

Keep me a short three months more,
Then I'll be sated too.
– Heinrich Heine

It is our own mediocrity that makes us let go of love, makes us renounce it. True love doesn't know the meaning of renunciation . . .
– Eugène Ionesco, *The Hermit*

I pray thee leave, love me no more
    Call home the heart you gave me.
– Michael Drayton, 'To His Coy Love'

I am tired of love.
– Hilaire Belloc, 'Fatigue'

We must in tears
Unwind a love knit up in many years.
In this last kiss I here surrender thee
Back to thyself, so thou again art free;
Thou in another, sad as that, resend
The truest heart that lover e'er did lend.
– Henry King, Bishop of Chichester, 'The Surrender'

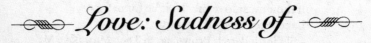 *Love: Sadness of*

A pity beyond all telling
Is hid in the heart of love.
– W.B. Yeats, 'The Pity of Love'

Love and Marriage

Love is often the fruit of marriage.
– Molière

One should always be in love. That is the reason one should not marry.
– Oscar Wilde, *A Woman of No Importance*

Love is so much better when you are not married.
– Maria Callas (attributed)

Love is an ideal thing, marriage is a real thing; a confusion of the real with the ideal never goes unpunished.
– Johann Wolfgang von Goethe

Love and marriage, love and marriage,
Go together like a horse and carriage,
This I tell ya, brother
You can't have one without the other.
– Sammy Cahn, 'Love and Marriage' (music by James Van Heusen)

'Love, shmove,' Papa used to say, 'I love blintzes; did I marry one?'
– Sammy Levinson, *One Era & Out the Other*

People marry for a variety of other reasons and with varying results; but to marry for love is to invite inevitable tragedy.
– James Branch Cabell, *The Cream of the Jest*

On the whole, I haven't found men unduly loath to say, 'I love you.' The real trick is to get them to say, 'Will you marry me?'
– Ilka Chase, in *This Week*, 5 February 1956

Love and Money

Money cannot buy
the fuel of love
but is excellent kindling.
– W.H. Auden

Love lasteth as long as the money endureth.
– William Caxton, *The Game of Chesse*

Even a bald head
A pretty girl can hold
If he is willing
To pay his weight in gold.
– English song

Money can't buy love – but it certainly puts you in a wonderful
bargaining position.
– Harrison Baker (attributed)

I don't pop my cork for every guy I see.
Hey! big spender, spend a little time with me.
– Dorothy Fields, 'Big Spender' (music by Cy Coleman)

Her beauty was sold for an old man's gold –
She's a bird in a gilded cage.
– Arthur J. Lamb, 'A Bird in a Gilded Cage'

A poor beauty finds more lovers than husbands.
– George Herbert, *Outlandish Proverbs*

Love and Poverty

Lips, however rosy, must be fed.
– A.B. Cheales, *Proverbial Folklore*

Love and Sex

You mustn't force sex to do the work of love or love to do the work of sex.
  – Mary McCarthy, *The Group*

Love is the self-delusion we manufacture to justify the trouble we take to have sex.
  – Dan Greenberg

Nobody dies from the lack of sex. It's lack of love we die from.
  – Margaret Atwood, *The Handmaid's Tale*

  Sex is a momentary itch
  Love never lets you go.
  – Kingsley Amis, 'An Ever-Fixed Mark'

It is not until sex has died out between a man and a woman that they can really love.
  – Enid Bagnold, *Autobiography*

Lust is what makes you keep wanting it, even when you have no desire to be with each other. Love is what makes you keep wanting to be with each other, even when you have no desire to do it.
  – Judith Viorst

You don't get high-quality sex without love . . .
  – Alex Comfort, *The Joy of Sex*

Love Letters

Love makes me write what shame forbids me speak.
  – Robert Herrick, 'What Shame Forbids to Speak'

I am two fools, I know,
For loving, and for saying so
In whining poetry.
– John Donne, 'The Triple Fool'

At the touch of love everyone becomes a poet.
– Plato, *Symposium*

And oft the pangs of absence to remove
By letters, soft interpreters of love.
– Matthew Prior, 'Henry and Emma'

But a woman's sayings to her lover,
Should be in wind and runnng water writ.
– Catullus, *Carmina* (trans. by Sir W. Marris)

I don't know what you want or what I am! You write to me like
a love, you treat me like a casual acquaintance!
– Edith Wharton, letter to W. Morton Fullerton

I look down the tracks and see you coming – and out of the haze
& mist your darling rumpled trousers are hurrying to me.
– Zelda Fitzgerald, letter to F. Scott Fitzgerald

Write to me . . . And let not the ink serve as a mask.
– Manuel Ugarte, letter to Delmira Agustini

They [lovers] read every word three ways; they read between
the lines and in the margins . . . They even take punctuation into
account.
– Mortimer J. Adler, in *Quote*, 26 December 1961

Sir, more than kisses, letters mingle souls.
– John Donne, verse letter to Sir Henry Wotton

A woman's best love letters are always written to the man she is
betraying.
– Lawrence Durrell, *Clea*

LOVE LETTERS

Lovemaking

I remember lovemaking as an exploration of a sadness so deep that people must go in pairs, one cannot go alone . . .
  – John Updike, *Couples*

It was lovemaking, Doctor, even though it was nasty. Maybe especially because it was nasty. Love is a smutty business, you know.
  – Tom Robbins, *Even Cowgirls Get the Blues*

We no longer make love. We occasionally fuck . . .
  – Walter Abish, 'Parting Shot'

Here we'll strip and cool our fire
In cream below, in milk-baths higher;
And when all wells are drawn dry,
I'll drink a tear out of thine eye.
  – Richard Lovelace, 'To Amarantha, That She Would
    Dishevel Her Hair'

Love can be made, using materials no more ethereal than an erect penis, a moist vagina, and a warm heart . . .
  – Tom Robbins, *Even Cowgirls Get the Blues*

. . . we lie together
after making love, quiet,
    touching along the length of our bodies,
familiar touch of the long-married.
  – Galway Kinnell, 'After Making Love We Hear Footsteps'

Lovemaking is radical, while marriage is conservative.
  – Eric Hoffer

In lovemaking, as in other arts, those who do it best cannot tell how it is done.
  – J.M. Barrie

Making love to a woman too many times is like scratching a place that doesn't itch any more.
— Anonymous

> Amo, amas
> I loved a lass
> And she was tall and slender
> Amas, amat
> I laid her flat
> And tickled her feminine gender.
> — Old schoolboy's rhyme

The prerequisite for making love is to like someone enormously.
— Helen Gurley Brown (attributed)

> It's time to make love. Douse the glim.
> The fireflies twinkle and dim.
> The stars lean together
> Like birds of a feather
> And the loin lies down with the limb.
> — Conrad Aiken, *A Seizure of Limericks*

See also: COPULATION; FORNICATION; SEXUAL INTERCOURSE.

Lover

A whining lover is a sorry fool.
— Alexander Ratcliff, 'A Satire Against Love'

WOMAN: You are the greatest lover I have ever known.
ALLEN: Well, I practise a lot when I am alone.
— Woody Allen

You are the very one I've searched for
    In many lands in every weather.
You are my sort; you understand me;
    As equals we can talk together.
– Heinrich Heine, 'Ich Liebe Solche Weissen Glieder' (trans.
  by Louis Untermeyer)

The sweeter the apple, the blacker the core,
Scratch a lover and find a foe.
– Dorothy Parker, 'Ballade of Great Weariness'

Lover, lunatic.
    – Plautus, *Mercater*

Lover, beware your lover, might well be an old maxim.
    – Maxwell Anderson, *Elizabeth the Queen*

We were no longer friend and friend
    But only lover and lover.
– Elinor Wylie, 'The Puritan's Ballad'

My lover is mine and I am his.
    – The Bible: Song of Songs

Notoriously, women tolerate qualities in a lover – moodiness, selfishness, unreliability, brutality – that they would never countenance in a husband, in return for excitement, an infusioin of intense feeling.
    – Susan Sontag, quoted in the *Village Voice* (New York),
      16 April 1982

Lover: Care of

Pluck me/pot me/peat me/feed me/water me/talk to me/weed me/seed me/deflower me/prune me/light me/tend me. HOURLY.

> – S. Wellbank, 'Why So Many of Them Die' (Your houseplant is a delicate thing. Follow these instructions carefully and it will bring you years of pleasure.)

Lover: Change of

Before you're off with the old lover
It's best to be on with the new.
– Anonymous, 'It's Gude to be Merry and Wise'

Gonna truck on down and spend my moo
Get some short-vamp shoes and a new guy too
'Cause I'm tired, mighty tired of you.
– Roberts and Fisher, 'Tired'

Lover: Choice of

Are you the new person drawn to me?
To begin with, take warning, I am surely
    far different from what you suppose.
. . .
Do you suppose you will find in me your ideal
Do you think it is so easy to have me become your
    lover?
– Walt Whitman, 'Are You the New Person Drawn to Me?'

He'd have given me rolling lands.
    House of marble and billowing farms
. . .
You – you'd only a lilting song
    Only a melody, happy and high
. . .
He'd have given me laces rare,
    Dresses that glimmered with frosty sheen
. . .
You – you'd only to whistle low,
    Gaily I followed wherever you led.
I took you and let him go –
    Someone ought to examine my head.
    – Dorothy Parker, 'The Choice'

I can love both fair and brown;
Her whom abundance melts, and her whom want
    betrays,
Her who loves loneness best, and her who masks and
    plays,
Her whom the country form'd and whom the town,
Her who believes, and her who tries,
Her who still weeps with spongy eyes,
And her who is dry cork, and never cries,
I can love her, and her, and you and you,
I can love any, so she be not true.
    – John Donne, 'The Indifferent'

Your true jilt uses men like chessmen, she never dwells so long on any single man as to overlook another who may prove more advantageous; nor gives one another's place, until she has seen that it is in for her interest; but if one is more useful to her than others, brings him in over the heads of all others.
    – Alexander Pope, *Thoughts on Various Subjects*

Every man needs two women, a quiet home-maker, and a thrilling nymph.
> – Iris Murdoch

Everybody winds up kissing the wrong person goodnight.
> – Andy Warhol, *From A to B and Back Again*

> When I am dead, you'll find it hard, says he
> To ever find another like me.
> What makes you think, as I suppose you do,
> I'll ever want another man like you?
> – Eugene T. Ware, 'He and She'

Finding a man is like finding a job; it's easier to find one when you already have one.
> – Paige Mitchell (attributed)

You need somebody to love while you're looking for someone to love.
> – Shelagh Delaney, *A Taste of Honey*

Lover: Deceiver

> I hear my daddy callin' some other woman's name.
> I know he don't mean me; I'm gonna answer jes de same.
> – Blues song

Lover: Defects in

She has the bear's ethereal grace,
　　The bland hyena's laugh,
The footstep of the elephant,
　　The neck of the giraffe,
I love her still, believe me,
　　Though my heart its passion hides;
'She's all my fancy painted her,'
　　But oh, how much besides.
– Lewis Carroll, *College Rhymes*: 'My Fancy'

The man I love got lowdown ways for true,
Well, I'm hinkty and lowdown too.
– W.C. Handy, 'The Basement Blues'

You're so mean and evil, you do things you ought not
　　do.
But you've got my brand of honey, so I guess I'll have
　　to put up with you.
– Jimmy Rushing and Count Basie, 'Going to Chicago Blues'

In faith, I do not love thee with mine eyes,
For they in thee a thousand errors note,
But 'tis my heart that loves what they despise.
– William Shakespeare, 'Sonnet 141'

Lover: Faults of

Love sees no faults.
　　– Thomas Fuller, *Gnomologia: Adagies and Proverbs*

Be to her virtues very kind
Be to her faults a little blind.
　　– Matthew Prior, 'An English Padlock'

Lover: Good

He's a deep-sea diver with a stroke that can't go wrong,
He's a deep-sea diver with a stroke that can't go wrong,
He can touch bottom and his wind holds out so long.
– Bessie Smith, 'Empty Bed Blues'

Just like a snail: that man of mine
He never likes to hurry; he takes his time.
– Trixie Smith, 'He Likes it Slow'

Lover: Inept

Even when they made love . . . it was perfunctory, as if he were
listening for something else, a phone call, a footfall. He was
scratching himself. She was like his hand.
– Margaret Atwood

He fell on me like a wave. But like a wave he washed away,
leaving no sign that he had been there.
– Louise Erdrich

Lovers are always in a hurry . . . like a racing river.
– Ben Ames Williams

He don't perform his duties like he used to.
He never hauls my ashes less I tell him to.
Before he gets to work, he says he's through.
My handy man ain't handy no more.
– Edith Wilson, 'My Handy Man'

Lover: Longing for

I am a lover and have not found my thing to love.
— Sherwood Anderson, *Winesburg, Ohio*

She denies me her bed. Half her body to love.
She has given half to Prudence.
    I die between.
— Paulus Silentarius, *Tantalos* (trans. by Dudley Fitts)

It was the promise of men, that around each corner there was yet another man, more wonderful than the last, that sustained me. You see, I had men confused with life . . . You can't get what you want from a man, not in this life.
— Nancy Friday, *My Mother, My Self*

Lover: Loss of

Though his suit was rejected,
He sadly reflected,
    That a lover forsaken
    A new love may get;
But a neck that's once broken
    Can never be set.
— Sir Walter Scott, *Peveril of the Peak*

Lover: Old

Yet still I love thee without art,
Ancient person of my heart.
— John Wilmot, Earl of Rochester, 'A Song of a Young Lady
  to Her Ancient Lover'

Come back to me in dreams, that I may give
Pulse for pulse, breath for breath:
Speak low, lean low,
As long ago, my love, how long ago.
– Christina Rossetti, 'Echo'

Look in my face; my name is Might-have-been;
I am also called No-more, Too-late, Farewell.
– Dante Gabriel Rossetti, *The House of Life*: 'A Superscription'

Lover: Quest for

O, beauty, are you not enough?
Why am I crying after love?
– Sarah Teasdale, *Rivers to the Sea*: 'Spring Night'

Somewhere there must be one
    Made for this soul, to move it;
– William Johnson Cory, *Amaturus*

Lover: Unknown

Unremembered and afar
I watched you as I watched a star,
Through darkness struggling into view
And I loved you better than you knew.
– Elizabeth Akers Allen

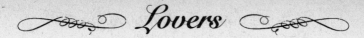

Lovers

Lovers behave far more respectably than married couples. Have you ever heard of a mistress-swapping party?
– Jilly Cooper, *Men and Super Men*

This maiden she lived with no other thought
    Than to love and be loved by me.
– Edgar Allan Poe, 'Annabel Lee'

The world will always welcome lovers
As time goes by.
– Herman Hupfeld, 'As Time Goes By'

She whom I love is hard to catch and conquer,
Hard, but O the glory of the winning were she won!
– George Meredith, *Love in the Valley*

I would not leave my little wooden hut for you!
I've got one lover and I don't want two.
– Thomas Mellor, 'I Wouldn't Leave My Little Wooden Hut
  for You'

    Love lasts or – or doesn't last.
. . .
Lovers must never crumple like cissies
or break down or cry about their wrongs.
If girls are sugar, God holds the sugar tongs.
– Gavin Ewart, 'Ella Mi Fu Rapita!'

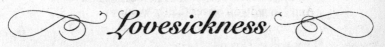

Lovesickness

If you shall find my lover, what shall you say to him? Tell him I am sick with love.
    – The Bible: Song of Songs

Love Songs

A love song is just a caress set to music.
— Sigmund Romberg (attributed)

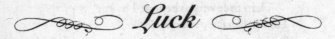

Luck

Greater luck hath no man than this, that he lay down his wife at the right moment.
— Samuel Butler

Lust

The expense of spirit in a waste of shame
Is lust in action; and till action, lust
Is perjured, murderous, bloody, full of blame,
Savage, extreme, rude, cruel, not to trust.
— William Shakespeare, 'Sonnet 129'

Love comforteth like sunshine after rain,
But Lust's effect is tempest after sun;
Love's gentle spring doth always fresh remain,
Lust's winter comes ere summer half be done;
Love surfeits not, Lust like a glutton dies,
Love is all truth, Lust full of forged lies.
— William Shakespeare, *Venus and Adonis*

Lust will not keep.
Something must be done about it.
— Inscription on the entrance gate to the Yoshiwara (the red light district of feudal Tokyo)

I was absolutely wild for her when she was a girl and I was a boy, absolutely off of my head with volcanic lust. I wanted to come, come, come.

> – Joseph Heller, *Something Happened*

So lust, though to a radiant angel link'd,
Will sate itself in a celestial bed
    And prey on garbage.

> – William Shakespeare, *Hamlet*

Thou deemest luste and love convertible.

> – Thomas Hoccleve, *De Regimine Principum*

The new lust gives the lecher the new thrill.

> – John Masefield, 'The Widow in Bye Street'

And concerning lust . . . it is a short pleasure, bought with long pain, a honeyed poison, a gulf of shame, a pickpurse, a breeder of diseases, a gall to the conscience, a corrosive to the heart, turning man's wit to foolish madness, the body's bane, and the soul's perdition.

> – John Taylor, *The Unnatural Father*

. . . wars, fires, plagues have not done that mischief to mankind as this burning lust, this brutish passion.

> – Robert Burton, *The Anatomy of Melancholy*

The most malignant of thy enemies is the lust that abides within thee.

> – Sa'dī, *Gulistān*

Lust is more abstract than logic; it seeks (hope triumphing over experience) for some purely sexual, hence purely imaginary, conjunction of an impossible maleness with an impossible femaleness.

> – C.S. Lewis, *The Allegory of Love*

The lust of the goat is the bounty of God.
– William Blake, *The Marriage of Heaven and Hell*

Our lust is brief.
– James Joyce, *Ulysses*

> Men triumph over women still,
> Men trample women's rights at will,
> And man's lust roves the world untamed.
> – John Masefield, 'C.L.M.'

Let my lusts be my ruin, then, since all else is a fake and a mockery.
– Hart Crane

> O sick, insatiable
> And constant lust.
> – Roy Fuller, 'Spring 1942'

. . . that blind goat-kicking lust, which would debase females, make all women cunts . . .
– Norman Mailer, *The Prisoner of Sex*

> But when lust
> By unchaste looks, loose gestures, and foul talk,
> But most by lewd and lavish act of sin,
> Lets in defilement to the inward parts,
> The soul grows clotted by contagion . . .
> – John Milton, *Comus*

I've looked at a lot of women with lust. I've committed adultery in my heart many times. This is something God recognizes I will do – and I have done it – and God forgives me.
– Jimmy Carter

> For forty years I shunned the lust
>   Inherent in my clay.

Death only was so amorous
    I let him have his way.
– Countee Cullen, 'For A Virgin Lady'

I'd call it love if love
didn't take so many years
but lust too is a jewel
a sweet flower . . .
– Adrienne Rich, *Necessities of Life*

Oh the monotonous meanness of his lust . . .
– Robert Lowell, 'To Speak of Woe That Is In Marriage'

Machismo

But machismo is about the conquest and humiliation of women.
    – V.S. Naipaul, *The Return of Eva Peron*

They fear women, so hate them, but as most are latently homo-
sexual they fear that more, so fifty times a day boastfully and
loudly proclaim for each other's benefit that they would hump a
rockpile if they thought a snake were underneath it.
    – Alexander Theroux, *Darconville's Cat*

While in the west machismo may not have the same connot-
ations as in Latin America – with regard to man's reproductive
capacity or wife-battering – it applies, in a more often attenuated
form, to men who fundamentally despise women, either boss-
ing them around, continually criticizing and seeking to 'put
them right', or affecting to love them while, in practice, abusing
and betraying them.
    – Amanda Hopkinson

Macho does not prove mucho.
    – Zsa Zsa Gabor (attributed)

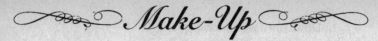

Make-Up

Give me a look, give me a face,
That makes simplicity a grace;
Robes loosely flowing, hair as free;
Such sweet neglect more taketh me
Than all the adulteries of art;
They strike mine eyes, but not my heart.
– Ben Jonson, 'Epicoene; or, The Silent Woman'

Male and Female

The two sexes mutually corrupt and improve each other.
– Mary Wollstonecraft, *A Vindication of the Rights of Woman*

And forget the He and She.
– John Donne, 'The Undertaking'

A woman is a woman until the day she dies, but a man is only a man as long as he can.
– Moms Mabley (attributed)

Blessings are found only where male and female are together.
– The Kabbalah

There never will be any rest between male and female so long as more than one of each exists upon earth or anywhere else.
– Charles Bukowski, 'Back-Up'

For men at most differ as Heaven and Earth
But women, worst and best, as Heaven and Hell.
– Alfred, Lord Tennyson, *Idylls of the King*

What is it men in women require?
The lineaments of gratified desire.
What is it women do in men require?
The lineaments of gratified desire.
– William Blake, 'A Question Answered'

We are told that the social gap of the sexes is narrowing, but I can only report that having . . . experienced life in both roles, there seems to be no aspect of existence, no moment of the day, no contact, no arrangement, no response, which is not different for men and women.
– Jan Morris, *Conundrum*

Men and women, women and men. It will never work.
– Erica Jong

Why can't a woman be more like a man?
– Alan J. Lerner, *My Fair Lady*

Nothing can vex
Like the opposite sex.
– George Starbuck Galbraith, in *Reader's Digest*,
November 1956

It takes all sorts to make a sex.
– Saki (attributed)

Male and female sexuality exist like 'His' and 'Hers' sweaters. The measurable difference is slight but it is highly significant . . .
– Beatrice Faust, *Women, Sex and Pornography*

Another American conspiracy of recent vintage holds that women are as highly sexed as men. This is the insane side of equality . . . the female sex drive is sixty per cent vanity, thirty per cent curiosity, and ten per cent physical. I didn't masturbate

until I was seventeen – find me a man who can make that statement.
– Florence King in J. Winokur, *The Portable Curmudgeon Redux*

See also: LOVE: DIFFERENCES BETWEEN MEN AND WOMEN.

Male Chauvinism

The male whale's penis is over six feet long . . . Whenever there is a particularly obnoxious male chauvinist doing his thing, the thought always dashes through my head: 'What would you say if I made you aware at this very moment that you are no bigger than a whale's "hard–on"?'
– Judianne Densen-Gerber, *Walk in My Shoes*

Like all rogues, he was a great calumniator of the fair sex.
– Sir Walter Scott, *The Heart of Midlothian*

Marital Conflict

I'm not living with you. We occupy the same cage.
– Tennessee Williams, *Cat on a Hot Tin Roof*

The best part of married life are the fights. The rest is merely so–so.
– Thornton Wilder, *The Matchmaker*

Wallpaper design for the marital bedroom:
EXCUSE ME COULD YOU PLEASE SAY THAT AGAIN I DON'T BELIEVE I HEARD YOU CORRECTLY LISTEN JUST WHO THE HELL DO YOU THINK YOU ARE FOR GOD'S SAKE WHAT AM I SUPPOSED TO BE YOUR

SERVANT DON'T YOU DARE TALK TO ME IN THAT TONE OF VOICE I GUESS WE JUST AREN'T MEANT TO BE TOGETHER THAT'S ALL I'VE HAD IT UP TO HERE WITH YOU THAT'S RIGHT YOU HEARD ME THAT'S NOT MEANT TO BE A THREAT WE'RE JUST IN DIFFERENT TIMES IN OUR LIFE O.K. GO AHEAD AND LEAVE I'LL HELP YOU PACK YOUR BAGS I GUESS WE DON'T NEED TO BE TOGETHER OH THAT'S CUTE REAL CUTE

> – Dan Greenberg and Suzanne O'Malley, *How to Survive Love and Marriage*

> My hopped up husband drops his home disputes,
> and hits the streets to cruise for prostitutes.
> – Robert Lowell, 'To Speak of Woe That Is In Marriage'

They waste their strength in venereal strife.
> – Lucretius, *De Rerum Natura*

The life of a wife and husband who love each other is never at rest. Whether the marriage is true or false, the marriage portion is the same: elemental discord.
> – Jean Giraudoux, *Tiger at the Gates*

Don't look back in anger, look forward in fury.
> – Anonymous

With women the heart argues, not the mind.
> – Matthew Arnold

Almost all married people fight, although many are ashamed to admit it. Actually, a marriage in which no quarrelling takes place may well be one that is dead or dying from emotional undernourishment. If you care, you probably fight.
> – Flora Davis, in *Glamour*, March 1969

In every house of marriage there's room for an interpreter.
> – Stanley Kunitz, *Route Six*

> Your old-fashioned tirade –
> loving, rapid, merciless –
> breaks like the Atlantic Ocean over my head.
> – Robert Lowell, 'Man and Wife'

Marriage is like life in this – that it is a field of battle and not a bed of roses.
> – Robert Louis Stevenson, *Virginibus Puerisque*

A Lexicon for Fighting Marital Fights, Arranged According to Subject:

Amnesia: 'Who do you think you ARE?'

Apology: 'PARdon me for LIVing.'

Family Tree: 'She's YOUR mother, not mine.'

Hearing impairment: 'Could you speak up a little? They can't hear you in Europe.'

Language barrier: 'What's the matter, you don't understand English?'

Mining: 'I hadn't realized we'd descended to that level.'

Wildlife: 'That's right, use physical violence. That's all an animal like you knows anyway.'
> – Dan Greenberg and Suzanne O'Malley, *How to Survive Love and Marriage*

Marriage accustomed one to the good things, so one came to take them for granted, but it magnified the bad things, so they came to feel as painful as a grain in one's eye. An open window, a forgotten quart of milk, a TV set left blaring, socks on the bathroom floor could become occasions for incredible rage.
> – Marilyn French, *The Women's Room*

All married couples should learn the art of battle as they should learn the art of making love. Good battle is objective and honest – never vicious and cruel. Good battle is healthy and constructive, and brings to the marriage the principle of equal partnership.

– Ann Landers, *Ann Landers Says Truth is Stranger*

In saying what is obvious, never choose cunning. Yelling works better.

– Cynthia Ozick, in *The First Ms. Reader*

I find my wife hath something in her gizzard that only waits for an opportunity of being provoked to bring up; but I will not, for my content–sake, give it.

– Samuel Pepys, *Diary*

I say, when there are spats, kiss and make up before the day is done and live to fight another day.

– Rev. Randolph Ray, in the *New York World Telegram and Sun*

Marriage

Strange to say what delight we married people have to see poor fools decoyed into our condition.

– Samuel Pepys, *Diary*

One should always marry in the same way as one dies; that is, only when it impossible to do otherwise.

– Leo Tolstoy (attributed)

It takes two to make a marriage a success and only one a failure.

– Herbert Louis Samuel, *A Book of Quotations*

> To keep your marriage brimming
> With love in the loving cup,
> Whenever you're wrong, admit it;
> Whenever you're right, shut up.
> – Ogden Nash, 'A Word to Husbands'

I know many married men; I even know a few happily married men; but I don't know one who wouldn't fall down the first open coal-hole running after the first pretty girl who gave him a wink.
– George Jean Nathan, 'Women as Playthings'

I can't fall in love. That's probably what holds my marriage together.
– Joseph Heller, *Something Happened*

Nor shall I presume to judge the marriage. Not only is one chap's meat another man's poison, but what nourishes at twenty may nauseate at forty, and vice versa.
– John Barth, *Letters*

A good marriage is one that can survive the ninety-day euphoria of romantic love.
– Edward Abbey, in John Winokur, *A Curmudgeon's Garden of Love*

There are good marriages, but there are no delicious ones.
– François, duc de La Rochefoucauld, *Réflexions ou sentences et maximes morales*

Oh, bring me gifts, or beg me gifts,
    And wed me if you will!
I'd make a man a good wife,
    Sensible and still.
– Edna St Vincent Millay, 'Sonnet'

If I were a girl, I'd despair; the supply of good women far exceeds that of the men who deserve them.
– Robert Graves

If you want to sacrifice the admiration of many men for the criticism of one, go ahead and get married.
– Katharine Houghton Hepburn, to her daughter Katherine, quoted in Anne Edwards, *A Remarkable Woman*

The only thing about marriage that appealed to me was sex without scandal: husbands could be counted on not to ask 'How come you let me go all the way?'
– Florence King, *Confessions of a Failed Southern Lady*

Marriage is our last, best chance to grow up.
– Rev. Joseph Barth, in *Ladies Home Journal*, April 1961

By all means marry; if you get a good wife, you'll become happy; if you get a bad one, you'll become a philosopher.
– Socrates

A good marriage is that in which each appoints the other guardian of his solitude.
– Rainer Maria Rilke, *Letters* (trans. by Jane Barnard Greene and M.D. Herter Norton)

Is this an age to buckle with a bride?
– Juvenal, *Sixth Satire* (trans. by John Dryden)

Girls, leave matrimony alone; it's the hardest way on earth to get a living.
– Fanny Fern, in C. Kramarae and P.A. Treichler, *Feminist Dictionary*

'Thus grief still treads upon the heels of pleasure:
Marry'd in haste, we may repent in leisure.'

'Some by experience find these words misplac'd:
At leisure marry'd, they repent in haste.'
– William Congreve, *The Old Bachelor*

I wonder what Adam and Eve
think about it by this time.
– Marianne Moore, *Collected Poems*: 'Marriage'

Except for poverty, incompatibility, opposition of parents, absence of love on one side and of desire to marry on both, nothing stands in the way of our happy union.

– Cyril Connolly, in D. Pryce-Jones, *Cyril Connolly: Journal and Memoir*

Marriage: Choice of Partner

A living doll, everywhere you look.
It can sew, it can cook,
It can talk, talk, talk.

It works, there is nothing wrong with it.
You have a hole, it's a poultice.
You have an eye, it's an image.
My boy, it's your last resort.
Will you marry it, marry it, marry it.

– Sylvia Plath, *Ariel*: 'The Applicant'

The people people work with best
    Are often very queer,
The people people own by birth
    Quite shock your first idea;
The people people choose for friends
    Your common sense appal
But the people people marry
    Are the queerest ones of all.

– Charlotte Perkins Gilman

There was once a bishop who was asked what he thought of sin. He said simply he was against it, and my answer to anyone who asked me the same question of marriage and family life would be equally simple. I am for it.

– Elizabeth II, on her silver wedding anniversary

Hail wedded love, mysterious law, true source
Of human offspring, sole propriety,
In Paradise of all things common else.
— John Milton, *Comus*

I married beneath me. All women do.
— Nancy Astor, quoted in *The Dictionary of National Biography*

I love being married. It's so great to find the one special person
you want to annoy for the rest of your life.
— Ruth Rudner, comedy routine

Where I love, I must not marry;
Where I marry, cannot love.
— Thomas Moore, *Juvenile Poems*: 'Love and Marriage'

Marriage: Con

It doesn't much signify whom one marries, for one is sure to
find out the next morning it was someone else.
— Will Rogers (attributed)

The music of a wedding procession always reminds me of the
music of soldiers going into battle.
— Heinrich Heine (attributed)

Marriage is a mantrap baited with simulated accomplishments
and delusive idealizations.
— George Bernard Shaw, *Man and Superman*

Marriage is a bribe to make a housekeeper think she is a house-
holder.
— Thornton Wilder, *The Matchmaker*

The surest way to be alone is to get married.
> – Gloria Steinem

Marry?
. . .
Better drain a cup of shame
Than play the wedding-game.
Better wallow in the mud
Than spill the hymeneal blood.
Never shall a wife rob me
Of my treasured liberty.
> – François Rabelais, *Gargantua and Pantagruel*

Marriage may be compared to a cage: the birds outside despair to get in; those within despair to get out.
> – Michel de Montaigne, *Essays*

Hanging and wiving go by destiny.
> – John Heywood, *A Dialogue containing the number in effect of all the Proverbs in the English Tongue*

Marriage always demands the greatest understanding of the art of insincerity possible between two human beings.
> – Vicki Baum, *And Life Goes On*

Marriage is like pantyhose. It all depends on what you put into it.
> – Phyllis Schlafly, in the *Boston Globe*, 16 July 1974

Take my wife . . . Please.
> – Henny Youngman, comedy routine

Why did He not marry? Could the answer be that Jesus was not by nature the marrying kind?
> – Hugh Montefiore, Anglican clergyman, later Bishop, at a conference, Oxford, 20 July 1967

I have always thought that every woman should marry and no man.
> – Benjamin Disraeli, *Lothair*

Of all serious things, marriage is the most ludicrous.
> – Beaumarchais (Pierre-Augustin Caron), *The Marriage of Figaro*

The only charm of marriage is that it makes a life of deception necessary for both parties.
> – Oscar Wilde

So they were married – to be the more together –
And found they were never again so much together,
    Divided by the morning tea,
    By the evening paper,
    By children and tradesmen's bills.
> – Louis MacNeice, *Plant and Phantom*: 'Les Sylphides'

All my friends at school grew up and settled down
Then they mortgaged up their lives
. . .
They just got married 'cos there's nothing else to do.
> – Mick Jagger and Keith Richard, 'Sitting on a Fence'

You study one another for three weeks, you love each other for three months, you fight for three years and you tolerate the situation for thirty.
> – André de Misson

Married. It was like a dream come true for Donna. Just think, soon her little girl would have unpaid bills, unplanned babies, calls from the bank, and sub-standard housing. All the things a mother dreams for her child.
> – Erma Bombeck

Marriage is rather a silly habit.
> – John Osborne (attributed)

For the crown of our life as it closes
Is darkness, the fruit thereof of dust
No thorns go as deep as a rose's
And love is more cruel than lust.
Time turns the old days to derision
Our love into corpses or wives
And marriage and death and division
Make barren our lives.
– A.C. Swinburne, 'Dolores'

Two by two in the ark of
the ache of it.
– Denise Levertov, 'The Ache of Marriage'

What revolution can appear so strange,
As such a lecher, such a life to change?
A rank, notorious whoremaster, to choose
To thrust his neck into the marriage noose!
– Juvenal, *Sixth Satire* (trans. by John Dryden)

Marriage is a step so grave and decisive that it attracts light-headed, variable men by its very awfulness.

. . .

Times are changed with him who marries; there are no more by-path meadows, where you may innocently linger, but the road lies long and straight and dusty to the grave.
– Robert Louis Stevenson, *Virginibus Puerisque*

Marriage. The beginning and end are wonderful. The middle part is hell.
– Edith Bagnold, *The Chalk Garden*

'I don't hate him,' Athenaise answered . . . 'It's jus' being married that I detes' an' despise.'
– Kate Chopin, 'Athenaise'

I'll hug. I'll kiss. I'll play
And, cock-like, hens I'll tread,
And sport in any way
But not in the bridal bed.
– Robert Herrick

Marriage: Definitions of

Marriage is a lottery.
> – English proverb

Marriage is a covenant which hath nothing free but the entrance.
> – Michel de Montaigne, *Essays*

Marriage: The state or condition of a community consisting of a master, a mistress and two slaves, making in all, two.
> – Ambrose Bierce, *The Devil's Dictionary*

Marriage is difficult enough; just plain monogamy. Polygamy is more difficult. And group marriage is just too difficult for anybody.
> – Margaret Mead

Marriage: End of

We lov'd, and we lov'd, as long as we could
'Til our love was lov'd out in us both;
But our marriage is dead, when the pleasure has fled:
'Twas pleasure that made it an oath.
– John Dryden, 'Marriage à la Mode'

Love leads to marriage; marriage then
Slays love, and by new love is slain;
So round and round the two are led
The dead extinguishing the dead.
– W.R.E. (Waldo Espy), *Another Almanac of Words at Play*

See also: DIVORCE.

Marriage: Failure of

I see no marriages fail sooner, or more troubled, than such as
are concluded for beauty's sake, and huddled up for amorous
desires.
– Michel de Montaigne, *Essays*

Lovers lying two and two
    Ask not whom they sleep beside,
And the bridegroom all night through
    Never turns him to the bride.
– A.E. Housman, *A Shropshire Lad*

Marriage: Pro

The peace of God came into my life when I wedded her.
– Alfred, Lord Tennyson (attributed), about his wife

Reverend and honourable matrimony,
Mother of lawful sweets, unashamed mornings,
Dangerous pleasures.
– Thomas Middleton, *The Phoenix*

Marriage: Reasons for

Some pray to marry the man they love
   My prayer will somewhat vary:
I humbly pray to heaven above
   That I love the man I marry.
   – Rose Pastor Stokes, 'My Prayer'

I am wanton and lascivious,
And cannot live without a wife.
   – Christopher Marlowe, *Dr Faustus*

. . . I suspect unless one promised her marriage, it'd have been harder to plug her than to sneak daybreak past a rooster.
   – Alexander Theroux, *Darconville's Cat*

Should I get married? Should I be good?
. . .
Because what if I'm 60 years old and not married
All alone in a furnished room with pee stains on my
   underwear
And everybody else is married! All the universe married
   but me!
   – Gregory Corso, 'Marriage'

His pulse beats matrimony.
   – John Ray, *English Proverbs*

. . . the sad fact is that most marriages are not undertaken in the West, still today, for reasons of romantic love but rather out of crude self-interest: the girl or woman in order to have her own home and social position, to be able to have children she biologically wants, in a protected way, and to get out of her family's control (and possibly off the work-market as well); the man in order not to keep eating in restaurants all his life, to have a wife to keep home for him, and to show off to other men, and to have a 'steady lay'.
   – Gershon Legman, *Rationale of the Dirty Joke*

The women who take husbands not out of love but out of greed, to get their bills paid, to get a fine house and clothes and jewels; the women who marry to get out of a tiresome job, or to get away from disagreeable relatives, or to avoid being called an old maid – these are the whores in everything but name. The only difference between them and my girls is that my girls give a man his money's worth.

> – Polly Adler, *A House is Not a Home*

Why the hell should I get a wife when the man next door's got one?

> – Furry Lewis, 87-year-old blues artist, when asked why he never married

Marriage is the price men pay for sex; sex is the price women pay for marriage.

> – Anonymous

Stan Waltz has decided to take unto himself a wife but he hasn't yet decided whose . . .

> – Peter De Vries, *Let Me Count the Ways*

Marriage begins with a bang and ends in a whimper.

> – Lin Field, *Mrs Murphy's Law*

Marriage: Yes or No

You may marry or you may not. In today's world that is no longer the big question for women. Those who glom on to men so that they can collapse with relief, spend the rest of their days shining up their status symbol and figure they never have to reach, stretch, learn, grow, face dragons or make a living again are the ones to be pitied. They, in my opinion, are the unfulfilled ones.

> – Helen Gurley Brown, *Sex and the Single Girl*

Advice to persons about to marry – 'Don't'.
– *Punch* (London), 1845

Marriage and Children

The value of marriage is not that adults produce children but that children produce adults.
– Peter De Vries, *The Tunnel of Love*

Marriage and Poverty

First thrive, then wive.
– John Clarke, *Paroemiologia Anglo-Latina*

Marriage and Sex

I was about to cross legs with legs.
– Lucilius, *Satires*

If four bare legs in bed were the main thing, mighty few marriages would last.
– Anonymous

Sex is the foundation of marriage.
– Th. Van de Velde, *Ideal Marriage*

It is a weak man who marries for love.
– Samuel Johnson, quoted in James Boswell's *The Life of Samuel Johnson*

Better to sit up all night than to go to bed with a dragon.
— Jeremy Taylor, *Holy Living*

Mighty is love, but most in naked wedlock.
— Sextus Aurelius Propertius

Here's to woman! Would that we could fall into her arms without falling into her hands.
— Ambrose Bierce (attributed)

Marriage Partner

I've looked around enough to know that you're the one I want to go through time with.
— Jim Croce, 'Time in a Bottle'

Married Men

Lady, lady, should you meet
One whose ways are all discreet,
One who murmurs that his wife
Is the lodestar of his life,
One who keeps assuring you
That he was never untrue,
Never loved another one . . .
Lady, lady, better run.
— Dorothy Parker, 'Social Note'

Masochism

I had to give up masochism – I was enjoying it too much.
  – Mel Calman, *Mel Calman's Dictionary of Psychoanalysis*

Masturbation

Sophisticated persons masturbate without compunction. They do it for reasons of health, privacy, thrift, and because of the remarkable perfection of invisible partners.
  – P.J. O'Rourke, *Modern Manners*

Masturbation: the primary sexual activity of mankind. In the nineteenth century it was a disease; in the twentieth, it's a cure.
  – Thomas Szasz, *The Second Sin*: 'Sex'

Don't knock masturbation. It is sex with someone I love.
  – Woody Allen and Marshall Brickman, from the film
  Annie Hall

If God had intended us not to masturbate he would have made our arms shorter.
  – George Carlin, comedy routine

My father said, 'Mike, if you masturbate, you'll go blind.' I said, 'Dad, I'm over here.'
  – Mike Binder, comedy routine

Recently, when I am alone I try to talk myself out of masturbation. I ask myself why can't I just be friends with myself.
  – Richard Lewis, comedy routine

Masturbation is the thinking man's television.
  – Christopher Hampton (attributed)

i learned how
to masturbate
through the new york times
— Sonia Sanchez, 'Summary', in *Black Fire*

See also: SOLITARY SEX.

Mate-Swapping

O curse of marriage!
That we can call these delicate creatures ours
And not their appetites. I had rather be a toad,
And live upon the vapour of a dungeon,
Than keep a corner in the thing I love
For others' uses.
— William Shakespeare, *Othello*

Freddy was all heart and as American as apple pie and swapsies.
— John Updike, *Couples*

May and December Relationships

Crabbed age and youth cannot live together;
Youth is full of pleasance, age is full of care;
Youth like summer morn, age like winter weather;
Youth like summer brave, age like winter bare.
— William Shakespeare, *The Passionate Pilgrim*

Night crows on tombs, owl sits on carcass dead,
So lies a wench with Sophocles in bed.
— Alciati, in R. Burton, *Anatomy of Melancholy*

Old and young cattle plough not well together.
> – Ovid, in R. Burton, *Anatomy of Melancholy*

> Will you love me in December as you do in May,
> Will you love me in the good old-fashioned way?
> When my hair has all turned to grey,
> Will you kiss me then and say
> That you love me in December as you did in May?
> – James J. Walker, 'Will You Love Me in December as You
>   Do in May' (music by Ernest R. Bell)

I was aware at the time that some people noted a certain discrepancy in our ages – a bridegroom is not usually thirty years older than his father-in-law.
> – Pablo Casals, on his marriage as an octogenarian to a 30-
>   year-old woman

Memory

Lovers remember everything.
> – Ovid, *Heroides*

Wolves lose their teeth but not their memory.
> – Thomas Draxe, *Bibliotheca*

> April is the cruellest month, breeding
> Lilacs out of the dead land, mixing
> Memory and desire, stirring
> Dull roots with spring rain.
> – T.S. Eliot, 'The Waste Land'

> Old as I am, for ladies' love unfit,
> The power of beauty I remember yet.
> – John Dryden, 'Cymon and Iphigenia'

Remember me when I am gone away
    Gone far away into the silent land.

. . . .

Better by far you should forget and smile
Than that you should remember and be sad.
– Christina Rossetti, 'Remember'

Hast thou forgotten ere I forget?
– A.C. Swinburne, 'Itylus'

What lips my lips have kissed, and where, and why,
I have forgotten . . .
. . .
I can not say what loves have come and gone;
I only know that summer sang in me
A little while, that in me sings no more.
– Edna St Vincent Millay, 'What My Lips Have Kissed'

 *Men*

. . . cocksure, cocky gamecock.
    – Luis Raphael Sanchez, *Macho Camacho's Beat*

Man is the only animal that eats when he is not hungry, drinks
when he is not thirsty, and makes love at all seasons.
    – Anonymous

Man is the only animal who injures his mate.
    – Ludovico Ariosto, *Orlando Furioso*

Some men break your heart in two,
Some men fawn and flatter,
Some men never look at you,
And that cleans up the matter.
– Dorothy Parker, 'Experience'

Middle Age

all that we might have been,
all that we were – fire, tears,
wit, taste, martyred ambition –
stirs like the memory of refused adultery
the drained and flagging bosom of our middle years.
– Adrienne Rich, 'Snapshots of a Daughter-in-Law'

Oh, come in Middle Age, come in, come in!
Come close to me, give me your hand, let me look on
your face . . . Oh . . . Is that what you really look like?
Oh God help me . . . help me.
– Dorothy Parker, *The Middle or Blue Period*

On his bold visage middle age
Had slightly press'd its signet sage, ·
Yet had not quenched the open truth
And fiery vehemence of youth;
Forward and frolic glee was there
The will to do, the soul to dare.
– Sir Walter Scott, *The Lady of the Lake*

When I was young I used to have successes with women because
I was young. Now I have successes with women because I am
old. Middle age is the hardest part.
– Arthur Rubinstein (attributed)

Older women are best because they always think they may be
doing it for the last time.
– Ian Fleming (attributed)

The Mind

Adulterers and customers of whores
And cunning takers of virginities
Caper from bed to bed, but not because
The flesh is pricked to infidelities.

The body is content with homely fare
It is the avid, curious mind that craves
New pungent sauce and strips the larder bare,
The palate and not hunger enslaves.
– John Press, 'Womanizers'

The mind is an erogenous zone.
– David Frost (attributed)

Modest woman chooses a man by the mind, not the eye.
– Publilius Syrus, *Sententiae*

When beauty fires the blood, how love exalts the mind.
– John Dryden, 'Cymon and Iphigenia'

And love's the noblest frailty of the mind.
– John Dryden, *The Indian Emperor*

I must have women. There is nothing unbends the mind like them.
– John Gay, *The Beggar's Opera*

Beauty's the thing that counts
In women: red lips
And black eyes are better than brains.
– Mary J. Elmendorf, 'Beauty's the Thing'

There are no chaste minds. Minds copulate wherever they meet.
– Eric Hoffer, *Reflections on the Human Condition*

The human mind is capable of excitement without the application of gross and violent stimulants; and he must have a very faint perception of its beauty and dignity who does not know this.
– William Wordsworth, *Lyrical Ballads*: Preface

People will begin to explore all the sidestreets of sexual experience, but they will do this intellectually ... Sex won't take place in the bed, necessarily – it will take place in the head!
– J.G. Ballard, in *Penthouse*, September 1980

I like them fluffy
. . .
not huffy or stuffy, not tiny or tall,
But fluffy, just fluffy, with no brains at all.
– A.P. Herbert, 'I Like Them Fluffy'

 *Mistresses*

Let's face it, I have been momentary,
A luxury. A bright red sloop in the harbour.
– Anne Sexton, 'For My Lover: Returning to His Wife'

People often say that, by pointing out to a man the faults of his mistress, you succeed only in strengthening his attachment to her, because he does not believe you; yet how much more if he does!
– Marcel Proust, *Remembrance of Things Past: Swann in Love*

Coquettes know how to please, not how to love, that is why men love them so.
– Pierre Marivaux, *Lettres sur les habitants de Paris*

Tell him it's all a lie,
I love him as much as my life;
He wouldn't be jealous of me –
I love him and loathe his wife.
– Author unknown, 'A Learned Mistress' (trans. by Frank
   O'Connor), in Edna O'Brien, *Some Irish Loving*

The trouble of finding a husband for one's mistress, is that no other man seems quite good enough.
– William Cooper, *Scenes from Provincial Life*

What is the worst portion in this mortal life?
A pensive mistress, and a yelping wife.
– Theodore Roethke, 'The Marrow'

So mistresses tend to get a steady diet of whipped cream, but no meat and potatoes, and wives often get the reverse, when both would like a bit of each.
– Merle Shain, *Some Men are More Perfect Than Others*

Chaste to her husband, frank to all beside,
A teeming mistress, but a barren bride.
– Alexander Pope, *Moral Essays*

Buy old masters. They fetch a better price than old mistresses.
– Lord Beaverbrook (attributed)

When you marry your mistress, you create a job vacancy.
– Sir James Goldsmith (attributed)

Every man wants a woman to appeal to his better side, his nobler instincts and his higher nature, and another woman to help him forget them.
– Helen Rowland

No, make me mistress to the man I love
If there be yet another name more free
More fond than mistress, make me that to thee!
– Alexander Pope, 'Eloisa to Abelard'

The Western custom of one wife and hardly any mistresses.
– Saki, *Reginald in Russia*

While tearing off
A game of golf
I may make a play for the caddy.
But when I do
I don't follow through
'Cause my heart belongs to Daddy.
– Cole Porter, 'My Heart Belongs to Daddy', from the
musical *Leave It to Me*

Since mistress presupposes wife
It means a doubly costly life.
– Peter De Vries, 'To His Impassionate Mistress'

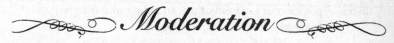

Moderation

A great soul prefers moderation to excess.
– Seneca, *Epistulae morales*

It is good trying the sack before it is full.
– George Herbert, *Jacula Prudentum*

Shear the sheep but don't flay them.
– Dutch proverb

Too much spoils, too little does not satisfy.
– James Howell, *Proverbs*

Therefore love moderately; long love doth so;
Too swift arrives as tardy as too slow.
    – William Shakespeare, *Romeo and Juliet*

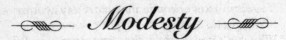

Modesty

Suit the action to the word, the word to the action; with this special observance, that you o'er step not the modesty of nature.
    – William Shakespeare, *Hamlet*

Modesty died when clothes were born.
    – Mark Twain (attributed)

Modesty is ruin to a harlot.
    – *The Hitopsdesa*

A woman who goes to bed with a man ought to lay aside her modesty with her skirt and put it on again with her petticoat.
    – Michel de Montaigne, *Essays*

Modesty is hardly to be described as a virtue. It is a feeling rather than a disposition. It is a kind of fear of falling into disrepute.
    – Aristotle, *The Nochomachean Ethics*

Have you no modesty, no maiden shame?
    – William Shakespeare, *A Midsummer Night's Dream*

Women commend a modest man, but like him not.
    – Thomas Fuller, *Gnomologia: Adagies and Proverbs*

Modesty, which is regarded as a feminine characteristic *par excellence*, but is far more a matter of convention than one would think, was, in our opinion, originally designed to hide the deficiency in her genitals.
    – Sigmund Freud, *New Introductory Lecture on Psychoanalysis*

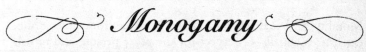

Money

Money is the sinew of love as well as war.
— Thomas Fuller, *Gnomologia: Adagies and Proverbs*

You sittin' down wonderin' what it's all about,
If you got no money, they'll put you out,
Why don't you do right like some other men do?
Get out of here, and get me some money too.
— Joe McCoy, 'Why Don't You Do Right'

All matters of the heart cost money. Marriage does. Affairs do. Divorce costs most of all.
— Jonathan Gathorne-Hardy, Marriage, Love, Sex, Divorce

Brigands demand your money or your life; women demand both.
— Samuel Butler (attributed)

Monogamy

Love has been in perpetual strife with monogamy.
— Ellen Kay (attributed)

It is politically incorrect
          to demand monogamous
          relationships
. . .
          Me i am
totally opposed to
monogamous relationships
          unless
          i'm
in love.
— Pat Parker, 'A Small Contradiction'

Go sow your wild oats
And reap as you will
I hoe in one furrow.
– Eve Merriam, 'Monogomania'

We tried to smash monogamy, but it was ourselves who crashed, to slink off to coupledom and middle age.
– Linda Grant, *Sexing the Millennium*

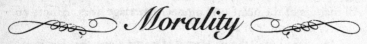

Morality

The so-called new morality is the old immorality condoned.
– Lord Shawcross, in the *Observer,* 17 November 1963

As soon as one is unhappy one becomes moral.
– Marcel Proust, *Remembrance of Things Past: Within a Budding Grove*

Morality in sexual relations, when it is free from superstition, consists essentially of respect for the other person, and unwillingness to use that person solely as a means of personal gratification, without regard to his or her desires.
– Bertrand Russell, *Marriage and Morals*

Love is moral without legal marrriage, but marriage is immoral without love.
– Ellen Kay, *The Morality of Woman and Other*

What is beautiful is moral, that is all there is to it.
– Gustave Flaubert, letter to Guy de Maupassant

We are told by moralists with the plainest faces that immorality will spoil our looks.
– Logan Pearsall Smith

~ Mouth ~

Your golden-lipped mouth is not in mine to laugh.
  – Paul Éluard, *Capitale de la douleur*

She had the eyes of a poetess, the nose of an aristocrat, the chin
of a noble woman, and the mouth of a suck artist in a Tijuana
pony show.
  – Tom Robbins, *Even Cowgirls Get the Blues*

Sweet red splendid kissing mouth.
  – A.C. Swinburne, *Translations from Villon*

~ Movement ~

Ladies never move.
  – George Nathaniel Curzon, to his second wife, on
    lovemaking

Wives have no need at all
For loose and limber motions, pelvic thrusts,
Abdominal gyrations . . .
  – Lucretius, *The Way Things Are* (trans. by Rolfe Humphries)

A difficult achievement for true lovers
Is to lie mute, without embrace or kiss,
Without a rustle or smothered sigh,
Basking each in the other's glory.
  – Robert Graves, 'The Starred Coverlet'

Music

Music is an incitement to love.
> – Latin proverb

The lascivious pleasing of a lute.
– William Shakespeare, *Richard III*

> Music, moody food
of us that trade in love.
– William Shakespeare, *Antony and Cleopatra*

To jizz–jazzm–spasm
She had her orgasm.
– Anonymous, in Gershon Legman, *The Limerick*

Low, raunchy music: A hard, mean fuck you! sound.
. . .
. . . cock-stroking rock 'n roll.
> – Albert Goldman, *Ladies and Gentlemen, Lenny Bruce*

My music isn't supposed to make you wanna riot! My music is
supposed to make you wanna fuck!
> – Janis Joplin (attributed)

Mutuality

Love's chemistry thrives best in equal heat.
> – John Wilmot, Earl of Rochester, 'The Imperfect Enjoyment'

Nakedness

No woman so naked as one you can see to be naked underneath her clothes.
— Michael Frayn, *Constructions*

I wasn't really naked. I simply didn't have any clothes on.
— Josephine Baker, on her dancing at the Folies Bergères

Man is the sole animal whose nudities offend his companions and the only one who, in his natural actions, withdraws and hides himself from his own kind.
— Michel de Montaigne, *Essays*

As souls unbodied, bodies uncloth'd must be,
To taste whole joys

. . .

To teach thee, I am naked first; why then
What need'st thou have more covering than a man.
— John Donne, 'To His Mistress Going to Bed'

The body of someone we love is not altogether naked, but is clothed and framed in our feelings.
— Anatole Boyard, in *The New York Times*, 4 July 1979

Is nakedness indecent? No, not inherently. It is your thought, your sophistication, your fear, your respectability, that is indecent. There come moods when these clothes of ours are not only irksome to wear, but are themselves indecent.
— Walt Whitman, *Specimen Days*

In naked beauty most adorned.
— John Milton, *Paradise Lost*

The pride of the peacock is the glory of God
The lust of the goat is the bounty of God
The wrath of the lion is the wisdom of God
The nakedness of women is the work of God.
– William Blake, 'Proverbs of Hell'

. . . the very sight of naked parts causes enormous, exceeding concupiscence, and stirs up both men and women to burning lust.
– Robert Burton, *The Anatomy of Melancholy*

She shall pull off her clothing, laying bare her ripeness . . .
– *The Epic of Gilgamesh*

It is hard to be a snob when you are bare-assed.
– *Playboy*, April 1969

A nudist resort in Benares
Took a midget in unawares
But he made members weep
For he just couldn't keep
His nose out private affairs.
– Anonymous Limerick

A woman is truly beautiful only when she is naked and she knows it.
– André Courrèges, in the *Metropolitan Museum of Modern Art Bulletin*

Show me thy feet; show me thy legs, thy thighs;
Show me those fleshy principalities;
Show me that hill (where smiling love doth sit),
Having a living fountain under it;
Show me thy waist, then let me therewithal,
By the ascension of thy lawn, see all.
– Robert Herrick, 'To Diareme'

NAKEDNESS

Naked I came, and naked I leave the scene,
And naked was my pastime in between.
– James Vincent Cunningham, 'Five Epigrams'

How idiotic civilization is! Why be given a body if you have to
keep it shut up in a case like a rare, rare fiddle?
– Katherine Mansfield, *Bliss and Other Stories*

Narcissism

A narcissist is someone who is better looking than you.
– Gore Vidal (attributed)

Natural and Unnatural

If nature permits it, it is natural. If nature does not permit it, it
cannnot be done.
– Buckminster Fuller, *Architecture As Ultra Invisible Reality*

Nature of Love

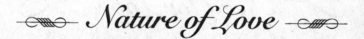

It is to be all made of sighs and tears; –
. . .
It is to be all made of faith and service; –
. . .
It is to be all made of fantasy,
All made of passion, and all made of wishes;
All adoration, duty, and observance;

All humbleness, all patience, and impatience;
All purity, all trial, all obeisance.
  – William Shakespeare, *As You Like It*

OPHELIA: 'Tis brief, my lord.
HAMLET: As woman's love.
  – William Shakespeare, *Hamlet*

Love is begot by fancy, bred
    By ignorance, by expectation fed,
Destroyed by knowledge, and at best
    Lost in the moment 'tis possessed.
  – George Granville, Baron Lansdowne, 'Love'

Necking

Whoever called it necking was a poor judge of anatomy.
  – Groucho Marx

See also: FOREPLAY; PETTING.

Need for Love

    if the soul
is to know itself
it must look
into a soul
  – George Seferis, 'Mythistoreme: Poem IV'

Neglect

Love does not brook neglect.
    – Menander, *Fragments*

New Love

Love will come again, but in circuitous paths.
    – Willie Morris, *New York Days*

Night

    The night
Shows stars and women in a better light.
    – George Gordon, Lord Byron, *Don Juan*

They say a moonshine night is good to run away with another
man's wife.
    – William Rowley, *A Match at Midnight*

Ninety Years of Age

I always felt that a woman has the right to treat the subject of her
age with ambiguity until, perhaps, she passes into the realm of
over ninety. Then it is better she be candid with herself and with
the world.
    – Helena Rubinstein, *My Life for Beauty*

What I wouldn't give to be seventy again.
> – Oliver Wendell Holmes (attributed) at age 92, upon seeing a
> pretty girl struggle with her skirts in the wind

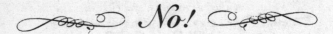

No!

To think is to say No.
> – Alain (Émile Chartier), *Le Citoyen contre les pouvoirs*

> It's not 'cause I shouldn't,
> It's not 'cause I wouldn't,
> It's not 'cause I couldn't,
> It's simply because I am the laziest girl in town.
> – Cole Porter, 'Laziest Girl in Town'

I must say . . . a fast word about oral contraception. I asked a girl
to go to bed with me and she said 'no'.
> – Woody Allen, at a nightclub, Washington D.C., April 1965

> All those illegitimate babies . . .
> Oh girls, girls
> Silly little cheap things
> Why don't you put some value on yourselves,
> Learn to say No?
> Did nobody teach you?
> Nobody teaches anybody to say No nowadays
> People should teach people to say No.
> – Stevie Smith, 'Valuable'

Say No, and you'll never be married.
> – James Kelly, *Complete Collection of Scottish Proverbs*

Pray, don't say no, until you are asked.
> – Jonathan Swift, *Polite Conversations*

When the denial becomes fainter and fainter,
And her eyes give what her tongue does deny,
Ah what a trembling I feel when I venture,
Ah what a trembling does usher my Joy!
– John Dryden, 'Love's Fancy'

But fast she holds my hands, and close her thighs,
And what she longs to do, with frowns denies.
– The Duke of Buckingham, 'The Happy Night'

Chloe blush'd and frown'd and swore,
    And pushed me rudely from her;
I call'd her Faithless, Jilting Whore,
    To talk to me of honour;
But when I arose and would be gone,
    She cried, wither go ye?
– Nicholas Rowe, 'Chloe Blush'd and Frown'd and Swore'

Saying no the maiden shakes her head up and down.
    – Japanese proverb

When Venus said 'Spell no for me.'
'N-O,' Dan Cupid wrote with glee,
And smiled at his success.
'Ah child' said Venus, laughing low.
'We women do not spell it so.
We spell it Y–E–S.'
– Carolyn Wells, 'The Spelling Lesson'

Have you not heard it said full oft
A woman's nay doth stand for naught.
– William Shakespeare, *The Passionate Pilgrim*

Fabulla, sweet virgin, you have learned your lesson too
    well,
I warned you to hold off impetuous lovers,
To say 'No' once, twice, even three times.

NO!
_____

311

> But, dear girl for whom I hunger and pine away,
> I did not tell you to say 'No' forever,
> And to me.
> – Martial, 'The Too Literal Pupil' (trans. by Louis
>   Untermeyer)

> The swain did woo, she was nice,
> Following fashion nayed him twice.
> – Robert Greene, *The Shepherd's Ode*

> Or if thou think'st I am too quickly won,
> I'll frown and be perverse and say thee nay.
> – William Shakespeare, *Romeo and Juliet*

Girls are so queer you never know what they mean. They say No when they mean Yes, and drive a man out of his wits for the fun of it.
> – Louisa May Alcott, *Little Women*

A man assumes that a woman's refusal is just part of a game. Or, at any rate, a lot of men assume that. When a man says no, it's no. When a woman says no, it's yes, or at least maybe. There's even a joke to that effect. And little by little, women begin to believe in this view of themselves.
> – Erica Jong, *Fear of Flying*

> . . . cannot go
> From yes to no
> For no is not love, no is no . . .
> – W.H. Auden, 'Too Dear, Too Vague'

A woman's 'No' is said with one mouth only.
> – Proverb

NO!
────────

Since maids, in modesty, say 'No' to
    that
Which they would have the profferer con
    strue 'aye'.
– William Shakespeare, *Two Gentlemen of Verona*

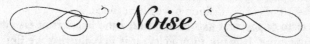

Noise

your sex squeaked like a billiard–cue
chalking itself, as not to make an error
with twists spontaneously methodical
    – e.e. cummings, *Collected Poems*

Nonconformity

Nonconformity and lust stalking hand in hand through the
country, wasting and ravaging.
    – Evelyn Waugh, *Decline and Fall*

Normality

There is no norm in sex. Norm is the name of a guy who lives in
Brooklyn.
    – Alex Comfort, quoted in Thomas Szasz, *Sex by Prescription*

Novelty

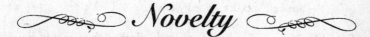

Men are by nature fond of novelty.
    – Pliny the Elder, *Natural History*

The principal quality of a woman is never beauty nor charm nor intelligence, it is novelty.
– Jacques Baroche, *The Sexual Behavior of the Married Man in France*

Novelty always appears handsome.
– H.G. Bohn, *Handbook of Proverbs*

The taste of the first kiss disappointed me like a fruit tasted for the first time. It is not in novelty, it is in habit that we find the greatest pleasures.
– Raymond Radiguet, *Le Diable au corps*

By nature, men love newfangledness.
– Geoffrey Chaucer, *The Canterbury Tales*

Nude

. . . no nude, however abstract, should fail to arouse in the spectator some vestige of erotic feeling, even if it be only the faintest shadow – and if it does not do so it is bad art and false morals.
– Kenneth Clark, *The Nude*

a pretty girl who is naked
is worth a million statues.
– e.e. cummings, *Collected Poems*

Bare like nude giant girls that have no secret.
– Stephen Spender, 'The Pylons'

If God had meant for people to wear clothes they would have been born that way.
– Ad in the *Village Voice* (New York)

Nudity

For me, the naked and nude
(By lexicographers construed
As synonyms that should express
The same deficiency of dress
Or shelter) stand as wide apart
As love from lies, or truth from art.
   – Robert Graves, 'The Naked and the Nude'

Then she rode forth, clothed on with chastity.
   – Alfred, Lord Tennyson, 'Godiva'

To be naked is to be oneself. To be nude is to be seen naked by others, and yet not recognized for oneself . . . Nudity is a form of dress.
   – John Berger, *Ways of Seeing*

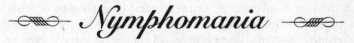

Nymphomania

There's an oversexed lady named White
Who insists on a dozen a night.
    A fellow named Fedder
    Had the brashness to wed her –
His chances of survival are slight.
   – Anonymous Limerick

A nymphomaniac is a woman who has just a little more sex tension than her partner.
   – Wardell Pomeroy, in N. Lehrman, *Masters and Johnson Explained*

Obscenity

I have left out those words which, a little daring, might have offended eyes and ears; young girls as well as ladies who are truly virtuous and wear out three lovers might have blushed and become indignant.

> – Honoré de Balzac, *Contes drolatiques*

Obscene is not the picture of a naked woman who exposes her pubic hair but that of a fully clothed general who exposes his medals awarded in a war of aggression.

> – Herbert Marcuse (attributed)

I know that the wiser sort of men will consider, and I wish the ignorant sort would learn, how it is not the baseness or homeliness, either of words or matters, that makes them foul and obscene, but their base minds, filthy conceits, or lewd intents that handle them.

> – John Harington, *The Metamorphosis of Ajax*

I think it is disgusting, shameful, and damaging to all things American. But if I were 22, with a great body, it would be artistic, tasteful, patriotic, and a progressive religious experience.

> – Shelley Winters, comments on seeing Kenneth Tynan's nude revue 'Oh, Calcutta!'

Obsessions

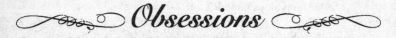

I spy on ladies
And I think of naught but filth, though there is no faster
Road for a chap to Hades.

> – Roy Fuller, 'Faust's Servant'

Obstacles to Love

You know that love
Will creep in service where it cannot go.
– William Shakespeare, *Two Gentlemen of Verona*

Oedipus Complex

I want a girl just like the girl that married dear old Dad.
– William Dillon, title of song (music by Harry van Tilzer)

For many a man has seen himself in dreams
His mother's mate, but he who gives no heed
To such matters bears the easier fate.
– Sophocles, *Oedipus Tyrannus*

Old Love

Dawn love is silver
    Wait for the west:
Old love is gold love
    Old love is best.
– Katherine Lee Bates, 'For a Golden Wedding'

Old Lover

Young I was, but now am old,
But I am not yet grown cold;
I can play and I can twine
'Bout a virgin like a vine:
In her lap I can lie

Melting, and in fancy die
And return to life, if she
Clasps my cheek, or kisseth me;
Thus, and thus it appears
That our love outlasts our years.
– Robert Herrick, *Hesperides*

Old foxes want no tutors.
. . .
Old porridge is sooner warmed than new made.
– Thomas Fuller, *Gnomologia: Adagies and Proverbs*

See also: AGE AND AGEING.

One-Night Stands

'you'll have to go now
ive a lot of work to do
& i cant have a man around
here are yr pants
there's coffee on the stove
it's been very nice
but i can't see you again
you got what you came for
didn't you'
& she smiled
he wd either mumble curses bout crazy bitches
or sit dumbfounded
. . .
'i cdnt possibly wake up
with a strange man in my bed
why don't you go home'
– Ntozake Shange, 'for colored girls who have considered
suicide when the rainbow is enuf'

Would you care to stay till sunrise
it's completely your decision
it's just that night cuts through me like a knife
would you care to stay awhile and save my life?
– Dory Previn, 'The Lady With the Braid'

How do you do
would you like to be friends?
No I just want a bed for the night
Someone to tell me they care.
You can fake it. That's all right
in the morning I won't be here.
– Janis Ian, 'The Come-on'

Do not exploit. Do not be exploited. Remember that sex is not out there, but in here, in the deepest layer of your own being. There is not only the morning after – there are also lots of days and years afterward.
– Jacob Neusner

A man has missed something if he has never woken up in an anonymous bed beside a face he'll never see again . . .
– Gustave Flaubert (attributed)

Open Marriage

Open marriage means an honest and open relationship between two people based on equal freedom and identity of both partners.
– George and Nena O'Neill

Open marriage is nature's way of telling you you need a divorce.
– Marshall Brickman

Edwina and I spent all our married lives getting into other people's beds.
– Earl Mountbatten of Burma, quoted in P. Ziegler, *Mountbatten*

I haven't known any open marriages, though quite a few have been ajar.

> – Zsa Zsa Gabor (attributed)

Some people ask the secret of our long marriage. We take time to go to a restaurant two times a week. A little candlelight, dinner, music and dancing. She goes on Tuesdays. I go Fridays.

> – Henny Youngman, comedy routine

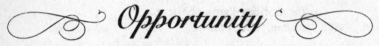

Opportunity

Opportunity is whoredom's bawd.

> – William Camden, *Remains Concerning Britain*

Optimist and Pessimist

An optimist is a girl who mistakes a bulge for a curve.

> – Ring Lardner (attributed)

A pessimist is a man who thinks all women are bad. An optimist is one who hopes they are.

> – Chauncey M. Depew (attributed)

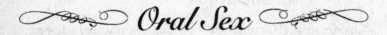

Oral Sex

I regret to say that we of the FBI are powerless to act in cases of oral–genital intimacy, unless it has in some way obstructed interstate commerce.

> –J. Edgar Hoover

Oral–genital sex definitely limits the amount of loving verbal communication that the husband and wife can have as they make love.
> – Ed and Gaye Wheat, 'Intended for Pleasure', in *Newsweek*,
> 1 February 1982

He loves roast beef well who licks the spit.
> – John Ray, *English Proverbs*

A sip is the most that mortals are permitted from any goblet of delight.
> – A.B. Alcott, *Table Talk: Habits*

. . . the business which the younger generation has graced with the unisex term 'giving head' . . . Wives who wanted head from their husbands and didn't get it, wives who got it and hated it, wives who didn't mind getting it if they did not have to give it, wives who loved giving head so much their clitorises indeed seemed to be, like the freckled-faced blue movie star, at the back of their throats.
> – John Updike, *A Month of Sundays*

The only thing wrong with oral sex is the view.
> – John Gregory Dunne, *Dutch Shea, Jr*

> Graze on my lips; and if these hills be dry,
> Stray lower, where the pleasant fountains lie.
> – William Shakespeare, *Venus and Adonis*

His idea of oral sex is talking about himself.
> – Lin Field, *Mrs Murphy's Laws*

As for the topsy-turvy tangle called soixante-neuf, personally I have always felt it maddeningly confusing – like trying to pat your head and rub your stomach at the same time.
> – Helen Lawrenson, *Whistling Girl*

ORAL SEX

As the old saying goes, so it is today: upside down and downside up.
> – Menander, *The Widow*

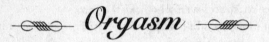 ## Orgasm

Hurry to your goal together. That is full bliss when man and woman lie equally conquered.
> – Ovid

> (cccome? said he
> ummm said she)
> you're divine! said he
> (you are Mine said she)
> – e.e. cummings, 'may i feel said he'

On the brink of being satiated, desire still appears to be infinite.
> – Jean Rostand, *Journal d'un caractère*

> Seç my lips tremble, and my eye-balls roll
> Suck my last breath, and catch my flying soul.
> – Alexander Pope, 'Eloisa to Abelard'

. . . she used to come just from sitting on a vibrating subway seat, never the IRT, on the IND. Took at least five stops.
> – John Updike, *Bech: A Book* [Note: IRT and IND are various underground lines in New York City.]

. . . the tyranny of the orgasm.
> – Cyril Connolly, quoted in Rollo May, *Love and Will*

> Did you?
> Did you? You did, didn't you?

Yes, I'm afraid, I – oh, I'm sorry, I am sorry. I know
    how it makes you feel.
Oh, don't worry about it. I'm sure I'll quiet down after
    a while.
I'm so sorry, dearest. Let me help you.
I'd rather you didn't.
. . .
Please, couldn't we just forget it? For now the thing is
    done, finished.
Besides, it's not really that important. My tension
    always wears off eventually. And, anyway – maybe
    next time it will be different.
Oh, it will, I know it will. Next time I won't be so tired
    or so eager. I'll make sure of that. Next time it's
    going to be fine . . .
    But about tonight – I'm sorry dear.
– Leslie H. Farber, 'I'm Sorry, Dear', in McGrady,
    The Love Doctors

My back aches; my penis is sore.
I simply can't do it any more.
    I'm dripping with sweat
    And you haven't come yet;
And my God! It's a quarter to four!
– Gershon Legman, *The Limerick*

Hit the ball over the fence and you can take your time going
around the bases.
    – John W. Rapt, 'What the World Needs'

Where, then, does vaginal orgasm come from? People say it is
learned. And by God you'd better learn it, lady, especially if you
are with a liberal man; you'd better learn to shuffle, nigger,
because if you don't you won't get the job. And you want to eat,
don't you? Why should she learn vaginal orgasm? Because that is
what men want.
    – Ti-Grace Atkinson, *Amazon Odyssey*

ORGASM
———————
323

Normally
      I can't come
And when I can well then
      for some dim reason
      usually I don't
Although once I did
      almost.
  – Norman Mailer, *Advertisements for Myself*

Orgasm is like a slight case of apoplexy.
  – Democritus

He always has an orgasm and doesn't wait for me. It's unfair.
  – Lorena Bobbitt, in a statement to police on being asked why
   she cut off her husband's penis, quoted in *Esquire*,
   February 1994

It's rather like a sneeze.
  – Truman Capote (attributed)

One orgasm in the bush is worth two in the hand.
  – Graffito, in R. Reisner, *Encyclopedia of Graffiti*

He said, 'Maria . . . I feel as though I wanted to die when I am
  loving thee.'
'Oh,' she said, 'I die each time. Do you not die?'
'No. Almost. But did thee feel the earth move?'
  – Ernest Hemingway, *For Whom the Bells Tolls*

The orgasm has replaced the Cross as the focus of longing and
the image of fulfilment.
  – Malcom Muggeridge, *The Most of Malcolm Muggeridge*:
   'Down With Sex'

It is naive in the extreme for women to expect to be regarded as
equals by men . . . so long as they persist in a sub-human (i.e.,
animal-like) behaviour during sexual intercourse. I am referring
. . . to the outlandish PANTING, MOANING, SOBBING,

WRITHING, SCRATCHING, BITING, SCREAMING con-
niptions, and the seemingly invariable 'OH MY GOD . . . OH
MY GOD . . . OH MY GOD' all so predictably integral to pre-,
post-, and orgasmic stages of sexual intercourse.
  – Terry Southern

I was in bed one night when my boy friend Ernie said, 'How
come you never tell me when you're having an orgasm?' I said
to him, 'Ernie, you're never around.'
  – Bette Midler, comedy routine

Instead of fulfilling the promise of orgiastic bliss, sex in America
of the feminine mystique is becoming a strangely joyless
national compulsion, if not a contemptuous mockery.
  – Betty Friedan, *The Feminine Mystique*

I finally had an orgasm and my doctor told me it was the wrong
kind.
  – Woody Allen, from the film *Manhattan*

The modern erotic ideal: man and woman in loving sexual
embrace experiencing simultaneous orgasm through genital
intercourse. This is a psychiatric-sexual myth useful in forcing
feelings of sexual inadequacy and personal inferiority. It is also a
rich source of 'psychiatric patients'.
  – Thomas Szasz, *The Second Sin*

And was it good for you?
. . .
Oh very. Of course, it always is.
  – Eve Merriam, 'The Love-Making: His and Hers'

'Are you nearly there?'
'It's hard to say.'
'If you imagine it as a journey from here to China, where would
    you be?'
'The kitchen.'
  – Jenny Lecoat, quoted in J. Levine, *My Enemy, My Love*

Love's climax should never be rushed, I say,
But worked up slowly, lingering all the way.
– Ovid, *Ars Amatoria*

O love! for love I could not speak,
It left me winded, wilting, weak.
– Sir John Betjeman, 'The Licorice Fields at Pontefract'

Orgy

Home is heaven and orgies are vile,
But you need an orgy once in a while.
– Ogden Nash, 'Home is 99⁴⁴/₁₀₀% Sweet Home'

I did not suspect it was an orgy until three days later.
– S.J. Perelman, *Cloudlane Revisited:* 'Sodom in the Suburbs'

Things are pretty bad when you can't even get laid at an orgy.
– Paul Krasner, 'I Just Got Back From An Orgy'

I know I've had wet dreams that are more delicious and satis-
fying than anything I've ever experienced at complicated orgies
I've attended . . . and much less trouble.
– Joseph Heller, *Something Happened*

You get a better class of person at orgies, because people have to
keep in trim more. There is an awful lot of going around
holding in your stomach, you know. Everybody is very polite
to each other. The conversation isn't very good but you can't
have everything.
– Gore Vidal, on London Weekend Television, 1972

I believe that sex is a beautiful thing between two people.
Between five it is fantastic.
– Woody Allen, *The Night Club Years* (record)

The Other Woman

If Marilyn is in love with my husband, it proves she has good taste, for I am in love with him, too.
> – Simone Signoret, on rumours linking her husband Yves Montand with actress Marilyn Monroe, quoted in *New York Journal-American*, 14 November 1960

It's hard to love another woman's man.
You can't get him when you want him,
You got to catch him when you can.
– Bessie Smith, 'Sorrowful Blues'

Pain

Only I discern –
Infinite passion, and the pain
Of finite hearts that yearn.
– Robert Browning, 'Two in the Campagna'

Pains of love be sweeter far
Then all other pleasures are.
– John Dryden, 'Tyrannic Love'

Pains are the wages of ill pleasures.
> – Thomas Fuller, *Gnomologia: Adagies and Proverbs*

And painful pleasure turns to pleasing pain.
– Edmund Spenser, *The Faerie Queene*

To love is to suffer, to be loved is to cause suffering.
> – Comtesse Diane, *Maximes de la vie*

See also: TORMENT.

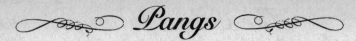

Pangs

O girl – please listen close! – do you know the pang that shoots through men like arrows at the sight of you when you but flash your wisps?
> – Seymour Krim, *Views of a Nearsighted Canonneer*

The pangs of dispriz'd love.
> – William Shakespeare, *Hamlet*

Panic

Anxiety is the first time you can't do it a second time; panic is the time you can't do it the first time.
> – American saying, in William A. Nolen, 'Impotence', *Esquire* (New York), November 1981

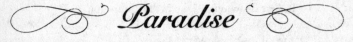

Paradise

He that will enter into paradise, must have a good key.
> – George Herbert, *Jacula Prudentum*

Paradox

People who can hardly bear each other have sex which is often by mutual consensus sensational . . . whereas the nicest love of two fine minds in two fine bodies can come to nothing via fornication.
> – Norman Mailer, *The Prisoner of Love*

Pardon

Men craving pardon will uplift their hands;
Women pray pardon with their legs on high.
– *A Thousand and One Nights* (trans. by Richard F. Burton)

Parting

Eyes, look your last!
Arms, take your last embrace.
– William Shakespeare, *Romeo and Juliet*

When we two parted
    In silence and tears
Half broken–hearted
    To sever for years.
. . .

If I should meet thee
    After long years
How should I greet thee?
    With silence and tears.
– George Gordon, Lord Byron, 'When We Two Parted'

Only two months since you stood here!
    Two short months! then tell me why
Voices are harsher than they were
    And tears are longer ere they dry.
– Walter Savage Landor, 'What News'

Oh, seek my love, your newer way;
    I'll not be left in sorrow.
So long as I have yesterday
    Go take your damned tomorrows.
– Dorothy Parker, *Enough Rope*: 'Godspeed'

I will not let thee go.
Ends all our month-long love in this?
Can it be summed up so
Quit in a single kiss?
I will not let thee go.

. . .

Thou sayest farewell, and lo!
I have thee by the hand
And I will not let thee go.
– Robert Bridges, 'I Will Not Let Thee Go'

I knew you once; But in Paradise
If we meet, I will pass or turn my face.
– Robert Browning, 'The Worst of It'

Maid of Athens, ere we part!
Give, oh give me back my heart.
– George Gordon, Lord Byron, 'Maid of Athens'

All's over then: does truth sound bitter
    As one at first believes?
– Robert Browning, 'The Lost Mistress'

Abandon me to stammering, and go,
If you have tears, prepare to cry elsewhere –
I know of no emotion we can share,
Your intellectual protests are a bore.
– Thomas Gunn, 'Carnal Knowledge'

With all my will, but much against my heart,
We two now part.
– Coventry Patmore, 'A Farewell'

It is seldom indeed that one parts on good terms, because if one
were on good terms one would not part.
    – Marcel Proust, *Remembrance of Things Past: The Fugitive*

To meet, to know, to love – and then to part,
Is the sad tale of many a heart.
– Samuel Taylor Coleridge, 'Couplet Written in a Volume of
Poems'

We'll meet again, don't know where,
Don't know when,
But I know we'll meet again some sunny day.
– Ross Parker and Hugh Charles, 'We'll Meet Again'

'Where shall I go? What shall I do?'
'Frankly my dear, I don't give a damn.'
– Sidney Howard, from the film *Gone With the Wind*, based on
the novel by Margaret Mitchell (Spoken by Rhett Butler to
Scarlett O'Hara)

I'll see you again
When spring breaks through again.
– Noel Coward, 'Bittersweet'

Parting is not sweet sorrow but a dry panic.
– John Steinbeck, letter to Elaine Scott

Get your tongue out of my mouth, I'm kissing you good-bye.
– Cynthia Heimel, Title of book

Ah, who will shoe your feet, my love
And who will glove your hands
And who will kiss your red, rosy lips
When I am gone to the foreign land?
– Anonymous, 'The Lover's Lament'

The time has come: for us to part
. . .
You're like an old shoe I must throw away,
You're just an old has-been: like a worn-out joke.
– Ida Cox, 'Worn-Down Daddy Blues'

Partying

College men are at their hormonal peak. A woman going to a fraternity party is walking into Testosterone Flats, full of prickly cacti and blazing guns.
– Camille Paglia, *Sex, Art, and American Culture*

Passes

Men seldom make passes
At girls who wear glasses.
But a girl on a sofa
Is easily won ofa.
– Dorothy Parker, *Enough Rope*: 'News Item'

Boys don't make passes at female smartasses.
– Letty Cottin Pogrebin, *Down With Sexist Upbringing*

Men seldom make passes at a girl who surpasses.
– Franklin P. Jones (attributed)

An observant young man of the West
Said, 'I've found out by personal test,
    That men who make passes
    At girls who wear glasses.
Make out just as good as the rest.
– Anonymous Limerick

I'll tell you something
I think you'll understand
Then I'll say that something
I want to hold your hand.
– John Lennon and Paul McCartney, 'I Want To Hold Your Hand'

Women don't make passes
At men who are asses.
– Jane Bartlett, in *Ms Bartlett's Familiar Quotations*

Passion

A man who has not passed through the inferno of his passions has not overcome them.
– Carl Gustav Jung, *Memories, Dreams, Reflections*

Eternal passion!
Eternal pain!
– Matthew Arnold, 'Philomela'

The duration of passion is proportionate to the original resistance of the woman.
– Honoré de Balzac (attributed)

Love cannot grow without passion.
– Greek proverb

We fly to the sensation of sex in order to avoid the passion of eros.
– Rollo May, *Love and Will*

Our passions are true phoenixes; as the old burn out the new straight rise up from the ashes.
. . .
Passions are vices and virtues in their highest powers.
– Johann Wolfgang von Goethe

It is with our passions as with fire and water,
they are good servants, but bad masters.
– Roger L'Estrange, *Aesop's Fables*

One man's mate is another man's passion.
>   – Eugene Healy, *Mr Sandman Loves His Life*

The natural man has only two primal passions, to get and beget.
>   – William Osler, *Science and Immortality*

All passions exaggerate: it is because they do
that they are passions.
>   – Nicolas Chamfort

Wise people may say what they will
but one passion is not cured by another.
>   – Lord Chesterfield

> My passions hound me like an enemy,
> from youth to withered old age.
>   – Judah Halevi, 'Lord, All My Longing is Before You

It is only with scent and silk and artifices that we raise love from
an instinct to a passion.
>   – George Moore

Sexual passion is the cause of war and the end of peace, the basis
of what is serious, the inexhaustible source of wit, the key to all
allusions ... sexual passion is kernel of the will to live, and
consequently the concentration of all desire ...
>   – Arthur Schopenhauer, quoted in Rollo May, *Love and Will*

> What's called 'passion', you'll learn, may be
>   'overriding'.
> But not in me it doesn't: I'm that smart,
> I can give everything and keep my heart.
> Kisses are kisses. No need for souls to mingle.
>   – Jonathan Price, 'A Considered Reply to a Child'

If passion drives, let reason hold the reins.
>   – Benjamin Franklin, *Poor Richard's Almanac*

PASSION

I pray . . .
That I may seem, though I die old,
A foolish, passionate man.
– W.B. Yeats

'Twas the usual saying of a very ingenuous person that
passionate men, like Yorkshire hounds, are apt to overrun the
scent.
– Sir T.P. Blount, *Essays*

How well do I remember the aged poet,
Sophocles, when in answer to the question,
'How does love suit with age – are you
still the man you were?' replied,
'Peace, most gladly have I escaped the thing
of which you speak; I feel as if I had escaped
from a mad and furious master.'
– Plato

When passion entereth at the fore-gate, wisdom goeth out the
poster.
– Thomas Fuller, *Gnomologia: Adagies and Proverbs*

A man in passion rides a horse that runs away with him.
– C.H. Spurgeon, *Ploughman's Pictures*

For one heat, all know, doth drive out another,
One passion doth expel another still.
– George Chapman, *Monsieur D'Olive*

Passion often turns the cleverest men into idiots
and makes the greatest blockheads clever.
– François, duc de La Rochefoucauld, *Réflexions ou sentences et
maximes morales*

It is difficult to overcome one's passions, and impossible to satisfy them.
– Marguerite de La Sablière, *Pensées chrétiennes*

The only sin passion can commit is to be joyless.
– Dorothy L. Sayers

Ecstasy affords
the occasion and expediency determines the form.
– Marianne Moore, 'The Past and the Present'

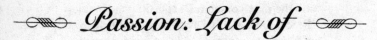

Passion: Lack of

Lukewarmness I account a sin
As great in love as in religion.
– Abraham Cowley, 'The Request'

Paternity

It's a wise child who knows its own father.
– English proverb

It is a wise father who knows his own child.
– William Shakespeare, *The Merchant of Venice*

Since strangers lodge their arrows in thy quiver,
Dear dame, I pray you yet the cause deliver,
If you can tell the cause and not dissemble,
How all our children me so much resemble?
The lady blushed and yet this answer made,

Though I have used some traffic in the trade,
And must confess, as you have touched before
My bark was sometimes steered with foreign oar.
    Yet sowed I no man's stuff but first persuaded
    The bottom with your ballast full was laded.
– Sir John Harington, 'Of an Heroical Answer of a Great Lady
   to Her Husband'

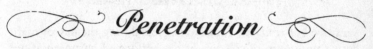

Penetration

And he came into her at once, to enter the peace on earth of her soft, quiescent body. It was the moment of pure peace for him, the entry into the body of a woman.
– D.H. Lawrence, *Lady Chatterley's Lover*

Why look at sexual intercourse as penetration? I have always considered my partner enveloped. I'd rather make a toast to all the great envelopes of the world. What say you ladies?
– Judianne Densen-Gerber, *Walking in My Shoes*

The moment of greatest significance in love-making is not the moment of orgasm. It is rather the moment of entrance, the moment of penetration . . . This is the moment that shakes us, that has within it the great wonder, tremendous and tremulous as it may be – or disappointing and despairing, which says the same thing from the opposite point of view.
– Rollo May, *Love and Will*

And when I entered you
It seemed that great happiness
Could be measured with the precision
Of sharp pain. Quick and bitter.
– Yehuda Amichai, 'Quick and Bitter' (trans. from the
   Hebrew by Assia Gutmann)

Bury me, bury me
Deeper, ever so deeper.
– Alfred, Lord Tennyson, 'Maud'

See also: SEXUAL INTERCOURSE; TECHNIQUE.

Penis

Sensitive but resilient, equally available during the day or night with a minimum of coaxing, it has performed purposely if not skilfully for an eternity of centuries, endlessly searching, sensing, expanding, probing, penetrating, throbbing, wilting and wanting more.
– Gay Talese, *Thy Neighbor's Wife*

His penis ... filled him with quizzical wonder, with gentle skepticism. For the sake of those few inches of skin and muscle, a man could ruin his reputation, his work, his life. Absurd.
– Alan Lelchuk, *Shrinking: The Beginning of My Ending*

I wonder why men can get serious at all. They have this delicate long thing hanging outside their bodies, which goes up and down by its own will ... If I were a man I would always be laughing at myself.
– Yoko Ono, in *On Film* (1967)

It's not the size of the ship; it's the size of the waves.
– Little Richard (attributed)

... the penis ... has its own disposition, it goes where it will ... A man may want to study ... or go on an errand to do a kindness to an aged woman, but this tyrant wants to discharge because ... a wench has just stooped over to gather her laundry.
– Edward Dahlberg, *The Sorrows of Priapus*

Don't let that little frankfurter ruin your life.
　　　– Bruce Jay Friedman, *Steam Bath*

. . . it is man's most honest organ.
　　　– Gay Talese, *Thy Neighbor's Wife*

The penis is the only muscle man has he cannot flex . . . It is the only extremity he cannot control . . . But even worse, as it affects the dignity of its owner, is its seeming obedience to that inferior thing, woman. It rises at the sight, or even the thought of a woman.
　　　– Elizabeth Gould Davis, in *Scold*

　　O what a peacemaker is a guid wee-willy pintle,
　　It is the mediator, the guarantee, the umpire,
　　the bond of union, the solemn league and covenant,
　　the plenipotentiary, the Aaron's rod, the Jacob's staff,
　　the prophet Elisha's pot of oil, the Ahasuerus' sceptre.
　　the sword of mercy, the philosopher's stone, the horn
　　of plenty, and the Tree of Life between Man and
　　Woman.
　　　– Robert Burns, *The Merry Muses of Caledonia*

One called it her darling little faucet, another her corking pin, a third her coral branch, a fourth her bung peg, a fifth her stop-gap. Others named it variously their ramrod, their spikebit, their swagdangle, their trunnion, their private hardware, their lever, their borer, their little ruddy sausage, their nutty little booby prize.
　　　– François Rabelais, *Gargantua and Pantagruel*

　　A maiden's mouth shows the make of her chose
　　And a man's mentula one knows by the length of his
　　　nose.
　　　– *A Thousand and One Nights* (trans. by Sir Richard Burton)

From a little spark may burst a mighty flame.
– Dante Alighieri, *The Divine Comedy*

Men are not measured in inches.
– Thomas Fuller, *Gnomologia: Adagies and Proverbs*

He [Homo sapiens] is proud of the fact that he has the biggest brain of all the primates, but attempts to conceal the fact that he also has the biggest penis.
– Desmond Morris, *The Naked Ape*

John Thomas says good-night to Lady Jane, a little droopingly, but with a hopeful heart.
– D.H. Lawrence, *Lady Chatterley's Lover*

His sex beat about like the cane of a furious blind man.
– Amos Oz (attributed)

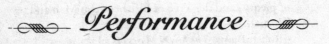

Performance

Is it not strange that desire should so many years outlive performance?
– William Shakespeare, *Henry IV, Part II*

All words,
And no performance!
– Philip Massinger, *Parliament of Love*

Perfume

Purple the sails, and so perfumed that
The winds were love-sick with them . . .
– William Shakespeare, *Antony and Cleopatra*

A woman smells best when she hath no perfume at all.
> – Robert Burton, *The Anatomy of Melancholy*

Oh, what perfumes, what evaporations to coprocontaminate and scatoscandalize the pretty little snouts of adolescent punks.
> – François Rabelais, *Gargantua and Pantagruel*

Perfume: any smell that is used to drown a worse one.
> – Elbert Hubbard (attributed)

It is a sad woman who buys her own perfume.
> – Lena Jaeger, in the *Observer*, 25 November 1955

The woman one loves always smells good.
> – Rémy de Gourmont (attributed)

Her honeyish pungent female smell monopolized the warm bed.
> – John Updike, *Couples*

'Where should one use perfume?' a young woman asked. 'Wherever one wants to be kissed.' I said.
> – Gabrielle 'Coco' Chanel (attributed)

Why are women wearing perfumes that smell like flowers? Men don't like flowers. I've been wearing a great scent. It's called New Car Interior.
> – Rita Rudner, comedy routine

> I've grown accustomed to the trace
> Of something in the air
> Accustomed to her face.
> – Alan Jay Lerner, 'I've Grown Accustomed to Her Face'
>   (music by Frederick Lowe)

Perversion

The only abnormality is the incapacity to love.
> – Anaïs Nin (attributed)

Unnatural vices
Are fathered by our heroism.
> – T.S. Eliot, *Gerontion*

My own belief is that there is hardly anyone whose sexual life, if it were broadcast, would not fill the world at large with surprise and horror.
> – W. Somerset Maugham (attributed)

. . . every man in love is a sex pervert.
> – Billy Wilder (attributed)

Be creative, invent a sexual perversion.
> – Graffito

If you want to know what I think, I think you're some kind of deviated prevert.
> – Peter George, Stanley Kubrick and Terry Southern, quoted in A. Walker, *Stanley Kubrick Directs*

But where's the extreme of vice, was ne'er agreed:
Ask where's th' North? at York, 'tis on the Tweed;
In Scotland, at the Orcades; and there
At Greenland, Zembia, or Lord knows where.
> – Alexander Pope, *An Essay on Man*

Petting

Valerie fondles lovers
like a mousetrap fondles mice.
– Roger McGough, *The Mersey Sound*: 'Discretion'

. . . [he] twisted my nipples as though tuning a radio.
– Lisa Alther, *Kinflicks*

Half the time, if you really want to know the truth, when I am
horsing around with a girl I have a hellova lot of trouble finding
what I am looking for . . . Take this girl I just missed having
sexual intercourse with, that I told you about. It took me about
an hour just to get her goddam brassiere off. By the time I did
get it off, she was about ready to spit in my eye.
– J.D. Salinger, *Catcher in the Rye*

She saw the men eager, but was at a loss,
What they meant by their sighing and kissing so close;
    By their praying and whining,
    And clasping and twining,
    And panting and wishing,
And sighing and kissing,
And sighing and kissing so close.
– John Dryden, 'Song'

He who fondles you more than usual has either deceived you or
wants to do so.
– French proverb

The boys and girls are one tonight.
They unbutton blouses. They unzip flies.
They take off shoes. They turn off the light.
The glimmering creatures are full of lies.
– Author unknown

Sylvia the fair, in bloom at Fifteen,
Felt an innocent warmth, as she lay on the green;
She heard of a pleasure, and something she guessed,
By the towzing and tumbling and touching her Breast.
– John Dryden, 'A New Song'

Phallic Symbols

. . . guns which they always handle silently with phallic reverence.

> – Alexander Theroux, *Darconville's Cat*

Sometimes a cigar is just a cigar.

> – Sigmund Freud (attributed)

Nobody we know, dear.

> – Coral Browne, to a companion when an enormous phallus
> was revealed as the centrepiece of the National Theatre
> (London) production of *Oedipus*

Pick-Ups

Peace rallies used to be
great for cruising.
Then the war ended.
– Rod McKuen, *A Field Guide to Cruising Cont'd*

Despite his appearance, he [Dylan Thomas] enjoyed considerable sexual success among suggestible college girls, whom he would approach with the honest unappealing inquiry, 'Can I jump you?'

> – Brendan Gill, in *Here at the New Yorker*

Platonic Love

I was that silly thing that once was wrought
To practise this thin love;
I climbed from sex to soul, from soul to thought;
But thinking there to move,
Headlong I rolled from thought to soul, and then
From soul I lighted at the sex again.
– William Cartwright, 'No Platonic Love'

Platonic affection, or more exactly Reciprocal Platonism, is discernible only among married people.
– Edgar Saltus

I am convinced, and always was, that Platonic love is Platonic nonsense.
– Samuel Richardson, *Pamela*

Platonic friendship: the short interval between introduction and seduction.
– Anonymous

Of course a platonic relationship is possible – but only between a husband and wife.
– Irving Kristol (attributed)

Platonic love is love from the neck up.
– Thyra Samter Winslow (attributed)

If there is such a thing as Platonic love between a man and a woman, it is the result of some profound misunderstanding, a stifling of their true and authentic impulses.
– Ivan Mestrovic

What I cannot love, I overlook. Is that real friendship?
– Anaïs Nin, *Diary*

Pleasure

Pleasure's a sin and sometimes sin's
a pleasure.
– George Gordon, Lord Byron, *Don Juan*

Short pleasure, long lament.
– English proverb

Ever let the fancy roam
Pleasure never is at home.
– John Keats, 'Fancy'

Pains of love be sweeter far
Than all other pleasures are.
– John Dryden, 'Tyrannic Love'

Stolen pleasures are the sweetest.
– English proverb

When a man says he had pleasure with a woman, he doesn't
mean conversation.
– Samuel Johnson

The best pleasures of this world are not quite pure.
– Johann Wolfgang von Goethe, *Clavigo*

Pleasure is said by her votaries to consist of the memory of the
past, the enjoyment of the present, and the hope of future
delights.
– Philo, *De Simniis*

The pleasure that is the safest is the least pleasure.
– Ovid, *Ars Amatoria*

No pleasure is risk-free.
– Johann Wolfgang von Goethe

No pleasure lasts long enough.
>   – Sextus Aurelius Propertius, *Elegies*

Vice poisons pleasure, passion falsifies it,
temperance sharpens it, innocence purifies it,
beneficence doubles it, friendship multiplies it.
>   – Chinese proverb

Pleasure is the object, the duty, the goal
Of all rational creatures.
>   – Voltaire, *Epître à Madame de G.*

Most men pursue pleasure with such breathless haste that they
hurry past it.
>   – Søren Kierkegaard, *Either/Or*

There is a sting in the tail of all unlawful pleasures.
>   – Oswald Dykes, *English Proverbs*

Fly the pleasure that bites tomorrow.
>   – George Herbert, *Outlandish Proverbs*

Politeness

Politenesss is a pleasant way for a man to get nowhere with a
girl.
>   – Author unknown

Polygamy

In pious times, e'er Priest-craft did begin,
Before Polygamy was made a sin.
>   – John Dryden, *Absalom and Achitophel*

Polygamy, n.: A house of atonement, or expiatory chapel, fitted with several stools of repentance, distinguished from monogamy, which has but one.
> – Ambrose Bierce, *The Devil's Dictionary*

Polygamy may well be held in dread,
Not only as a sin, but as a bore.
> – George Gordon, Lord Byron, *Don Juan*

Marriage with more than one wife is like a man attached to more churches than one, whereby his faith is so distracted that it becomes no faith.
> – Emanuel Swedenborg, *Heaven and Hell*

In every port he finds a wife.
> – Isaac Bickerstaffe, *Thomas and Sally*

I don't see why we can't get along with a polygamist who doesn't polyg as we do with a lot of monogamists who don't monog.
> – Theodore Roosevelt (attributed)

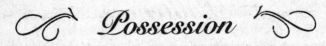

Possession

You can't possess anything but yourself. Let me loose.
> – Vicki Sears, 'Sticktalk', in Irene Zahava, *Hear the Silence*

No man worth possessing can be quite possessed.
> – Sara Teasdale, quoted in *Reader's Digest*, May 1960

Post-Coital Tristesse

. . . post-coital remorse surging in like the tide . . . .
>   – John Barth, *Letters*

Every animal is sad after intercourse. (*Omne animal post coitum triste est.*)
>   – Latin proverb

Every animal is sad after coitus except the human female and the rooster. (*Triste est animal post coitum praeter mulierem gallumque.*)
>   – Galen

. . . the Augustinian saying, *Omne animal post coitum triste est* is true for me only if I fail to delight her. Otherwise, I can crow.
>   – Alan Watts, *In My Own Way: An Autobiography*

Satiety begets distaste.
>   – Michel de Montaigne, *Essays*

The only time human beings are sane is the ten minutes after intercourse.
>   – Eric Berne, *Games People Play*

Minutes pass in silence. It is those few minutes that pass after we make love that are most mysterious to me, uncanny.
>   – Joyce Carol Oates, *The Wheel of Love and Other Stories:*
>   'Unmailed, Unwritten Letters'

. . . every lover will experience a marvellous disillusion after the pleasure he has at last attained . . .
>   – Arthur Schopenhauer

. . . peace follows, the work done, we may sleep, letting an arm grow numb rather than wake a sleeping head cushioned there . . .
>   – Malcolm Muggeridge, *Chronicles of Wasted Time*

And all this dirt for just three minutes of rapture.
> – Jules Laforgue, *For the Book of Love*

Nothing is so good as it seemed before.
> – George Eliot, *Silas Marner*

> What to ourselves in passion we propose,
> The passion ending, doth the purpose lose.
> – William Shakespeare, *Hamlet*

> Come here, lie with me
> And take away the pain
> Then go away
> I never want to see you again.
> – Anonymous, quoted in Linda Grant, *Sexing the Millennium*

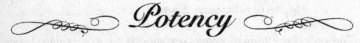

Potency

It's not the men in my life that count – it's the life in my men.
> – Mae West, in the film *I'm no Angel*

Women think of being a man as a gift. It is a duty. Even love making can be a duty. A man has always to get it up, and love isn't always enough.
> – Norman Mailer, in *Nova* magazine

The most distressing fact of growing older is that I find my private parts shrinking.
> – Cecil Beaton (attributed)

See also: IMPOTENCE.

Poverty

Love can't last around poverty. Neither can a woman's looks.
 – Kristin Hunter, *The Landlord*

Romance without finance is no good.
 – Willie 'the Lion' Smith, in *Esquire*, 1964

Love conquers all except poverty and a toothache.
 – Mae West (attributed)

Power

She who would long retain her power must use her lover ill.
 – Ovid, *Amores*

Women run the world, God dealt them all the cards between their legs.
 – James Jones, *From Here to Eternity*

She knows her man, and when you rant and swear,
Can draw you to her with a single hair.
 – John Dryden, *Persius, Satires*

One hair of a woman can draw more than a hundred pair of oxen.
 – James Howell, *Familiar Letters*

She stoops to conquer.
 – Oliver Goldsmith, Title of play

Where love rules there is no will to power; and where power predominates, there love is lacking. The one is the shadow of the other.

 – Carl Gustav Jung, *Psychological Reflections: A Jung Anthology*

Disguise our bondage as we will,
'Tis woman, woman, rules us still.
– Thomas Moore, *Miscellaneous Poems*: 'Sovereign Woman'

In men, we various ruling passions find;
In women, two almost divide the kind;
Those, only fixed, they first or last obey,
The love of pleasure and the love of sway.
– Alexander Pope, *Moral Essays*

The more developed sexual passion, in both sexes, is very largely an emotion of power, domination, or appropriation. There is no state of feeling that says 'mine, mine' more fiercely.
– Charles Horton Cooley, *Human Nature and the Social Order*

The penis is mightier than the sword.
– Mark Twain (attributed)

I know there are nights when I have the power, when I could put on something and walk in somewhere, and if there is a man who doesn't look at me, it's because he's gay.
– Kathleen Turner (attributed)

Men are brought up to command, women to seduce.
– Sally Kempton (attributed)

Do not put such unlimited power in the hands of husbands. Remember all men would be tyrants if they could.
– Abigail Adams, a plea to her husband John Adams, quoted in S. Friedman, *Secret Loves*

If you live with a man, you must conquer him every day. Otherwise he will go to another woman.
– Brigitte Bardot

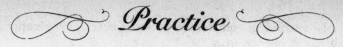

Practice

There was a young lady named Flo
Whose lover was almighty slow.
    So they tried it all night
    'Til he got it just right,
For practice makes pregnant, you know.
– Anonymous Limerick

Predator: Sexual

He swept through her like a great ragged hawk on its journey to another prey.
    – John Le Carré

He regarded women in the way little girls regard their dolls, as toys to be dressed and undressed.
    – Frank Swinnerton

She runs through men like a fever.
    – Anonymous

He ran through women like a child through growing hay.
    – Louis MacNeice, 'The Libertine'

Pregnancy

The menace of another pregnancy hung like a sword over the head of every poor woman.
    – Margaret Sanger, *My Fight For Birth Control*

. . . he yearned to embrace, to possess forever, this luxurious ball, this swollen woman . . .
– John Updike, *Couples*

Except for women, few pregnant animals copulate.
– Pliny the Elder, *Natural History*

Once I wore my apron low
. . .
Now I wear my apron high.
– Anonymous, 'Love, Oh Love, Oh Careless Love'

Congratulations: we all knew you had it in you.
– Dorothy Parker, telegram to a friend on giving birth

Well, okay, this man on the beach said Hi, I said Hi, He said Hi, I totally wasn't into this heavy conversation . . . So he said Okay? so I said Okay, so everything okay, okay? And I got totally with child like Mary with Jesus, except I know who the father is.
– Whoopi Goldberg, comedy routine

In the dark,
Defiant even now, it tugs and moans
To be untangled from the mother's bones.
– Genevieve Taggard, 'With Child'

The best prescription for a discontented female is to have a child.
– Pablo Picasso (attributed)

Her small belly fattened, the breasts he had taught
  her were beautiful
Swelled like melons, the nipples darkened. A
  turmoil
Churned inside her, sharp and hard . . .
Something of her but alien.
– Beth Bentley, 'The Birthday'

No way. My womb, like my fist,
is clenched against the world.
  – Martha Shelby, 'The Tree of Begats'

She was a crazy mathematics major from the Wharton School of Business who could not count to twenty-eight each month without getting into trouble.
  – Joseph Heller, *Catch-22*

Give me children or I shall die.
  – The Bible: Genesis (Rachel to Jacob)

A ship under sail, a man in complete armour, and a woman with a big belly, are the three handsomest sights in the world.
  – James Howell, *Proverbs*

My bigness is horrible or a new form of beauty – which?
  – John Updike, *Couples*

Love me lots
Love me little
Only leave me not
Fatter in the middle.
  – Leonard Louis Levinson, *Bartlett's Unfamiliar Quotations*

Don't litter, stop the population explosion.
  – Graffito

. . . lovers reading the instructions in comic books
Are turning out babies according to the instructions.
  – Howard Nemerov, 'Make Love Not War'

The great pod of her belly swelled and grew.
  – A.D. Hope, 'Imperial Adam'

Premarital Sex

My genuine advice to a girl is to try him out in bed first because that's where it goes or doesn't. If it goes, you've got a chance. If it doesn't, God help you. Everything else is propaganda.
> – George M. Williams, *The Camp*

To take meat before grace.
> – Scottish saying

There was a young parson of Harwich,
Tried to grind his betrothed in a carriage.
    She said, 'No, you young goose,
    Just try self-abuse,
And the other we'll try after marriage.'
> – Anonymous Limerick

I was born in 1896 and my parents were married in 1919.
> – J.R. Ackerley, *My Father and Myself,*

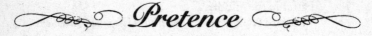

Pretence

In youth, it was a way I had,
    To do my best to please.
And change, with every passing lad
    To suit his theories.

But now I know the things I know.
    And do the things I do,
And if you do not like me so,
    To hell, my love, with you.
> – Dorothy Parker, 'Indian Summer'

The Englishman can get along with sex quite perfectly as long as he can pretend that it isn't sex but something else.
–James Agate, *The Selective Ego*

I'll believe it when girls of twenty with money marry male paupers, turned sixty.
– Elbert Hubbard, *The Roycroft Dictionary and Book of Epigrams*

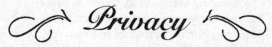

Privacy

Sex is such a personal thing. Why do we think of sharing it with another person?
– Lily Tomlin (attributed)

No act is so private it does not seek applause.
–John Updike, *Couples*

Love, in distinction from friendship, is killed, or rather extinguished, the moment it is displayed in public.
– Hannah Arendt

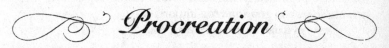

Procreation

The act of procreation and the members employed therein are so repulsive . . .
– Leonardo da Vinci, *Dell' Anatomia Fogli*

The procreation of mankind is a great marvel and mystery. Had God consulted me in the matter, I should have advised him to continue the generation by fashioning them out of clay, in the way Adam was fashioned.
– Martin Luther, *Table-Talk*

Urge, and urge, and urge:
Always the procreant urge of the world.
– Walt Whitman

If you can procreate without loving . . . I find you despicable.
– Mariama Ba, *So Long a Letter*

Love is only the dirty trick played on us to achieve continuation
of the species.
– W. Somerset Maugham, *A Writer's Notebook*

⊰≫— *Promiscuity* —≪⊱

And I shall sigh, when some will smile,
To see thy love to every one
Hath brought thee to be loved by none.
– Sir Robert Aytoun, 'To His Foresaken Mistress'

A pot that belongs to many is ill-stirred and worse boiled.
– Thomas Fuller, *Gnomologia: Adagies and Proverbs*

I consider promiscuity immoral. Not because sex is evil, but
because sex is too good and too important.
– Ayn Rand, quoted in *Playboy*, 1964

. . . the simple feat of keeping her legs crossed was a structural
impossibility.
– Maxwell Bodenheim, *Replenishing Jessica*

ELYOT: It doesn't suit women to be promiscuous.
AMANDA: It doesn't suit men for women to be promiscuous.
– Noël Coward, *Private Lives*

What is a promiscuous person? It's usually someone who is getting more sex than you are.
– Victor Lownes (attributed)

She who indulges, bulges.
– Graffito

You were born with your legs apart. They'll send you to the grave in a Y-shaped coffin.
– Joe Orton, *What the Butler Saw*

Don't love everybody – specialize.
– Anonymous

Votaries of the copulative cult.
– Aldous Huxley, 'Soles Occidere et Redire Possunt'

I don't screw around. If I'd done one third of what people said I have, if I'd had half the women, I'd be a great man. But I haven't. I wish I had.
– Dan Rather (attributed)

'Has it ever occurred to you that in your promiscuous pursuit of women you are merely trying to assuage your subconscious fears of sexual impotence?'
     'Yes, sir , it has.'
     'Then why do you do it?'
     'To assuage my fears of sexual impotence.'
– Joseph Heller, *Catch-22*

Promiscuous . . . That was a word I never applied to myself. Possibly no one ever does, for it is a sordid word, reducing many valuable moments to nothing more than dog-like copulation.
– Marya Mannes, *Message from a Stranger*

On a sofa upholstered in panther skin
Mona did research in original sin.
– William Plomer, 'Mews Flat Mona'

So do not think of helpful whores
as aberrational blots;
I could not love you half so well
without my practice shots.
– James Simmons, 'Cavalier Lyric'

Could you endure such promiscuity?
– Ezra Pound, 'Homage to Sextus Propertius'

There's nothing like a good dose of another woman to make a
man appreciate his wife.
– Clare Boothe Luce, quoted in L. and M. Cowan, *The Wit of
Women*

Your idea of fidelity is not having more than one man in bed at
the same time.
– From the film *Darling*

The only difference between a caprice and a lifelong passion is
that the caprice lasts a little longer.
– From the film *The Picture of Dorian Gray*

She could commit adultery at one end and weep for her sins at
the other, and enjoy both operations at once.
– Cecil Beaton (attributed)

I'm as pure as the driven slush.
– Tallulah Bankhead, in the *Saturday Evening Post*, 1947

Promises

Promises and pie-crust are made to be broken.
> – Jonathan Swift, *Polite Conversations*

Proposals

Whoever loves, if he do not propose
The right true end of love, he's one that goes
To sea for nothing but to make him sick.
> – John Donne, 'Love's Progress'

You were young – but that is scarcely to your credit
Pretty – as one expects the young to be.
And you were very much in love with me.
And half I lured it on, and half I fled it,
   Till honour turned its foolish face on mine
   Taking for allies music and good wine –
And told me what I ought to say: I said it.
> – Gerald Gould, 'Monogamy'

Will ye gang wi' me Lizzy Lindsay,
   Will ye gang to the Highlands wi' me?
Will ye gang wi' me Lizzy Lindsay,
   My bride and my darling to be.
> – Anonymous, 'Lizzy Lindsay'

Man proposes; woman forecloses.
> – Minna Antrim, *Naked Truth and Veiled Allusions*

Let us form, as Freud has said, a group of two. You are the best
thing this world can offer.
> – Randall Jarrell, 'Woman'

'I'd like to marry your daughter'
    'Have you seen my wife yet?'
        'Yes. I have. But I prefer your daughter.'
            – Anonymous

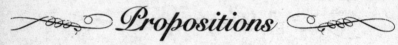 Propositions

Many things are lost for want of asking.
    – George Herbert, *Jacula Prudentum*

The bashful hog eats no pears.
    – Italian proverb

A maiden who listens is – like a besieged city that consents to
parlay – halfway towards surrender.
    – Adrien de Montluc, *La Comédie de proverbes*

> I wrong you not if my thoughts reveal,
> Saying how the beauty that your clothes conceal
> Is like a spark that sets afire my heart.
> I only ask that you then, for your part,
> Will be a saddle and let me ride,
> Just for this once.
>   . . .

Madame . . . it would prove beneficent to the commonwealth,
pleasurable to your person, honourable to your progeny, and
necessary to me that I cover you for the propagation of the race
. . .

    – François Rabelais, *Gargantua and Pantagruel*

> Come live with me, and be my love,
> And we will some new pleasures prove.
> – John Donne 'The Bait'

Come, let us go, while we are in our prime;
And take the harmless folly of the time.
– Robert Herrick, *Hesperides*

Refuse or not, they'll love you more for asking.
– Ovid, *Ars Amatoria*

Crave and have.
– Gabriel Harvey, *Marginalia*

I never ask for what I can buy.
– George Bernard Shaw, *Major Barbara*

One boon alone I languish for: to lay
My peacock, shoveller, cockerel, popinjay
Deep in the shelter of your downy nest.
    Sweet lady, once.
– François Rabelais, *Gargantua and Pantagruel*

Quit, quit for shame, this will not move,
    This cannot take her;
If of herself she will not love,
    Nothing can make her:
The Devil take her.
– Sir John Suckling, 'Song'

Take not the first refusal ill;
Tho' now she won't, anon she will.
– Thomas D'Urfey

Lie down, I think I love you.
– Graffito

Make love to every woman you meet. If you get five per cent on
your outlay, it's a good investment.
– Arnold Bennett, in *Reader's Digest*, June 1941

Where is the man who has the power and skill
To stem the torrent of a woman's will?
For if she will, she will, you may depend on't.
And if she won't, she won't; so there's the end on't.
– Anonymous inscription on a pillar in Canterbury

I hiss in your ear some vile suggestion,
Some delectable abomination
You smile at me indulgently: 'Men, Men!'
– Randall Jarrell, 'Woman'

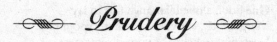

Prudery

What is prudery?
. . .
'tis a virgin hard of feature,
Old and void of all good nature;
Lean and fretful; would seem wise,
Yet play the fool before she dies.
– Alexander Pope, 'Answer to Mrs Howe'

. . . twenty, as everyone well knows , is not an age to play the prude.
– Molière, *The Misanthrope*

The perfect hostess will see that the works of male and female authors be properly separated on her book shelves. Their proximity, unless they happened to be married, should not be tolerated.
– Lady Gough, *Etiquette*

Puppy Love

I am fourteen
and my skin has betrayed me
the boy I cannot live without
still sucks his thumb
in secret.
– Audre Lorde, 'Hanging Fire'

You took my heart in your hand
With a friendly smile,
With a critical eye you scanned,
Then set it down,
And said: It is still unripe
Better wait awhile.
– Christina Rossetti, 'Twice'

The daughters of Albion
. . .
taking off their navy blue school drawers and putting on nylon
    panties for the night
       – Adrian Henri, 'Mrs Albion You've Got A Lovely Daughter'

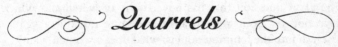

Quarrels

The quarrels of lovers are the renewal of love.
    – Horace, *Andria*

Love is a kind of warfare.
    – Ovid, *Ars Amatoria*

Never go to bed mad. Stay up and fight.
    – Phyllis Diller (attributed)

When a woman refuses to quarrel with a man, it means she is tired of him. True lovers fight back.
– Arthur Richman, in *Reader's Digest*, October 1951

Never argue with a woman when she is tired – or rested.
– H.C. Diefenbach, in *Reader's Digest*, November 1960

The way to fight a woman is with your hat. Grab it and run.
– John Barrymore, in *Reader's Digest*, July 1940

Love-quarrels oft in pleasing concord end.
– John Milton, *Samson Agonistes*

Thrice happy they, and more than thrice, whom an unbroken bond holds fast, and whom love, never torn asunder by foolish quarrellings, will not loose till life's last day.
– Horace, *Odes*

Questions that Have Yet to be Answered

The great question that has never been answered and which I have not yet been able to answer despite my thirty years of research into the feminine soul is: what does a woman want?
– Sigmund Freud

How big is the normal penis? That is the question of the century.
– David Reuben

When marriage ends, who is left to understand?
– Joyce Carol Oates, *The Wheel of Love and other Stories*:
'Unmailed, Unwritten Letters'

When a man grows old, and his balls grow cold,
And the head of his pecker turns blue,
And he goes to diddle, and it bends in the middle
    Did that ever happen to You?
– Richard Pallet, *Cobbes Prophecies*

Heaven and earth!
How is it that bodies join
but never meet?
– Beah Richards, *A Black Woman Speaks Her Mind and Other
  Poems*

For in what stupid age or nation
Was marriage ever out of fashion?
– Samuel Butler, *Hudibras*

Where's the man who could ease a heart
Like a satin gown?
– Dorothy Parker

Why can't a woman be more like a man?
Men are honest, so thoroughly square;
Eternally noble, historically fair;
Who, when you win, will always give your back a pat.
Why can't a woman be like that?
– Alan Jay Lerner, 'A Hymn to Him' (music by Frederick
  Loewe)

Why does free love cost so much?
    – Graffito, in R. Reisner, *Encyclopedia of Graffiti*

Tell me, you who know, what is this thing called love?
    – Lorenzo Da Ponte, Libretto for Mozart's *Marriage of Figaro*

Do we really know anybody? Who does not wear a face to hide
another?
    – Francis Marion, *Westward the Dream*

QUESTIONS THAT HAVE YET TO BE ANSWERED
———————

Aren't women prudes if they don't and prostitutes if they do?
> – Kate Millett, in a speech, 1975

> The sport being such, as both alike sweet try it,
> Why should one sell it and the other buy it?
> – Ovid, 'Elegia X'

All are good lasses, but whence come bad wives?
> – James Kelley, *Complete Collection of Scottish Proverbs*

How to they do it, the ones who make love without love?
> – Sharon Olds, 'Sex Without Love'

If I love you, what business is it of yours?
> – Johann Wolfgang von Goethe

Is sex necessary?
> – James Thurber and E.B. White, Title of book

What will happen to sex after [women's] liberation?
> – Nora Ephron, in *Esquire* (New York), July 1972

WHAT am I suffering from? Sexuality. Will it destroy me? How can I rid myself of sexuality?
> – Thomas Mann, quoted in M. Reich-Raqnicki, *Thomas Mann and His Family*

Why are women . . . so much more interesting to men than men are to women?
> – Virginia Woolf, *A Room of One's Own*

So who's deviant?
> – Lenny Bruce (attributed)

What else could we do, for we were in love?
> – Paul Éluard, 'Curfew' (trans. from the French by Quentin Stevenson)

QUESTIONS THAT HAVE YET TO BE ANSWERED

Alas! alas! who's injured by my love?
– John Donne, 'The Canonization'

How can I keep my maidenhead
Among so many men?
– Robert Burns, 'How Can I Keep My Maidenhead'

What makes men go crazy when a woman wear her
dress so tight?
– Muddy Waters, Blues song

How can I ever prove
What it is I love?
– Edwin Muir, 'In Love For Long'

When marriage ends, what is left to understand?
– Joyce Carol Oates, *The Wheel of Love and Other Stories*

If love be good, from whennes commeth my woo?
– Geoffrey Chaucer

Think'st thou one man is for woman meant?
– Juvenal, *Sixth Satire* (trans. by John Dryden)

Is it, in heav'n, a crime to love too well?
– Alexander Pope, 'Elegy to the Memory of an Unfortunate
    Lady'

When do I see thee most, beloved one?
– Dante Gabriel Rossetti, *The House of Life*: 'Lovesight'

What shall be the maiden's fate?
Who shall be the maiden's mate?
– Sir Walter Scott, *The Lay of the Last Minstrel*

QUESTIONS THAT HAVE YET TO BE ANSWERED

Is it too much to ask that women be spared the daily struggle for superhuman beauty in order to offer it to the caresses of a subhumanly ugly man?

    – Germaine Greer, *The Female Eunuch*

Isn't that the problem? That women have been swindled for centuries into substituting adornment for love, fashion (as it were) for passion?

    – Erica Jong, *How to Save Your Own Life*

Real Love

Is it an earthquake or merely a shock
Is it the good turtle soup or merely the mock
Is it a cocktail this feeling of joy
Or is what I feel the real McCoy?
Have I the right hunch or have I the wrong
Will it be Bach or just a Cole Porter song.
– Cole Porter, 'A Long Last Song'

Reasons

Something there is moves me to love, and I
Do know I love, but know not how or why.
– Alexander Brome, 'Love's Without Reason'

Kind souls, you wonder why, love you
    When you, you wonder why, love none
We love, Fool, for the good we do
    And not which unto us is done!
– Coventry Patmore, *The Angel in the House*: 'A Riddle
  Solved'

I loved him for himself alone.
> – Richard Brinsley Sheridan, *The Duenna*

We love being in love, that's the truth on't.
> – William Makepeace Thackeray, *The History of Henry Esmond*

> I do not love thee, Doctor Fell:
> The reason why I cannot tell;
> But this I know, and know full well:
> I do not love thee, Doctor Fell.
> – Sir Thomas Browne, impromptu translation of Martial's
> epigram

❧ Reconciliation ❧

The worst reconciliation is preferable to the best divorce.
> – Miguel de Cervantes

> Go, let the fatted calf be killed
>   My prodigal has come home at last;
> With noble resolutions filled
>   And filled with sorrow for the past
>   No more will burn with love or wine
> But quite has left his women and his swine.
> – Abraham Cowley, 'The Welcome'

Many promising reconciliations have broken down because, while both parties came prepared to forgive, neither party came prepared to be forgiven.
> – Charles Williams

I'll try, I'll try, really. I'll try again. The marriage. The baby. The house. The whole damn bore.
> – Anne Stevenson, 'From an Asylum: Kathy Chattle to her
> Mother, Ruth Arbeiter'

Will ye no come back again?
Better lo'ed ye canna be,
Will ye no come back again?
– Carolina, Baroness Nairne, *Life and Songs*: 'Bonnie Charlie's
   Now Awa''

Redheads

My son, I've travelled round the world
   And many maids I've met
There are two kinds you should avoid
The blonde and the brunette.
– Anonymous, 'A Warning'

Some American delusions:
. . .
5. That Americans are highly sexed and that redheads are more
highly sexed than others.
   – W. Somerset Maugham

A red–headed man will make a good stallion.
   – John Ray, *English Proverbs*

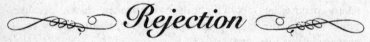

Rejection

Four times in one night
I know I can do.
But not once in four years,
Thelesilla, with you.
   – Martial, *Epigrams* (trans. by Rolfe Humphries)

Relationships

Can I ever know you
or you know me.
– Sara Teasdale, *Flame and Shadow*: 'The Mystery'

It is explained that all relationships require a little of give and take. This is untrue. Any particular partnership demands that we give and give and give and at the last, as we flop into our graves exhausted, we are told that we didn't give enough.
– Quentin Crisp, *How to Become a Virgin*

Almost all our relationships begin, and most of them continue as forms of mutual exploitation, a mental or physical barter, to be terminated when one or both run out of goods.
– W.H. Auden, *The Dyer's Hand*

Once the realization is accepted that even between the closest human beings infinite distances continue to exist, a wonderful living side by side can grow up, if they succeed in loving the distance between them which makes it possible to see the other whole against the sky.
– Rainer Maria Rilke, *Letters* (trans. by Jane Barnard Greene and M.D. Herter Norton)

Now the whole dizzying range of sexual possibilities has been boiled down to that one big, boring, bulimic word: RELATIONSHIP.
– Julie Burchill, *Arena* (London), 1988

I become through my relation to the Thou; as I become I, I say Thou. All real living is meeting.
– Martin Buber, *I-Thou*

I know loads of nice, interesting single women in their thirties and forties who would like a relationship, not necessarily marriage. But where are the equivalent men? They're usually married and living with Mrs Wrong or gay and with Mr Right.

> – Author unknown, quoted in, Linda Grant, *Sexing the Millennium*

Religion

Nothing makes religious people as nervous as sex or at least unregulated sex. Since each religion has its own regulations, people who go to different churches get nervous about different things.

> – Eric Berne, *Games People Play*

Sex is the ersatz, or substitute, religion of the 20th century.

> – Malcolm Muggeridge

Depending on one's sex and one's religious propensities, love can be . . . a single gaze on God.

> – Edna O'Brien, *Some Irish Loving*

To fall in love is to create a religion that has a fallible god.

> – Jorge Luis Borges, *Other Inquisitions*

Love, usually spelled s-e-x, replaced religion as the opiate of the masses.

> – Anonymous, in *Aphra*, Fall 1969

Remarriage

There is no fury like an ex-wife searching for a new husband.

> – Cyril Connolly, *The Unquiet Grave*

Shoot the second shaft, and perhaps thou mayst find again the first.
> – James Howell, *Proverbs*

He swapped his hen for a hooter (= owl)
A bad mistake.
> – Author unknown

He loves his bonds who, when the first are broke,
Submits his neck into a second yoke.
> – Robert Herrick, *Hesperides*

Many a man owes his success to his first wife, and his second wife to his success.
> – Jim Backus (attributed)

Over the years I have come down, rather to my surprise, on the side of marriage, although I suspect that for a number of people, including myself, it may be necessary to marry wrong before you can marry right.
> – A. Alvarez, *Life After Marriage: Love in the Age of Divorce*

The triumph of hope over experience.
> – Samuel Johnson, quoted in James Boswell, *The Life of Samuel Johnson*

Be wary how you marry one who hath cast her rider.
> – English proverb

I long for a way to accommodate second marriages.
> – Donald Coggan, Archbishop of Canterbury, in the *Observer*, 16 July 1978

Find a man of forty who heaves and moans over a woman in the manner of a poet, and you will behold either a man who has ceased to develop intellectually at twenty-four or thereabout, or

REMARRIAGE

a fraud who has an eye on the lands, tenements, and heriditaments of
the lady's first deceased husband.
– H.L. Mencken, *Prejudices*

There are four minds in the bed of a divorced man who marries a
divorced woman.
– *The Babylonian Talmud*

Most used husbands come with strings attached and the ghosts
of the past are nothing to the tangles of the present.
– Bettina Arndt, *All About Us*

Remembrance

I shall remember you with love, or season
My scorn with pity; let me make it plain:
I find this frenzy insufficient reason
For conversation when we meet again.
– Edna St Vincent Millay, 'Sonnet'

Remember me when I am gone away,
  Gone far away into the silent land;
  When you can no longer hold me by the hand
Nor half turn to go, yet turning stay.
– Christina Rossetti, 'Remember'

And if bad luck should lay my strength
Into the shallow grave,
Remember all the good you can;
Don't forget my love.
– John Cornford, 'Poem'

If I should go away,
Beloved, do not say

'He has forgotten me.'
For you abide,
A singing rib within my dreaming side;
You always stay.
– Alun Lewis, 'Postscript: for Gwen'

Rendezvous

You name the time and place
and swear that you'll be there.
– Martial *Select Epigrams of Martial* (trans. and adapted by
 Donald C. Goertz)

There is a witness everywhere.
 – Thomas Fuller, *Gnomologia: Adagies and Proverbs*

Renewal of Love

Love must be reinvented.
 – Arthur Rimbaud, *A Season In Hell*

Repentance

Short acquaintance brings repentance.
 – John Ray, English Proverbs

Repression

Better murder an infant in its cradle than nurse an unacted desire.
- William Blake

Repulsion

Anyone who is repelled by his sweetheart's farts has no business talking about love.
- Günter Grass, *The Flounder*

Reputation

In love, beauty counts more than reputation.
- Publilius Syrus, *Sententiae*

A bad reputation in a woman allures like the signs of heat in a bitch.
- Aldous Huxley, *Point Counter Point*

Respect

If he is cheeky
he doesn't respect you
for not punishing him
for not respecting you.
He won't respect you
if you don't punish him
for not respecting you.
- R.D. Laing, 'Knots'

Responsibility

No sex without responsibility.
— Lord Longford, in the *Observer*, 3 May 1954

Revenge

'Tis sweet to love, but when with scorn we meet,
Revenge supplies the loss with joys as great.
— George Granville, Baron Lansdowne, *The British Enchanters*

You are not permitted to kill a woman who has wronged you,
but nothing forbids you to reflect that she is growing older every
minute. You are avenged fourteen hundred and forty times a
day.

— Ambrose Bierce, *Epigrams*

Rivals

Perhaps she fancied you the man;
    And what care I a farthing?
You think she's false, I think she's kind,
    I take her body, you her mind,
Who has the better bargain?
— William Congreve, 'Song'

A snake lurks in the grass!
— Virgil, *Eclogue*

There will never be any rest between male and female as long as
more than one of each exists upon the earth or elsewhere.
— Charles Bukowski, 'Back-Up'

No throne or bed can brook a partnership.
> – Seneca, *Agamemnon*

> His movements were graceful and all girls he could
>   please,
> And my love he purloin'd.
– George le Bourne, 'The Flying Trapeze'

Romance

Some people claim that marriage interferes with romance.
There's no doubt about it. Anytime you have a romance, your
wife is bound to interfere.
> – Groucho Marx, *The Groucho Phile*

Girls and women can use romance to transform the more
crudely sexual relationship offered to them by boys and men and
make them more palatable for female consumption. That is,
romance stresses overall sensuality and gentlenesss rather than
straightforward genital sex, it demands softness rather than
aggression, sensitivity rather than 'screwing'.
> – Myra Connell *et al.*, *Feminism for Girls*

If there is to be any romance in marriage women must be given
every chance to earn a decent living at other occupations. Otherwise no man can be sure he is loved for himself and that his wife
did not come to the Registry Office because she had no luck at
the Labour Exchange.
> – Rebecca West, in the *Manchester Daily Dispatch*, 26
> November 1912

Women have tolerated miserable sexual relationships, faked
orgasms, and generally kept quiet about their needs, all in the
name of Romantic Love.
> – Eleanor Stephens, in Marsha Rowe, *Spare Rib Reader*

Romance, like the rabbit at the dog track, is the elusive, fake, and never-attained reward which for the benefit and amusement of our masters keeps us running and thinking in safe circles.
– Beverly James, in *The Florida Paper on Women's Liberation*

The concept of romantic love affords a means of emotional manipulation which the male is free to exploit, since love is the only circumstance in which the female is (ideologically) pardoned for sexual activity.
– Kate Millett, *Sexual Politics*

Nothing spoils a romance so much as a sense of humour in a woman.
– Oscar Wilde, *A Woman of No Importance*

 # *Sadism*

The Marquis de Sade and Genet
Are most highly thought of today,
But torture and treachery
Are not my sort of lechery.
– W.H. Auden, in *The New York Review of Books*, 1966

Why did the imagery of S/M become such a dominant motif in the eighties and nineties? Partly, of course, it had to do with safe sex. Penetration, thanks to AIDS, was out.
– Linda Grant, *Sexing the Millennium*

The colour is black, the material is leather, the seduction is beauty, the justification is honesty, the aim is ecstasy, the fantasy is death.
– Susan Sontag, 'Fascinating Fascism', in *Under The Sign of Saturn*

Safe Sex

Books is safe sex.
> – Kathy Acker, in Harriet Gilbert, *The Sexual Imagination from Acker to Zola*

If your newly found lover won't use a condom, you're in bed with a witless . . . and uncaring person.
> – Alex Comfort, *The New Joy of Sex*

Desire does not retreat. Despite the fear . . . and ignorance that mark the second decade of an AIDS epidemic, our bodies are still here. We feel the way people have felt always, wishing for the same sexual fulfilment and for passion to transform our days to magic, even as we work through a dilemma that is unique in our times . . . through safe sex, through research, through imagination unbound.
> – Dean Kuipes, in *Playboy*, March 1994

Life is still rich and sex should be abundant and sensitive. It is important that people don't feel that practising safe sex restricts pleasure.
> – Jeff Koons, in *Playboy*, March 1994

> My thoughts are crowded with death
> and it draws so oddly on the sexual
> that I am confused
> confused to be attracted
> by, in effect, my own annihilation.
> – Thom Gunn, 'In the Time of the Plague'

AIDS obliges people to think of sex as having, possibly, the direst consequences: suicide. Or murder.
> – Susan Sontag, *AIDS and its Metaphors*

No glove – no love.
> – Slogan

Saints and Sinners

Would she could make of me a saint or I of her a sinner.
– William Congreve, 'Song'

The greater the sinner the greater the saint.
– E. Hinchliffe, *Barthomley*

Satiety

There is satiety in all things, of sleep and love, of sweet song and the goodly dance.
– Homer, *The Iliad*

Even honey may cloy, and the gladsome flowers of Aphrodite's garden.
– Pindar, *Nemean Odes*

Full pigeons find cherries bitter.
– John Wodroephe, *The Spared Houres of a Souldier*

Satisfaction

Venus play tricks on lovers with her game of images which never satisfy.
– Lucretius, *De Rerum Natura* (trans. by Rolfe Humphries)

Love that is satisfied no longer charms.
– Thomas Corneille, *Le Festin de Pierre*

There is a great difference between satisfaction and satiation.
– Mary Jane Sherfey, 'A Theory on Female Sexuality', in the *Journal of the American Psychoanalitical Association*, 1966

Scandal

I've got these rubber models of all the reproductive organs of both sexes that I keep locked up in separate cabinets to avoid scandal.

> – Joseph Heller, *Catch-22*

Scolding

Husbands are in heaven whose wives scold not.

> – John Heywood, *A Dialogue containing the number in effect of all the Proverbs in the English Tongue*.

Scolding wives make the best housewives.

> – English proverb

If you would have a hen lay, you must bear with her cackling.

> – Thomas Fuller, *Gnomologia: Adagies and Proverbs*

If a hen does not prate, she will not lay.

> – Torriano, *Piazza Univ*

Scorn

After scorning comes catching.

> – Bethelson, *English–Danish Dictionary*.

Scorn at first makes after-love the more.

> – H.G. Bohn, *A Handbook of Proverbs*

To love a woman who scorns you is like licking honey from a thorn.

> – Welsh proverb

Search for Love

Follow love and it will flee;
Flee love and it will follow thee.
– T. Howell, *Devises*

Flee it and it will flee thee
Follow it and it will follow thee.
– John Ray, *English Proverbs*

O, beauty, are you not enough?
Why am I crying after love?
– Sara Teasdale, *Rivers to the Sea*: 'Spring Night'

Second Thoughts

Doing, a filthy pleasure is, and short.
And done, we straight repent us of the sport.
– Petronius (trans. from the Latin by John Dryden)

Secrecy

Stolen secrets are always sweeter,
Stolen kisses much completer.
– Leigh Hunt, 'Song of Fairies Robbing an Orchard'

A man who has no secrets from his wife either has no secrets or
no wife.
– Author unknown

Stolen sweets are the best.
> – Colley Cibber, *The Rival Fools*

Love ceases to be a pleasure,
When it ceases to be a secret.
> – Aphra Behn, *La Montre or The Lover's Watch, Four O'Clock*

He that kisseth his wife in the market-place shall have many teachers.
> – William Camden, *Remains Concerning Britain*

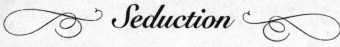 Seduction

All doors are open to courtesy.
> – Thomas Fuller, *Gnomologia: Adagies and Proverbs*

Don't compromise yourself. You are all you've got.
> – Janis Joplin, in *Reader's Digest*, 1973

It's a silly goose who comes to the fox's sermon.
> – English proverb

If a man entice a maid that is not betrothed, and lie with her, he shall surely endow her to be his wife.
> – The Bible: Exodus

Feather by feather the goose is plucked.
> – John Ray, *English Proverbs*

Ladies pretend a great skirmish at the first, yet are boarded willingly at the last.
> – John Lyly, *Euphues and His England*

                    . . . perplexed, confused
                    with love suffused
            She slowly sighed her legs apart.
            – Gershon Legman, *The New Limerick*

The main problem with honest women is not how to seduce them, but how to take them to a private place. Their virtue hinges on half-open doors.
            – Jean Giraudoux, *Amphitryon 38*

There are no unseductable women – only inept men.
            – Anonymous

A maid that laughs is half taken.
            – John Ray, *English Proverbs*

Nothing is more shameful than seducing an honest girl.
            – Wolfgang Amadeus Mozart, letter, 8 July 1778

Pursuit and seduction are the essence of sexuality. It's part of the sizzle.
            – Camille Paglia, *Sex, Art, and American Culture*

Seduction is often difficult to distinguish from rape. In seduction, the rapist often bothers to buy a bottle of wine.
            – Andrea Dworkin, *Letters from a War-Zone*

A wise woman never yields by appointment. It should always be an unforeseen happiness.
            – Stendhal, *On Love*

You have to penetrate a woman's defences. Getting into her head is a prerequisite to getting into her body.
            – Bob Guccione, quoted in W. Leigh, *Speaking Frankly*

Self-Love

He that is in love with himself has at least this advantage – he won't encounter many rivals in his love.
> – Georg Christoph Lichtenberg, *Aphorisms*

To love oneself is the beginning of a lifelong romance.
> – Oscar Wilde, *An Ideal Husband*

We stop loving ourselves when no one loves us.
> – Mme de Staël, *De l'Allemagne*

We had a lot in common. I loved him and he loved him.
> – Shelley Winters, quoted in Susan Steinberg, *Bittersweet*

He fell in love with himself at first sight and it is a passion to which he has always remained faithful.
. . .
Self-love is so often unrequited.
> – Anthony Powell, *Acceptance World*

The last time I saw him he was walking by himself down lovers' lane holding his own hand.
> – Fred Allen, *Much Ado About Me*

There is no one, no one, loves you like yourself.
> – Brendan Behan, *The Hostage*

View yourselves
In the deceiving mirror of self-love.
> – Philip Massinger, *Parliament of Love*

Separation

The only solid and lasting peace between a man and a woman is doubtless a separation.
– Lord Chesterfield

. . . and you can only stay if you start to understand . . .
– Holly Near, 'Started Out Fine'

What it is, I guess, is that I don't really miss *him*. I miss something that must have been *us*. Because we *were* something, in spite of each other. Weren't we.
– Lois Gould, *Such Good Friends*

Seventy Years of Age

Seventy . . . has no stamina, loves its sleep, will not stand without coaxing, draws aim more often than it fires – but it will go to't, smartly too, with the keener joy in what it can no longer take for granted.
– John Barth, *Letters*

Seventy is wormwood
Seventy is gall
But it is better to be seventy
Than not alive at all.
– Phyllis McGinley

. . . the only difference between a man of forty and one of seventy is thirty years of experience.
– Maurice Chevalier (attributed)

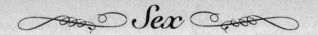

That pathetic short-cut suggested by Nature the supreme joker as a remedy for our loneliness, that ephemeral communion which we persuade ourselves to be of the spirit when it is in fact only of the body – durable not even in memory.

> – Vita Sackville-West, *No in the Sea*

Whatever else can be said about sex it cannot be called a dignified performance.

> – Helen Lawrenson

Sex is sacrament. Sex is sin. Sex is aerobics for the psyche. Sex is the major cause of oppression, and the major site of resistance.

> – Harriet Gilbert, *The Sexual Imagination from Acker to Zola*

No more about sex, it's too boring. Everyone's got one. Nastiness is a real stimulant – but poor honest sex, like dying, should be a private matter.

> – Lawrence Durrell, *Prospero's Cell*

No sex please – we're British.

> – Anthony Marriott and Alistair Foot, Title of play

There may be some things better than sex, and there may be some things worse. But there is nothing exactly like it.

> – W.C. Fields (attributed)

Once sex rears its ugly 'ead it's time to steer clear.

> – Margery Allingham, *The Fashion in Shrouds*

My mother used to say, Delia, if S-E-X ever rears its ugly head, close your eyes before you see the rest of it.

> – Alan Ayckbourn, *Bedroom Farce*

Sex may be a hallowing and renewing experience, but more often it will be distracting, coercive, playful, frivolous, discouraging, dutiful, or even boring.

    – Leslie H. Farber, *The Ways of the Will*

Sex as an institution, sex as a general notion, sex as a problem, sex as a platitude – all this I find too tedious for words. Let us skip sex.

    – Vladimir Nabokov, *Strong Opinions*

As we live, we are transmitters of life. And when we fail to transmit life, life fails to flow through us. This is part of the mystery of sex, it is a flow onwards. Sexless people transmit nothing.

    – D.H. Lawrence, 'We Are Transmitters'

There is no greater nor keener pleasure than that of bodily love – and none which is more irrational.

    – Plato, *The Republic*

. . . after nursing, sex is the most basic social arrangement for satisfying the pervasive and powerful human hunger for being needed/wanted and loved/satisfied.

. . .

Sex is a body-contact sport. It is safe to watch but more fun to play.

    – Thomas Szasz, *Sex By Prescription*

> Sex contains all, bodies, souls,
> Meanings, proofs, purities, delicacies, results,
>   promulgations,
> Songs, commands, health, pride, the maternal mystery,
>   the seminal milk,
> All hopes, benefactions, bestowals, all the passions,
>   loves, beauties, delights of the earth.

    – Walt Whitman, *Leaves of Grass*

Is sex dirty?
Only if it's done right.
– Woody Allen, from the film *Everything You've Ever Wanted to Know About Sex*

Jellyroll killed my pappy,
Drove my mamma stone blind.
– Blues song

Sex is wet . . . In fact it is more than wet, it is slippery.
– Eric Berne, *Games People Play*

Sex is one of the nine reasons for reincarnation . . . The other eight are unimportant.
– Henry Miller, *Big Sur and the Oranges of Hieronymus Bosch*

Sex is not something we do, it is something we are.
– Mary Calderone, quoted in Kogan, *Human Sexual Expression*

All that mystery about sex and then you discover that it is nothing – just a blank.
– Henry Miller, *Tropic of Cancer*

Sex: the thing that takes up the least amount of time and causes the most amount of trouble.
– John Barrymore (attributed)

Continental people have a sex life; the English have hot-water bottles.
– George Mikes, *How to Be an Alien*

These days, you fuck someone, your arm drops off.
– Bette Midler, quoted in the *Independent* (London), 12 November 1988

All I can say is that sex in Ireland is as yet in its infancy.
– Eamon De Valera, after visiting France

An appetite placed in humans to insure breeding. It has in turn bred, as a side product, interesting and often ludicrous customs. Its suppression has led to ugly perversions and cruelty.

> – Jonathan Benter

Sex is the great amateur sport. The professional, male or female, is frowned upon; he or she misses the whole point and spoils the show.

> · – David Cort, *Social Astonishments*

Sex, which ought to be an incident of life, is the obsession of the well-fed world.

> – Rebecca West, in *The Clarion*, 29 November 1912

It's pitch, sex is. Once you touch it, it clings to you.

> – Margery Allingham, *The Fashion in Shrouds*

It is depressing to have to insist that sex is not an unnecessary, morally dubious self-indulgence but a basic human need, no less for women than for men.

> – Ellen Willis, *Beginning to See the Light*

[Sex] can be a dreadful trap . . . There are women who become frigid, but that's not the worst thing that can happen to them. The worst thing is for women to find so much happiness in sexuality that they become more or less slaves of men and that strengthens the chain that binds them to their oppressor . . .

> – Simone de Beauvoir, in *Marie-Claire* (Paris), November
> 1976

Sex is really something I don't understand. You never know where the hell you are. I keep making up these sex rules for myself and then I break them right away.

> – J.D. Salinger, *Catcher in the Rye*

Sex hasn't been the same since women started to enjoy it.

> – Lewis Grizzard (attributed)

Leaving sex to the feminists is like letting your dog vacation at the taxidermist's.

. . .

Sex is dangerous – it's a dangerous sport.

. . .

I feel that sex is basically combat. I feel that the sexes are at war.
– Camille Paglia, *Sex, Art, and American Culture*

There are only two guidelines for good sex, 'Don't do anything you don't really enjoy', and 'Find out your partner's needs and don't balk at them if you can help it'.
– Alex Comfort, *The Joy of Sex*

Sex: Beginnings of

Amoebas at the start
Were not complex;
They tore themselves apart
And started sex.
– Arthur Guiterman

When you were a tadpole and I was a fish,
  In Paleozoic time,
And side by side on the ebbing tide,
  We sprawled through the ooze and the slime

. . .

My heart was rife with the joy of life.
  For I loved you even then.
– Langdon Smith, 'Evolution'

Sex: Need for

I need a little sugar in my bowl and a little hot dog between my roll.

> – Bessie Smith, 'Put a Little Sugar in My Bowl'

Never let us deny
The thing's necessity.
> – Robert Graves, 'Despite and Still'

Sex Appeal

That's it, baby. If you've got it, flaunt it.

> – Mel Brooks, from the film *The Producers*

Odd how the erotic appeal has swung away from the legs; today a smart girl takes her legs for granted and gets herself a good sweater.

> – Belle Livingstone, *Belle Out of Order*

Think of me as a sex symbol for the men who don't give a damn.

> – Phyllis Diller, comedy routine

Being a sex symbol has to do with an attitude, not looks. Most men think it's looks, most women know otherwise.

> – Kathleen Turner, in the *Observer* (London), 1986

Sex Drive

> Gored by the climacteric of his want
> he stalls above me like an elephant.
> – Robert Lowell, 'To Speak of Woe That Is In Marriage'

You put guys on a desert island and they'll do it to mud. Mud!
  – Lenny Bruce, in J. Cohen, *The Essential Lenny Bruce*

That seems forever the spermatozoon's ambition, out.
  – Gustav Eckstein, *The Body Has a Head*

. . . if they can't get rid of the seed, they cannot stop burning.
  – Robert Burton, *The Anatomy of Melancholy*

Man, we're all the same cats, we're all the same schmuck –
Johnson, me you every putz has got that one chick, he's yelling
like a dum-dum: 'Please touch it once. Touch it once, touch it
once.'

  – Lenny Bruce, in J. Cohen, *The Essential Lenny Bruce*

Sex Education

I am against sex ed in schools, because sex is more fun when it's
dirty and sinful.

  – Florence King, in J. Winokur, *The Portable Curmudgeon
  Redux*

Sexism

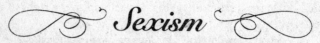

When two people marry they become in the eyes of the law one
person, and that person is the husband.

  – Shana Alexander, *State-by-State Guide to Women's Legal
  Rights*

The sexist notion that women are ... the acceptable prey of predatory males.
– John Irving, *The World According to Garp*

You've come a long way, baby.
– Slogan for Virginia Slims cigarettes

Sex Toys

There was a young man from Racine
Who invented a screwing machine.
    Concave or convex
    It would fit either sex
With attachments for those in-between.
– Adapted from Gershon Legman, *The Limerick*

Sexual Harassment

'You worked in an office once didn't you, Jill?' a feminist once asked me earnestly. 'Did men ever harass you?' 'Yes,' I replied, 'but not nearly enough.'
– Jilly Cooper, *Women and Super Women*

The gooser stands to the left of the ogler, the lip-smacker, the animal-noise maker and the verbal abuser and to the right of the rapist.
– Susan Brownmiller, 'On Goosing', in the *Village Voice* (New York), 15 April 1971

Today, on an Ivy League campus, if a guy tells a girl she has great tits, she can charge him with sexual harassment. Chickenshit stuff. Is this what strong women do?
– Camille Paglia, *Sex, Art, and American Culture*

There are women out there who equate a stranger's 'Hey, baby' with rape. You don't need a weatherman to know which way the wind is blowing; you need a good lawyer and at least five witnesses.
– Lynn Darling, in *Esquire*, February 1994

You have kindergarten harassers. We're reaching out and identifying them at the earliest grades.
– Edward 'Ted' Kennedy, in *Esquire*, February 1994

> Those groans men use
> passing a woman on the street
> or on the steps of the subway
>
> to tell her she is a female
> and their flesh knows it
> . . .
> Yet a woman, in spite of herself
>
> knows it's tribute
> if she were lacking all grace
> they'd pass her in silence
>
> She wants to throw the tribute away
> disgusted and can't.
> – Denise Levertov, 'The Mutes'

Sexual harassment . . . refers to the unwanted imposition of sexual requirements in the context of a relationship of unequal power. Central to the concept is the use of power derived from one social sphere to lever benefits or impose deprivations in another.

> – Catherine A. MacKinnon, *The Sexual Harassment of Working Women*

Sexual Identity

'Tits and ass,' mutter the girls, 'tits and ass. That's all we are around here.'

> – Thomas Pynchon, *Gravity's Rainbow*

I don't know what I am dahling. I've tried several varieties of sex. The conventional position makes me claustrophobic. And the others either give me a stiff neck or lockjaw.

> – Tallulah Bankhead, quoted in Israel, *Miss Tallulah Bankhead*

Sexual Intercourse

If we were to believe that sexual intercourse is repulsive, then we blaspheme God who made the genitals; hands can write a Sefer Torah [a scroll of the five books of Moses, the Pentateuch] and are then honourable and exalted. Hands can perform evil deeds, and are then ugly. Just so the genitals. Whatever use a man makes of them determines whether they are holy or unholy.

> – Rabbi Moses ben Nachman, quoted in Harriet Gilbert, *The Sexual Imagination from Acker to Zola*

Takes two to tango.

> – Al Hoffman and Dick Manning, Title of song

Anyone who calls it 'sexual intercourse' can't possibly be interested in doing it. You might as well announce you're ready for lunch by proclaiming, 'I'd like to do some masticating and enzyme secreting.'

    – Allan Sherman, comedy routine

The pleasure is momentary, the position is ridiculous, and the expense damnable.

    – Lord Chesterfield (attributed)

I think that in the sexual act, as delightful as it can be, the very physical part of it is, yes, a hammering away. So it has a certain brutality.

    – Louise Nevelson, *Dawn+Dusk*

I still could not picture it all taking place on the desk. There didn't seem to be enough room for a woman so tall. I have since discovered that a thimble is room enough when they really want to, and that the whole planet itself may prove too small when they really don't.

    – Joseph Heller, *Something Happened*

Be prepared mentally and physically for intercourse every night
. . .

    – Marabel Morgan, *The Total Woman*

> . . . may i move said he
> is it love said she)
> if you're willing said he
> (but you're killing said she
>
> but it's life said he
> but your wife said she
> now said he)
> ow said she

    – e.e. cummings, 'may i feel said he'

Did you know that the male bee is nothing but a slave of the queen? And once the male bee has – how should I say it – serviced the queen, the male dies. All in all, not a bad system.
– Cloris Leachman, on *The Mary Tyler Moore Show*

I am happy now that Charles calls on my bedchamber less frequently than of old. As it is, I can endure but two calls a week and when I hear his footsteps outside my door, I lie down on my bed, close my eyes, open my legs and think of England.
– Alice, Lady Hillingdon (attributed)

We do not go to bed in single pairs; even if we choose not to refer to them, we still drag there with us the cultural impediments of our social class, our parents' lives, our bank balances, our sexual and emotional expectations, our whole biographies – all the bits and pieces of our unique existences.
– Angela Carter, *The Sadeian Woman*

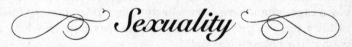

Sexuality

Sexuality throws no light on love, but only through love can we learn to understand sexuality.
– Eugen Rosenstock-Huessy

If my teacher could have influenced my sexuality, I would have turned out to be a nun.
– George Carlin, in *New York*, 24 July 1978

Sexuality is something, like nuclear energy, which may prove amenable to domestication . . . but then again may not.
– Susan Sontag, *Styles of Radical Will*

✦ *Sexual Organs* ✦

The sexual organs are the most sensitive organs of the human being. The eye or the ear seldom sabotage you. An eye will not stop seeing if it doesn't like what it sees, but the penis will stop functioning if he doesn't like what he sees. I would say that the sexual organs express the human soul more than any other limb of the body. They are not diplomats. They tell the truth ruthlessly. It is nice to deal with them and their caprices, but they are even more meshuga than the brain.

> – Isaac Bashevis Singer, in *The New York Times Magazine*, 26 November 1978

✦ *Sexual Revolution* ✦

I oversimplify but do not entirely misrepresent that supposed revolution if I describe it this way: Whereas an ideal woman in olden times might have given a dusty male wayfarer on the road of life a piece of pie – a modern woman may now give him a hand job or a blow job as well.

> – Kurt Vonnegut, Jr, *Palm Sunday*

Women's liberation calls it enslavement but the real truth about the sexual revolution is that it has made sex an almost chaotically limitless and therefore unmanageable realm in the life of women.

> – Midge Decter, *The New Chastity and Other Arguments Against Women's Liberation*

When the Sexual Revolution began, I tried to enlist. But I got a series of humiliating rejections. That was from the men. From the women came nothing but hysterical laughter.

> – Groucho Marx, in Richard J. Anobile, *Why a Duck?*

For most Americans, the sexual revolution was not a vast national orgy of swingers. There was never widespread approval of adultery or promiscuity. The revolution – evolution is a better word – appeared rather a massive questioning of the double standard and the sexual constraints we grew up with.

> – Ellen Goodman, 'Sex Education: A Curriculum of Fear', in the *Washington Post*, October 1980

Granted, the sexual revolution went too far, information-wise. When you find phrases like 'suck face' as a euphemism for 'kiss' it sort of takes the zing out of personal contact.

> – Ian Shoales, 'Single in the '80s'

The freedom that women were supposed to have found in the Sixties largely boiled down to easy contraception and abortion; things to make lifer easier for men, in fact.

> – Julie Burchill, *Damaged Goods*

The window of sexual freedom – between the Pill and AIDS – was quite short, about twenty years. That beautiful window! Along comes herpes, then Aids and it's all fucked up again. Every time it seems you can do this thing, something comes along and says no, you can't. I don't know whether it's a divine plot or a CIA plot or a right-wing Christian plot but something keeps poisoning the well.

> – Paul Ogar, quoted in Linda Grant, *Sexing the Millennium*

Sex without Love

Remember when you were a kid and the boys didn't like the girls? Only sissies liked girls? What I am trying to tell you is that nothing has changed. You think boys grow out of not liking girls, but we don't grow out of it. We just grow horny.

That's the problem. We mix up liking pussy for liking girls. Believe me, one couldn't have less to do with the other.
– Jules Feiffer

In real life women are always trying to mix something up with sex – religion or babies or hard cash; it is only men who long for sex separated out, without rings or strings.
– Katharine Whitehorn, 'Man's Ideal Woman', in the *Observer*, 20 December 1964

The zipless fuck is absolutely pure. It is free of ulterior motives. There is no power game. The man is not 'taking' and the woman is not 'giving'. No one is attempting to cuckold a husband or humiliate a wife. No one is trying to prove anything or get anything out of anyone. The zipless fuck is the purest thing there is. And it is rarer than the unicorn. And I have never had one.
– Erica Jong, *Fear of Flying*

Zipless experiences are pure present without past or future; no wonder they leave the participants empty. Such relationships please in fantasy but cannot fulfil in reality.
– Judianne Densen-Gerber, *Walk in My Shoes*

It is all this cold-hearted fucking that is death and idiocy.
– D.H. Lawrence, *Lady Chatterley's Lover*

Shame and Shamelessness

Where there is shame, there may in time be virtue.
– Samuel Johnson

An itching cunt feels no shame.
> – English proverb, in Eric Partridge, *A Dictionary of Catchphrases*

The more things a man is ashamed of, the more respectable he is.
> – George Bernard Shaw, *Man and Superman*

> Without shame the man I like knows and avows the
> deliciousness of his sex,
> Without shame the woman I like knows and avows
> hers.
> – Walt Whitman, *Leaves of Grass*: 'A Woman Waits for Me'

I never wonder to see men wicked, but I wonder to see them unashamed.
> – Jonathan Swift, *Reflections on Various Subjects*

Talk of shamelessness . . . I know a girl who lost her virginity on the night of Good Friday, at Jerusalem, just above the Church of the Holy Sepulchre.
> – Aldous Huxley, *Time Must Have Stopped*

I feel that the older I get, the more shameless I feel. And in a sense, more pure.
> – Maria Irene Fornes

Shotgun Wedding

Necessity never made a good bargain.
> – Benjamin Franklin, *Poor Richard's Almanac*

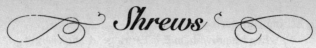

Shrews

Every man can rule a shrew save he that hath her.
– William C. Hazlitt, *English Proverbs*

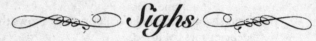

Sighs

The beginning, middle, and end of love is – a sigh.
– Arnold Haultain, *Hints for Lovers*

You must remember this, a kiss is still a kiss,
A sigh is just a sigh;
The fundamental things apply
As time goes by.
– Herman Hupfeld, 'As Time Goes By'

There's a sigh for yes and a sigh for no
And a sigh for I can't bear it!
O what can be done, shall we stay or run
Or cut the sweet apple and share it.
– John Keats, 'Sharing Eve's Apple'

If ever I kill my self for love, it shall be with a sigh, not a sword.
– John Lyly, *Euphues and His England*

Sin

The world's as ugly, ay, as sin
And almost as delightful.
– Frederick Locker-Lampson, 'The Jester's Plea'

That which we call sin in others is experiment for us.
    – Ralph Waldo Emerson

A sin that's hidden is half forgiven.
    – Boccaccio, *Decameron*

                    Their best conscience
Is not to leave 't undone, but to keep 't unknown.
    – William Shakespeare, *Othello*

Should we all confess our sins to one another we would all laugh
at one another for our lack of originality.
    – Kahlil Gibran, *Sand and Foam*

Don't worry kid, the wages of sin is birth.
    – Derek Walcott, 'Tales of the Islands'

For the sin you do by two and two
ye must pay for one by one!
    – Rudyard Kipling, 'Tomlinson'

This common tale, alas! few can prevent;
We first must sin, before we can repent.
    – Anonymous

A conscience cannot prevent sin. It only prevents you from
enjoying it.
    – Harry Hershfield, comedy routine

Fashions in sin change.
    – Lillian Hellman, *The Watch on the Rhine*

All sin tends to be addictive, and the terminal point of addiction
is damnation.
    – W.H. Auden, *A Certain World*: 'Hell'

Sincerity

Men are always sincere. They change sincerities, that's all.
– Tristan Bernard, *Ce que l'on dit aux Femmes*

Single Life

When my bed is empty
Makes me feel awful mean and blue
My springs are getting rusty
Living single like I do.
– Bessie Smith, 'Empty Bed Blues'

Scissors and string, scissors and string
When a man's single he lives like a king.
Needles and pins, needles and pins,
When a man marries, his troubles begin.
– Nursery rhyme

When I was single I went dressed so fine.
Now I am married, Lord, go ragged all the time.
Lord, I wish I was a single girl again.
Lord, I wish I was a single girl again.
– American folk song

I am anal retentive. I'm a workaholic. I have insomnia. And I am a control freak. That's why I'm not married. Who could stand me?

– Madonna, quoted in C. Anderson, *Madonna Unauthorized*

. . . that man is poor
Who hath but one of many,
But crowned is he with store
That, single, may have many.
– Robert Herrick

Down to Gehenna and up to the Throne
He travels the fastest who travels alone.
– Rudyard Kipling, 'The Winners'

Who travels alone, without lover or friend,
But hurries from nothing to nought at the end.
– Ella Wheeler Wilcox, 'Reply to Kipling'

He travels fastest who travels alone, and that goes double for
she. Real feminism is spinsterhood.
– Florence King, *Reflections in a Jaundiced Eye*

The race is run one by one and never two by two.
– Rudyard Kipling, 'Tomlinson'

Sisterhood

A woman should always stand by a woman.
– Euripides, *Helen*

Sixty Years of Age

Man comes of age at sixty, women at fifteen.
– James Stephens, in the *Observer* (London), 1 October 1944

I am sixty-one today
A year beyond the barrier,
And what was once the magic flute,
Is now a water carrier.
– Anonymous

When I get older, losing my hair . . .
Will you still be sending me a Valentine, birthday
greetings, bottle of wine?
. . .
Will you still need me, will you still feed me
When I'm sixty-four?
– John Lennon and Paul McCartney, 'When I'm Sixty-four'

You can take no credit for beauty at sixteen. But if you are
beautiful at sixty, it will be your own soul's doing.
– Marie Stopes

You must ask someone else. I am only sixty.
– Princess Metternich, when asked when a woman ceases
being capable of sexual love, quoted in Simone de Beauvoir,
The Second Sex

One starts to get young at sixty but then it is too late.
– Pablo Picasso (attributed)

The pleasures that once were heaven
Look silly at sixty-seven.
– Noel Coward, 'What's Going to Happen to the Tots?'

 *Skin*

I took off my tie
she took off her dress
I, my revolver belt
she her four bodices.
Not spikenard nor snail
have a skin so smooth,
nor do crystals shine
so brilliant in the moon.
– Federico Garcia Lorca, 'The Faithless Wife'

There isn't anything at all like a fine skin for putting splendour on a woman.
> – J.M. Synge, *The Well of the Saints*

Sleeping Together

And never, ever, no matter what else you do in your whole life, never sleep with anyone whose troubles are worse than your own.
> – Nelson Algren, quoted in H.E.F. Donohue, *Conversations with Nelson Algren*

Oh, come my lad, or go my lad,
    And love me if you like!
. . .
I might as well be easing you
    As lie alone in bed
And waste the night in wanting
    A cruel dark head!

You might as well be calling yours
    What never will be his,
And one of us be happy
    There's few enough as is.
> – Edna St Vincent Millay, 'Sonnet'

You're not just sleeping with one person, you're sleeping with everyone they [sic] ever slept with.
> – Theresa Crenshaw, *Men, Women, Sex, and AIDS*, on NBC-TV, 13 January 1987

I said, Baby! Baby!
Please don't snore so loud
. . .

You jest a little bit o' woman, baby
Sound like a great big crowd.
– Langston Hughes, 'Morning After'

Laugh and the world laughs with you; snore and you sleep alone.
– Anthony Burgess, *Inside Mr Enderby*

 ## *Solitary Sex*

I write in praise of the solitary act;
of not feeling a trespassing tongue
forced into one's mouth . . . Five minutes of solitude are
enough – in the bath, or to fill
the gap between the Sunday papers and lunch.
– Fleur Adcock, 'Against Coupling'

And while Ulysses snored, chaste Penelope
put her delicate hand to practical use
– Martial, *Select Epigrams of Martial* (trans. and adapted by
    Donald C. Goertz)

Never fail to have your wife's circlet tight about your middle
finger.
– François Rabelais, *Gargantua and Pantagruel*

See also: MASTURBATION.

Solitude

The physical union of the sexes only intensifies man's sense of
solitude.
– Nicholas Berdayev

We live, as we dream – alone.
  – Joseph Conrad, *Heart of Darkness*

Marriage is lonelier than solitude.
  – Adrienne Rich, *Poems*

Love is made by two people, in different kinds of solitude.
  – Louis Aragon, in José Pierre, *Recherches sur la sexualité*

Sorry

Love means never having to say you are sorry.
  – Erich Segal, *Love Story*

Vasectomy means not having to say you're sorry.
  – Larry Adler

'I'm sorry' ... he was always saying he's sorry. It was a schlemihl's [sic] stock line.
  – Thomas Pynchon, *V*

The premature ejaculator's favourite orgasm battle cry is, 'I'm coming. I'm sorry.'
  – Jerry Rubin and Mimi Leonard, *The War Between the Sheets*

Speech

But shall I tell thee what most thy suit advances?
Thy fair smooth words? No, no, thy fair smooth
    haunches.
  – Sir John Harington, 'The Author to His Wife, of a Woman's
    Eloquence'

Name it I would: but being blushing red,
The rest I'll speak, when we meet both in bed.
– Robert Herrick, 'What Shame Forbids to Speak'

Speak low, if you speak love.
– William Shakespeare, *Much Ado About Nothing*

Those who love most speak least.
– George Pettie, *Petite Palace of Pettie His Pleasure*

To speak of love is to make love.
– Honoré de Balzac, *The Physiology of Marriage*

And the words which carry most knives are the blind
Phrases searching to be kind.
– Stephen Spender, 'The Double Shame'

See also: COMMUNICATION; CONVERSATION; TALK.

Spoonerisms

The sight of her behind
Forces Pushkin from your mind –
'Forces Pushkin, Mr Gallagher?'
'Pushes foreskins, Mr Sheen.'
– Music hall routine quoted in Gershon Legman, *Rationale of the Dirty Joke*

Studs

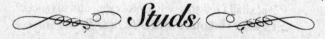

. . . the stud with a rock for a cock and a rock for a heart.
– Norman Mailer, *Genius and Lust*

. . . don't girls like a rake better than a milksop?
— William Makepeace Thackeray, *Vanity Fair*

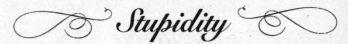

Stupidity

Stupidity always preserves beauty. It keeps away the wrinkles, it is the divine cosmetic.
— Charles Baudelaire, *Intimate Journals*

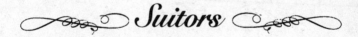

Suggestion

It is well known that we are susceptible only to those suggestions with which we are already secretly in accord.
— Carl Gustav Jung, *Modern Man in Search of a Soul*

Suitors

in your army of lovers
I am a private soldier.
— Gavin Ewart 'Love Song'

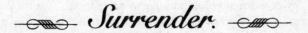

Surrender.

Above all else it is quite out of reason
That you should miserly be of your young limbs

That you should be niggardly of your sweet youth
My love, give me what you should not withhold.
– Jacob Cats 'Trou-Ring I'

Suspicion

It is the property of love to make us more distrustful and more credulous, to make us suspect the loved one, more readily than we should suspect anyone else, and be convinced more easily by her denials.

> – Marcel Proust, *Remembrance of Things Past: Cities of the Plain*

At the gate which suspicion cometh in, love goeth out.
> – Stefano Guazzo, *La civile Conversazione*

Love is sweetest seasoned with suspect.
> – George Clifford, 'To Cynthia'

Talk

The female and the fortress which begins to parlay is half-gain'd.
> – James Howell, *Parlay of Beasts*

For God's sake hold your tongue, and let me love.
> – John Donne, 'The Canonization'

For fewer women would indulge in copulation . . . if they could obtain in the vertical position the words of admiration which they need and which demand a bed.
> – André Malraux, *Man's Fate*

Whom we love best, to them we can say the least.
> – John Ray, *English Proverbs*

> Dont talk of June!
> Don't talk of Fall!
> Don't talk at all!
> Show me.
> – Alan Jay Lerner, *My Fair Lady*

If the art of conversation stood a little higher we would have a lower birthrate.
> – Stanislaw J. Lee

> I thought to undermine the heart
>   By whispering in the ear.
> – Sir John Suckling, 'Love's Siege'

> But words are words, I never yet did hear
> That the bruis'd heart was pierced through the ear.
> – William Shakespeare, *Othello*

You can't prevent a sexually transmitted epidemic without talking about sex.
> – Sam Puckert, in *New York*, 23 March 1987

. . . and used all speech which might provoke and stir.
> – Ovid, *Amores* (trans. by Christopher Marlowe)

'What are your views on love?'
>   'Love? I make it constantly but I never talk about it.'
> – Marcel Proust, *Remembrance of Things Past: The Guermantes Way*

You can stroke people with words.
> – F. Scott Fitzgerald, *The Crack-Up*

See also: COMMUNICATION; CONVERSATION; SPEECH.

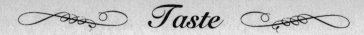

Taste

To each his own love, mine for me.
— Atilius, *Fragment*

Tears

I loved the very tears I made her shed.
— Jean Racine, *Britannicus*

There's nothing sooner dry than woman's tears.
— John Webster, *The White Devil*

She acts the jealous, And at will she cries;
For women's tears are but the sweat of eyes.
— Juvenal, *Sixth Satire* (trans. by John Dryden)

Beg her, with tears, thy warm desires to grant;
For tears will pierce a heart of adamant.
— Ovid, *Ars Amatoria* (trans. by John Dryden)

In woman's eye the unanswerable tear.
— George Gordon, Lord Byron, 'The Corsair'

Teasing

The bad thing about a cockteaser like Angela is that she turns her
man loose on the world and lets a lot of other women in for trouble.
— John Updike, *Couples*

... one of those artful little coquettes ... took me over all possible fraudulent jumps: breathing on my neck, tickling my sweaty palm with her fingertip, and insinuating her satin gown against my own with such resolute albeit counterfeit wantonness that only an almost saintly will power, after hours of this, forced me to break apart from the loathsome little vampire and make my swollen way into the night.
— William Styron, *Sophie's Choice*

Do me the favour to deny me at once.
— Benjamin Franklin, *Poor Richard's Almanac*

Desires are nourished by delays.
— Thomas Draxe, *Bibliotheca*

... allowing moist liberties but with steel-trap relentlessness withholding the big prize.
...
You ... teasers have turned millions of brave young men, many of whom died for your precious asses on the battlefields of the world, into a generation of sexual basket cases.
— William Styron, *Sophie's Choice*

I will kindle no more coals than I may well quench.
— Author unknown

Refuse me, Galla — teasing keeps love strong,
But don't refuse me, Galla, for too long.
— Martial, *Epigrams* (trans. by Rolfe Humphries)

Another thing missing from feminist discourse ... is that girls go after guys — that sexual sex and power and aggression are fused on both sides. Girls, in fact, are always manipulating men. It's called cockteasing.
— Camille Paglia, in *Esquire* (New York), February 1994

TEASING

Her left eye winks Yes
and her right stares No
and her smile smiles smiles.
– Alan Dugan, 'On Rape Unattempted'

Technique

It ain't what you do, it's the way that you do it.
– Thomas 'Fats' Waller, Title of song

Jane Mack does it like an angel, lithely, gracefully, daintily, and above all sweetly.
– John Barth, *Letters*

Mrs Murphy's Gresham's Law Modified: Bad screwing tends to drive out the good.
– Lin Field, *Mrs Murphy's Laws*

Much smoke, little fire.
– English proverb

The deeper the sweeter.
– Ben Jonson

Ignorance and bungling with love are better than wisdom and skill without.
– Henry David Thoreau, *A Week on the Concord and Merrimack Rivers*

He makes love to me expertly, mechanically, coldly . . . He's pressing all my buttons, as if I were a pocket calculator.
– Erica Jong, *How To Save Your Own Life*

The greatest strokes make not the best musick.
– John Ray, *English Proverbs*

Stop a little, to make an end the sooner.
      – Thomas Fuller, *Gnomologia: Adagies and Proverbs*

Fair and softly goes far in a day. He that goes softly, goes sure and also far. He that spurs on too fast at first setting out, tires before he comes to his journey's end.
      – John Ray, *English Proverbs*

Gently, gently goes far.
      – Portuguese proverb

    Now high, now low, now striking short and thick
    And diving deep, pierced to the quick.
    – Thomas Nashe, 'The Merrie Ballad of Nashe, His Dildo'

    (tip top said he
    don't stop said she
    oh no said he)
    go slow said she
    – e.e. cummings, 'may i feel said he'

I wouldn't be too ladylike in love if I were you.
      – A.P. Herbert, 'I Wouldn't Be Too Ladylike'

Never confuse movement with action.
      – Ernest Hemingway, in A.E. Hotchner, *Papa Hemingway*

    Tutti Frutti, good booty
    If you don't fit, don't force it.
    – Little Richard, 'Tutti Frutti'

    The sickle motion from the thighs
    Jackknifes upward at the knees
      Then straightens out from heel to hip.
    – T.S. Eliot, 'Sweeney Erect'

TECHNIQUE

All too many men still seem to believe, in a rather naive and egocentric way, that what feels good to them is automatically what feels good to women.

– Shere Hite, *The Hite Report*

Telephone

Please, God, let him telephone me now. Dear God, let him call me now . I won't ask anything else of you, truly I won't. It isn't much to ask. It would be so little to you, God, such a little, little thing. Only let him telephone now, God. Please, please, please.

– Dorothy Parker, 'The Telephone Company'

Temptation

Don't worry about avoiding temptation. As you grow older it will avoid you.

– Joey Adams

I generally avoid temptation unless I can't resist it.

– Mae West, in the film *My Little Chickadee*

If you can't be good, be careful.

– American proverb

The only way of getting rid of a temptation is to yield to it.

– Oscar Wilde, *The Picture of Dorian Gray*

> You may tempt the upper classes
> With your villainous demi-tasses
> But Heaven will protect the Working Girl.

– Edgar Smith, 'Heaven Will Protect the Working Girl'

I . . . beg you let me be quiet, for I am not over-fond of resisting temptation.
> – William Beckford, *Vathek*

I can resist everything except temptation.
> – Oscar Wilde, *Lady Windermere's Fan*

An open door may tempt a saint.
> – English proverb

Yield to temptation; it may not pass your way again.
> – R. A. Heinlein, *The Notebooks of Lazurus Long*

There are several good protections against temptations, but the surest is cowardice.
> – Mark Twain, *Pudd'nhead Wilson's Calendar*

> Is this her fault or mine?
> The tempter or tempted, who sins the most?
> – William Shakespeare, *Measure for Measure*

Temptation discovers what we are.
> – Thomas à Kempis, *De Imitatione Christi*

> Temptations offered I still scorn;
>   Denied, I cling them still;
> I'll neither glut mine appetite,
>   Nor seek to starve my will.
> – Thomas Heywood

'You oughn't to yield to temptation.'
> 'Well, somebody must, or the thing becomes absurd.'
> – Anthony Hope, *The Dolly Dialogues*

Tenderness

Tenderness is the repose of passion.
>   – Joseph Joulet, *Pensées*

> If you wish
> I shall be irreproachably tender:
> Not a man, but a cloud in pants.
>   – Vladimir Mayakovsky, 'Cloud in Pants'

Tension

Sex alleviates tension. Love causes it.
>   – Woody Allen

That experience called love and celebrated in poetry and prose of all peoples throughout human history – so transcends the physiological need for tension-relief that it can be spiritually satisfying even in the absence of providing relief of sexual tension.
>   – Thomas Szasz, *Sex By Prescription*

Testes

The boughs that bear the most hang the lowest.
>   – Thomas Fuller, *Gnomologia: Adagies and Proverbs*

. . . numb-headed hater, assassin dragging behind him a wrinkled sack, reproduction's two stooges.
>   – John Updike, 'Cunts (Upon Receiving the Swingers Life
>   Club Membership Solicitation)'

. . . Oh cod, riddled by dimples, hooded with wimples, lined with crimples, studded with pimples . . . Cod, herniary, varicose, and varicoceleous, septic, festering, carbuncled . . .
– François Rabelais, *Gargantua and Pantagruel*

Thighs

thy thighs are white horses yoked to chariot of kings
they are the striking of a good minstrel
between them is always a pleasant song.
– e.e. cummings, 'Song of Songs'

The happy dawning of her thigh.
– Robert Herrick, *Hesperides*

As spread thighs are to the libertine . . .
– Thomas Pynchon, *V*

. . . the eat-meat of inner thighs
– Seymour Krim, *Views of a Nearsighted Cannoneer*

Thirty Years of Age

no one touches
me anymore.
– Sonia Sanchez, 'Poem at Thirty'

Better than old beef is the tender veal
I want no woman thirty years of age.
– Geoffrey Chaucer, *The Canterbury Tales*

Women over thirty are at their best, but men over thirty are too old to recognize it.
  – Jean-Paul Belmondo (attributed)

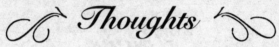

Thoughts

The secret thoughts of men run over all things, holy, profane, clean, obscene, grave and light, without shame or blame.
  – Thomas Hobbes, *Leviathan*

My thoughts are my trollops.
  – Denis Diderot

  We think about sex obsessively except
  During the act, when our minds tend to wander.
  – Howard Nemerov, 'Reading Pornography in Old Age'

Time

  Gather ye rosebuds while ye may,
      Old Time is still a-flying;
  And this same flower that smiles today
      Tomorrow will be dying
  . . .
  Then be not coy, but use your time;
      And while ye may, go marry;
  For having lost but once your prime,
      You may for ever tarry.
  – Robert Herrick, 'To the Virgins, To Make Much of Time'

Time, which strengthens friendships, weakens love.
  – Jean de La Bruyère, *On Women*

Any time not spent on love is wasted.
> – Torquato Tasso

When the frost is on the punkin'
That's the time for dicky dunkin'.
And when the weather is hot and sticky
That's the time for dunkin' dicky.
> – American folk poem, in Wilson, *Playboy's Book of Forbidden Words*

Straw-in-the fire love,
It's no morality play we're in,
Nor can we trick time,
Nor end where we began.
> – Jean Garrigue, 'To Speak My Influence'

Time walks at your side ma'am, unwilling to pass.
> – Christopher Fry

Laurel is green for a season, and love is sweet for a day;
But love grows bitter with treason, the laurel outlives
   not May.
> – A.C. Swinburne, 'Hymn to Proserpine'

All the while believe me, I prayed
Our night would last twice as long.
> – Sappho, 'One Night' (trans. by Willis Barnstone)

If you let slip time like a languished rose
It withers on the stalk with languished head.
> – John Milton, *Comus*

After three days men grow weary of a wench, a guest, and rainy weather.
> – Benjamin Franklin, *Poor Richard's Almanac*

Never fancy Time's before you,
Youth believe me, will away;
Then, alas! who will adore you,
  Or to wrinkles tribute pay?
– Matthew Prior, *Poems*: 'Lamentation for Dorinda'

Time, not the mind, puts an end to love.
  – Publilius Syrus, *Sententiae*

Love makes time pass; time makes love pass.
  – French proverb

  Oh, it's a long, long while
  From May to December,
  But the days grow short
  When you reach September.
  . . .
  Oh the days dwindle down
  To a precious few . . .
  And these few precious days
  I'll spend with you.
  – Maxwell Anderson, 'September Song' (music by Kurt
   Weill)

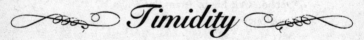 *Timidity*

If love be timid, it is not true.
  – Spanish proverb

He who begins timidly invites a refusal.
  – Seneca, *Hippolytus*

Togetherness

Let there be spaces in your togetherness.
— Kahlil Gibran, *The Prophet*

A wall between preserves love.
— Samuel Palmer, *Moral Essays on Proverbs*

Constant togetherness is fine – but only for Siamese twins.
— Victoria Billings, *The Woman's Book*

Tongue

For she has a tongue with a tang.
— William Shakespeare, *The Tempest*

The nimble tongue (love's lesser lightning) play'd
Within my mouth, and to my thoughts convey'd
Swift orders, that I should prepare to throw
The all–dissolving thunderbolt below.
— John Wilmot, Earl of Rochester, 'The Imperfect Enjoyment'

. . . alluring him with tongue in said George's mouth and said George's tongue in hers.
— Indictment of Anne Boleyn

Women whose tongues won't stay in their mouths are the sexiest.
— John Updike, *Couples*

His tongue is well-hung.
— English saying

A liquorish tongue, a lecherous tail.
— English proverb

Say, buddy, what
does that whore of yours
have to say?
Not your girl friend;
I mean your tongue.
– Martial, *Select Epigrams of Martial* (trans. and adapted by
   Donald C. Goertz)

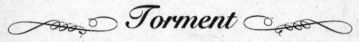

Torment

. . . love is a just another dirty lie. Love is ergoapiol pills to make
me come around because you were afraid to make me have a
baby. Love is that dirty aborting horror you took me to. Love is
my insides all messed up. It's half catheters and half whirling
douches. I know about love. Love always hangs up behind the
bathroom door. To hell with love.

– Ernest Hemingway, *To Have and Have Not*

Terminate torment
of love unsatisfied
The greater torment
of love satisfied.
– T.S. Eliot, 'Ash-Wednesday'

Love is a torment of the mind
   A tempest everlasting
– Samuel Daniel, 'Love is a Sickness'

'Will she
Or will she not
Give me her body?'
That is the question
That teases and torments you
And sends you reeling forth

Into the night
Singing to the stars.
Or striding angrily down dusty roads,
Striking off the heads
Of helpless flowers
With your cane.
– Zella Muriel Wright, *The Pagan Anthology*

See also: PAIN.

Touch

The most important of all senses in sexual matters, is *touch*.
– Th. Van de Velde, *Ideal Marriage*

It is good for man not to touch woman.
– St Paul, The Bible: 1 Corinthians

Trading Up

If you can kiss the mistress, never kiss the maid.
– English proverb

Triangles

One man;
Two loves.
No good ever comes of that.
– Euripides, *Andromache*

True Love

True love comes quietly, without banners of flashing lights. If you hear bells, get your ears checked.
— Erich Segal

Contrast with all loves that had failed or staled
Registered their own as love indeed.
— Robert Graves, 'Never Such Love'

Truth

There is nothing like desire for preventing the thing one says from bearing any resemblance to what one has in one's mind.
— Marcel Proust, *Remembrance of Things Past: The Guermantes Way*

Twenty Years of Age

I dated a twenty-one-year-old girl, took her to my apartment. Put on a record of Charlie Parker and Dizzy Gillespie playing a Cole Porter tune. She thought it was classical music.
— Woody Allen, in *The New York Times*, 12 January 1975

Ugliness

If you want to be happy for the rest of your life
Never make a pretty woman your wife.

> Just from my personal point of view
> Get an ugly girl to marry you.
> – Calypso song

Beautiful women usually fall to the lot of ugly men.
> – Italian proverb

Beauty is only skin deep, but ugly goes to the bone.
> – English proverb

> Now my hair is nappy and I don't wear no clothes of
>   silk,
> But the cow that's black and ugly has often got the
>   sweetest milk.
> – Sara Martin, 'Mean Tight Mama'

Beauty is still supposed to arouse desire. This is not the case. Beauty has nothing to do with the physical jerks under the coverlet. Ugliness is one of the most reliable stimulants.
> – Henri de Montherlant, 'The Goddess Cypris'

I ain't good-lookin', but I'm somebody's angel child.
> – Bessie Smith, quoted in E. Feinstein, *Bessie Smith*

No need to look at the mantlepiece when you are poking the fire.
> – English proverb

Desire beautifies what is ugly.
> – Alfred Henderson, *Latin Proverbs*

All the ugly ones fuck.
> – Thomas Pynchon, *V*

There are no ugly women, only lazy ones.
> – Helena Rubinstein, *My Life for Beauty*

Understanding

There is only one thing worse than a wife who doesn't understand her husband, and that's a wife who does.
— Anonymous

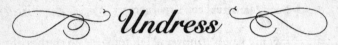

Undress

A man who enters his wife's dressing room is a sage of consummate wisdom – or an imbecile.
— Honoré de Balzac, *The Physiology of Marriage*

Abandoned déshabillé is one of the most sexually stimulating devices.
— M. Levy, *The Moons of Paradise*

Let me take you a button-hole lower.
— William Shakespeare, *Love's Labour's Lost*

> By degrees
> Her rich attire creeps rustling to her knees.
> — John Keats, 'The Eve of St Agnes'

> Come, madam, come
> . . .
> Off with that girdle, like heaven's Zone glistering,
> But a far fairer world encompassing.
> . . .
> Unlace yourself, for that harmonious chime
> Tells me from you, that now it is bedtime.
> . . .
> Now off with those shoes, and then safely tread
> In this love's hallow'd temple, this soft bed.
> — John Donne, 'To His Mistress Going to Bed'

A woman undressing, how dazzling. It is like the sun piercing the clouds . . .
  – August Rodin, in Robert Melville, *Erotic Art of the West*

With heavy breast the Dean undressed
The Bishop's wife to lie on.
She thought it crude, done in the nude
So he kept his old school tie on.
  – Anonymous, in Leon Kronenberger, *Animal, Vegetable, Mineral*

Take off your shell along with your clothes.
  – Alex Comfort, *The Joy of Sex*

Unfaithfulness

A man can have two, maybe three love affairs while he is married. After that, it is cheating.
  – Yves Montand (attributed)

I don't think there are any men who are faithful to their wives.
  – Jacqueline Kennedy Onassis (attributed)

Those who are faithful know only the trivial side of love; it is the faithless who know love's tragedies.
  – Oscar Wilde

Husbands are chiefly good lovers when they are betraying their wives.
  – Marilyn Monroe

For many young men will strive to deceive you,
And when they have had their will, straightway will
      leave you.
– Anonymous, *Roxburghe Ballads*: 'The Deluded Lass's
  Lamentation'

See also: BETRAYAL; INFIDELITY.

Union

When ye unite with another, do so with deep consciousness of
the greatness of the dignity of that which you do! Give yourself
to this work of love; with your souls and with your minds, even
as with your flesh.
– Omar Haleby, *El Ktab*

[Love] can be intimacy and attachment, the wedding of two
solids by the heat of passion in a union that may endure forever,
if it does not crack under the hammer of blows of life or waste
away under the monotonous drip of ever-haunting trivia.
– Eric Berne, *Games People Play*

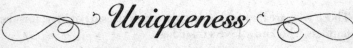

Uniqueness

For words of rapture groping, they
'Never such love,' swore 'ever before was!'
– Robert Graves, 'Never Such Love'

How many loved your moments of glad grace,
And loved your beauty with love false and true,
But one man loved the pilgrim soul in you
And loved the sorrows of your changing face.
– W.B. Yeats, 'When You Are Old'

Tell me no more how fair she is,
I have no mind to hear
The story of that distant bliss
I never shall come near:
By sad experience I have found
That her perfection is my wound.
– Henry King, Bishop of Chichester, 'Tell me no more how
  fair she is'

She gave the wound, and she alone can cure it.
– Walter Davison, 'Ode'

Unjust

. . . for man to man so oft unjust
is always so to women.
– George Gordon, Lord Byron, *Don Juan*

Unorthodox Sex

When a man and woman of unorthodox tastes make love the
man could be said to be introducing his foible into her quirk.
– Kenneth Tynan, in the *Guardian*, 1975

Unrequited Love

The wages of scorned love is baneful hate.
– Beaumont and Fletcher, *The Knight of Malta*

We shall find no fiend in hell can match the fury of a disappointed woman – scorned, slighted, dismissed without a parting pang.

> – Colley Cibber, *Love's Last Shift*

To prove that you love her, though she doesn't give a fig for you, you're supposed to spend a lifetime in silence with only a handful of glorious memories to keep you from madness?

> – Alexander Theroux, *Darconville's Cat*

Unwritten Law

The day that Sheila's Papa finds out that Sheila's Mama is cheating on him he's going to have an attack of the Mexican Charro syndrome and Sheila's Mama and whoever is rooting around with her are going to end up with more holes in them than a square yard of wire mesh.

> – Luis Raphael Sanchez, *Macho Camacho's Beat*

Urgency of Sex

The life of the universe depends upon the pudendum. As soon as the Word was made flesh, man was unable to be quiet, or work, or think, until he had dropped his seed.

> – Edward Dahlberg

What am I suffering from? Sexuality . . . Will it destroy me? How can I rid myself of sexuality?

> – Thomas Mann

Uxoriousness

Uxoriousness: A perverted affection that has strayed to one's own wife.

— Ambrose Bierce, *The Devil's Dictionary*

Sissy's mother used the vaginal wrench to slowly, gently turn her husband's objection down to a mere trickle.

— Tom Robbins, *Even Cowgirls Get the Blues*

Vagina

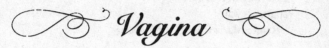

Glad tunnel of life, foretaste of resurrection,
slick applicant of appropriate friction.
springing loose the critical honey from the delirious bee.
. . .
Who put this mouse between my legs if not the Lord?
Who knocks to enter? Pigs of many stripes.

— John Updike, *Tossing and Turning*

By my life, this is my lady's hand! these be her C's, her U's, and her T's; and thus makes she her P's.

— William Shakespeare, *Twelfth Night*

No woman wants to find out that she has a twat like a horse-collar...

— Germaine Greer, *The Female Eunuch*

The vagina . . . in which men drop their grief, their complaints, their guilt.

— Alexander Theroux, *Darconville's Cat*

By swift degrees advancing — where
His daring hand that Altar seized,

Where Gods of Love do sacrifice:
That awful throne, that Paradice [sic]
Where Rage is calm'd, and Anger pleas'd;
That Fountain where Delight still flows,
And gives the Universe World Repose.
– Aphra Behn, 'The Disappointment'

Convince a woman that her vagina is beautiful and you have the makeup of an equal person. This I believe with all my heart.
– Nancy Friday, *My Mother, My Self*

that wonderful rare
space in you.
– Rainer Maria Rilke, *Phallic Poems*

It is like a purple flower of crimson, full of honey and perfume. It is like a hydra of the sea, living and soft, open at night. It is the humid grotto, the shelter always warm, the Asylum where man rests on his march toward death.
– Pierre Louÿs, *Aphrodite*

Their lives centre around their vaginas: what goes in and what comes out.
– Erica Abeel, 'Park Bench Mothers', in *New York*,
24 May 1971

There was a young man from Brighton
Who thought he'd at last found a tight 'un.
He said, 'O my love
It fits like a glove.'
Said she, 'You're not in the right 'un.'
– Anonymous Limerick

Snatches vary . . . No two are alike.
– Joseph Heller, *Something Happened*

Convolute cranny, hair and air, ambrosial chalice where seed can cling.

> – John Updike, *Couples*

The portions of a woman that appeal to a man's
     depravity
  Are constructed with considerable care,
And what at first appears to be a simple cavity
  Is in fact a most elaborate affair.

> – Author unknown, in Peter Fryer, *Mrs Grundy*

On this soft anvil all mankind was made.

> – John Wilmot, Earl of Rochester, *Sodom*

If you have a vagina and an attitude in this town, then that's a lethal combination.

> – Sharon Stone, in *Empire* (London), June 1992

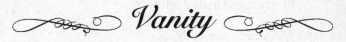

Vanity

Once love is purged of vanity, it resembles a feeble convalescent, hardly able to drag itself about.

> – Sébastien Chamfort

Statesmen and beauties are rarely sensible of the graduations of their decay.

> – Lord Chesterfield

My destiny has been cast among cocksure women. Perhaps when man begins to doubt himself, woman, who should be nice and peacefully hen-sure, becomes instinctively cocksure ... And woe betide everybody.

> – D.H. Lawrence, 'Women So Cocksure', in *Phoenix*

Variety

Age can not wither her, nor custom stale
Her infinite variety; other women cloy
The appetites they feed, but she makes hungry
Where she most satisfies.
– William Shakespeare, *Antony and Cleopatra*

Commit
The oldest sins the newest kind of way.
– William Shakespeare, *King Henry IV*

Variety is the soul of pleasure.
– Aphra Behn, *The Rover*

Every night should have its own menu.
– Honoré de Balzac

We did it in front of the mirror
And in the light. We did it in the darkness,
In water, and in the high grass.

We did it in honour of man
And in honour of beast and in honour of God.
But they didn't want to know about us,
They had already seen our sort.
– Yehuda Amichai, 'We Did It'

Men like new women. While women peform best with men
they know.
–John Updike, *Couples*

Yet still the meat's the same, the change does lie
All in the sauces' great variety.
–John Wilmot, Earl of Rochester, *Sodom*

Will no other vice content you?
– John Donne, 'The Indifferent'

Sour, sweet, bitter, pungent,
All must be tasted.
  – Chinese proverb

No pleasure lasts long unless there is variety in it.
  – Publilius Syrus, *Maxims*

  Variety's the very spice of life,
  That gives it all its flavour.
  – William Cowper, *The Task*: 'The Timepiece'

Variety's the source of joy below.
  – John Gay, *Epistle to Bernard Lintott*

Venery

Rarely use venery, but for health or offspring, never to dullness, weakness or the injury of your own or another's peace or reputation.
  – Benjamin Franklin, *Rules For His Own Conduct*

Vice

Vice is a monster of so frightful mien,
As to be hated needs but to be seen;
Yet seen too oft, familiar with her face,
We first endure, then pity, then embrace.
– Alexander Pope, *An Essay on Man*

He hasn't a single redeeming vice.
> – Oscar Wilde

Here's a rule I recommend. Never practise two vices at once.
> – Tallulah Bankhead (attributed)

Vice is its own reward.
> – Quentin Crisp (attributed)

It is the function of vice to keep virtue within bounds.
> – Samuel Butler, *Notebooks*

> Vice
> Is nice.
> But a little virtue
> Won't hurt you.
> – Felicia Lamport, 'Axioms to Grind'

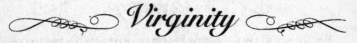

Virginity

Maidenheads are for ploughing.
> – Samuel Johnson (attributed)

She has cracked her pitcher or pipkin.
> – Francis Grose, *A Classical Dictionary of the Vulgar Tongue*

> A certain young sheik I'm not namin'
> Asked a flapper he thought he was tamin'
>   'Have you your maidenhead?'
>   'Don't be silly,' she said,
> 'But I still have the box it came in.'
> – Gershon Legman, *The Limerick*

I'll wager you that in ten years it will be fashionable again to be a virgin.
— Barbara Cartland, in the *Observer*, 20 June 1976

Do I still long
for my virginity?
— Sappho, 'Remorse'

My virginity weighed like a millstone round my neck. I was sick of it.
— Sylvia Plath, *The Bell Jar*

You have kissed and nibbled and poked and prodded and worried me there so often that my virginity was lost in the shuffle.
— Vladimir Nabokov, *Ida*

An isolated outbreak of virginity like
Lucinda's is a rash on the face of society.
It arouses only pity from the married, and
An embarrassment from the single.
— Charlotte Bingham, *Lucinda*

I may be dead tomorrow, uncaressed
    My lips have not touched a woman's, none
    Has given me a look in her soul, not one
Has ever held me swooning at her breast.
— Jules Laforgue, *For the Book of Love*

How can I keep my maidenhead,
    My maidenhead, maidenhead,
How can I keep my maidenhead,
    Among sae mony men, O.
— Robert Burns, 'How Can I Keep My Maidenhead'

To All You Virgins — Thanks for Nothing.
— Graffito

. . . the turnuppy cockuppy virgin.
> – François Rabelais, *Gargantua and Pantagruel*

You're such a virgin, a sweet perpetual virgin. You're so perfect you turn other people hard as ice . . .
> – Joyce Carol Oates, *Do With Me What You Will*

A well preserved virginity may signify a limited capacity to love.
> – Robert Shields, in the *Observer*, 13 June 1965

Oh the innocent girl
in her maiden teens
knows perfectly well
what everything means.

If she didn't she oughter;
it's a silly shame
to pretend that your daughter
is blank at the game.
> – D.H. Lawrence, *Pansies*: 'The Jeune Fille'

Losing her virginity – losing it? She'd taken it out for a walk in the woods and abandoned it.
> – Keith Waterhouse

Nature abhors a virgin – a frozen asset.
> – Clare Boothe Luce, in L. and M. Cowen, *The Wit of Wisdom*

Ladies, just a little more virginity, if you don't mind.
> – Sir Herbert Beerbohm Tree, to actresses auditioning for a
> show

What most men desire is a virgin who is a whore.
> – Edward Dahlberg, *Reasons of the Heart*

Maids often lose their maidenhead
Ere they set foot in nuptial bed.
– Robert Herrick, 'Love's Courtship'

Are there still virgins? One is tempted to answer no. There are only girls who have not yet crossed the line, because they want to preserve their market value . . . Call them virgins if you will, these travellers in transit.
 – François Giraud, quoted in *Coronet*, November 1960

Virginity is now a mere preamble or waiting room to be got out of as soon as possible . . .
 – Ursula Le Guin, 'The Space Crone', in *The Co-Evolution
 Quarterly*, Summer 1976

 *Virtue*

Woman's virtue is man's greatest invention.
 – Cornelia Otis Skinner, *Paris '90*

Most plain girls are virtuous because of the scarcity of opportunity to be otherwise.
 – Maya Angelou, *I Know Why the Caged Bird Sings*

Or do you on your mistress' virtue dote?
Tell me, I should be very glad to know it,
What virtue dwells beneath a petticoat?
– Alexander Ratcliff, 'A Satire Against Love'

The lady doth protest too much, me thinks.
– William Shakespeare, *Hamlet*

The virtues of society are the vices of the saint.
 – Ralph Waldo Emerson

Whether lust is homo- or hetero-sexual, virtue consists in dominating it.
> – André Gide, in A. Karlin, *Sexuality and Homosexuality*

The virtue which requires to be ever guarded is scarcely worth the sentinel.
> – Oliver Goldsmith

What is virtue but the Trade Unionism of the married.
> – George Bernard Shaw, *Man and Superman*

How unhappy is the woman who is in love and virtuous at the same time.
> – François, duc de La Rochefoucauld, *Maximes posthumes*

> To my flaming youth let virtue be as wax.
> – William Shakespeare, *Hamlet*

> Virtue is its own reward.
> – John Dryden, 'The Assignation'

Virtue which parlays is near surrender.
> – Nathaniel Bailey, *Dictionary*

Virtue is its own revenge.
> – E.Y. Harburg (attributed)

> . . . maiden virtue rudely strumpeted.
> – William Shakespeare, *Sonnets*

Voice

How well a soft and libertine voice will erect your member, it is as good as fingers . . .
> – Juvenal, *Sixth Satire*

His voice was intimate as the rustle of sheets, and he kissed easily.
— Dorothy Parker, *Dusk Before Fireworks*

Always I hear the milk tones of her voice, a virgin, a whore, a woman totally aware of every dark perversion, an innocent.
— Gilberto Sorrentino, *Mulligan's Stew*

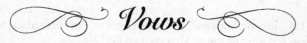 *Vows*

The vow of love-passion they say is no vow.
— Plato, *Symposium*

Men's vows are women's traitors.
— William Shakespeare, *Cymbeline*

Lovers' solemn oaths are much like solemn hodge-podge.
— Plautus, *Cistellaria*

Vows can't change nature.
— Robert Browning, 'Rabbi Ben Ezra'

Then talk not of inconstancy
    False hearts and broken vows;
If I, by miracle, can be
This live-long minute true to thee,
    'Tis all that Heav'n allows.
— John Wilmot, Earl of Rochester, 'Love and Love: A Song'

The lecher's vows in ashes I record.
— Sophocles, *Fragments*

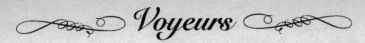

Voyeurs

... she saw him first, peeping mom, keeping her eye on the masculinery as always ...
> – Luis Raphael Sanchez, *Macho Camacho's Beat*

I am quite out of patience with their scurvy strictures ... by which his eyes are forbidden to look at that they most delight to see. What harm is there in beholding a man possess a woman?
> – Pietro Aretino, letter to Battista Zatti

... his blue eyes crossed and bulged from the meticulous maddening scrutiny of the golden twat of his beloved ...
> – Joseph Wambaugh, *The Choirboys*

Although man has learned through evolution to walk in an upright position, his eyes still swing from limb to limb.
> – Margaret Schooley, in *Reader's Digest*, January 1956

Oh! death will find me long before I tire
Of watching you.
> – Rupert Brooke, 'Sonnet'

Vulgarity

In every great king, in every loveliest flowery princess, in every poet most refined, every best dressed dandy, every holiest and spiritual teacher there lurks, waiting, waiting for the moment to emerge, an outcaste of outcastes, a dung carrier, a dog, lower than the lowest, bottomlessly vulgar.
> – Aldous Huxley, *Collected Essays*

Vulgarity is the garlic in the salad of taste.
> – Cyril Connolly

Be thou familiar, but by no means vulgar.
– William Shakespeare, *Hamlet*

It's worse than wicked. It's vulgar.
– *Punch* (London), 1876

INTERVIEWER: You've been accused of vulgarity.
MEL BROOKS: Bullshit!
– Mel Brooks, interview in *Playboy*, 1975

See also: FOUR-LETTER WORDS; OBSCENITY.

Wedding

Wedding, n.: A ceremony at which two persons undertake to become one, one undertakes to become nothing, and nothing undertakes to become supportable.
– Ambrose Bierce, *The Devil's Dictionary*

Wedlock

Wedlock is padlock.
– John Ray, *English Proverbs*

Wedlock is bedlock.
– Author unknown

The trouble with wedlock is, there's not enough wed and too much lock.
– Christopher Morley, *Kitty Foyle*

See also: MARRIAGE.

Don't lock me in wedlock, I want
marriage, an
encounter.
– Denise Levertov, 'About Marriage'

I was 32 and
    dying of
deadlocked wedlock.
– Erica Jong

What Goes Around Comes Around

Time wounds all heels.
— Jane Ace, in Goodman Ace, *The Fine Art of Hypochondria, or
How Are You?*

Widows and Widowers

A rich widow weeps with one eye and signals with the other.
— Portuguese proverb

The three merriest things in the world are a cat's kitten, a goat's
kid, and a young widow.
— Irish proverb

A buxom widow must either be married, buried, or shut up in a
convent.
— Spanish proverb

In my day, a college widow stood for something. She stood for plenty.
> – Groucho Marx, in the film *A Day at the Races*

He that would woo a maid must feign, lie, and flatter.
But he that woos a widow must down his breeches and
at her.
> – Nathaniel Smith, *Quakers Spiritual Court*

A good season for courtship is when the widow returns from the funeral.
> – Thomas Fuller, *Gnomologia: Adagies and Proverbs*

He that marries a widow and three children marries four thieves.
> – John Ray, *English Proverbs*

And yet – when asked what age of womanhood
Brings most delight, producing most good,
I turn to widowhood with tender touch,
And say: 'Stop here, for widows know so much.'
> – Anonymous, 'Boyhood', in *The Point of View*

The comfortable estate of widowhood is the only hope that keeps up a wife's spirits.
> – John Gay, *The Beggar's Opera*

Widow. The word consumes itself . . .
> – Sylvia Plath, 'Widow'

Be wery careful o' widders.
> – Charles Dickens, *Pickwick Papers*

Rich widows are only second-hand goods that sell for first-class prices.
> – Benjamin Franklin (attributed)

'Widow' is a harsh and hurtful word. It comes from the Sanskrit and it means 'empty'. I have been empty too long.
– Lynn Caine, *Widow*

Widows are divided into two classes – the bereaved and the relieved.
– Victor Robinson, *Truth Seeker*, 6 January 1906

He first deceased: she for a little tried
To live without him, liked it not, and died.
– Sir Henry Wotton, 'Death of Sir Albertus Moreton's Wife'

Will

Why did she love him? – Curious fool – be still –
Is human love the growth of human will?
– George Gordon, Lord Byron, 'Laura'

Wine, Women and Song

Who loves not wine, women or song
Remains a fool his whole life long.
– Martin Luther (attributed)

Without Bacchus and Ceres, Venus grows cold.
– Roman proverb

Wine makes old wives wenches.
– John Clarke, *Paroemiologia Anglo-Latina*

Warm wine, warm baths, warm women, onetime
    ladies,
Will take you down the easiest way to Hades.
– *The Greek Anthology*

See also: DRINKING.

Winking

The wink was not our best invention.
    – Ralph Hodgson

To wink with one eye and look with another.
    – Randle Cotgrave, *Dictionary*

    Wink and choose.
    – John Clarke, *Paroemiologia Anglo-Latina*

    He that winketh with one eye and looketh with the
        other,
    I will not trust him though he were my brother.
    – English proverb

A still-soliciting eye.
    – William Shakespeare, *King Lear*

Wives

Always seek a fellow's weak point in his wife.
    – James Joyce, *Ulysses*

Will you take this woman Matti Richards . . . to be your awful wedded wife?
> – Dylan Thomas, *Under Milk Wood*

Gentlemen, to the lady without whom I should never have survived to eighty, nor sixty, nor yet thirty years. Her smile has been my lyric, her understanding the rhythm of the stanza. She has been the spring where from I have drawn the words. She is the poem of my life.
> – Oliver Wendell Holmes (attributed)

My God, who wouldn't want a wife?
> – Judy Syfers, 'I Want a Wife'

Don't expect a wife to help you or hinder you. Don't expect anything. That is the golden rule of marriage.
> – Robertson Davies, *A Jig for the Gypsy*

Wife: One who knows everything except why she married you.
> – Anonymous

If wives were good, God would have one.
> – Russian proverb

The trouble with my wife is that she is a whore in the kitchen and a cook in bed.
> – Geoffrey Gorer (attributed)

A house-wife in bed, at table a slattern . . .
> – Jonathan Swift, *Portraits from Life*

One man's folly is another man's wife.
> – Helen Rowland, *Reflections of a Bachelor Girl*

The difference between a wife and a girlfriend is the difference between routine acquiescence and enthusiastic cooperation.
> – Anonymous

May you live out your life
Without hate, without grief
And your hair ever blaze,
In the sun, in the sun
When I am undone,
When I am no one.
– Theodore Roethke, 'Wish for a Young Wife'

She has always been there, my darling
She is, in fact, exquisite.
Fireworks in the dull middle of February
and as real as a cast-iron pot.
. . .
She is so naked and singular.
She is the sum of yourself and your dream.
Climb her like a monument, step by step.
She is solid.
– Anne Sexton, 'For My Lover: Returning to His Wife'

Who drags the fiery artist down?
Who keeps the pioneer in town?
Who hates to let the seaman roam?
It is the wife, it is the home.
– Clarence Day, Jr, 'Wife and Home'

Wife: A former sweetheart.
– H.L. Mencken

My old flame, my wife.
– Robert Lowell, 'The Old Flame'

Everyman gets the wife he deserves.
– *Midrash: Psalms Rabbah*

Think you if Laura had been Petrarch's wife
He would have written sonnets all his life.
– George Gordon, Lord Byron, *Don Juan*

I can nail my left palm
    to the left-hand cross–piece bar
I can't do everything myself
    I need a hand to nail my right
A help, a love, a you, a wife.
– Alan Dugan

Muse, momma, agent, promoter, domestic, peacemaker, and brow–mopper.
    – Paula Weideger, in S. Dowrick and S. Grundberg, *Why Children?*

Jill–of–all–trades
Lover, mother, housewife, friend, breadwinner . . .
– Genny Lim, 'Wonder Woman', in C. Moraga and G.
    Anzaldúa, *This Bridge Called My Back*

Wife and servant are the same,
But only differ in the name;
And when that fatal knot is tied,
Which nothing, nothing can divide;
When she the word obey has said,
And man by law supreme was made,
Then all that's kind is laid aside,
And nothing left but state and pride.
– Lady Mary Chudleigh, 'To the Ladies'

. . . wives are a dying need.
    – Una Stannard, *Mrs Man*

Honey you're awful lucky
I ever come home you're so homely
and the girls out there are so beautiful so
hell it must be love I guess.
– Al Purdy, 'Engraved on a Tomb'

Meek wifehood is no part of my profession;
I am your friend, but never your possession.
– Vera Brittain, *Married Love*

The clog of all pleasures, the luggage of life,
Is the best that can be said for a very good wife.
– John Wilmot, Earl of Rochester, 'On a Wife'

An ideal wife is any woman who has an ideal husband.
– Booth Tarkington, *Looking Forward and Others*

He shall hold thee,
when his passion shall have spent its novel force,
Something better than his dog,
a little dearer than his horse.
– Alfred, Lord Tennyson, 'Locksley Hall'

Women

I saw pale kings, and princes too,
Pale warriors, death pale were they all;
Who cried: 'La belle Dame sans merci
Hath thee in thrall!'
– John Keats, 'La Belle Dame sans Merci'

A fool there was and he made his prayer
(Even as you and I!)
To a rag and a bone and a hank of hair
(We called her the woman who didn't care),
But the fool he called her his lady fair
(Even as you and I!)
– Rudyard Kipling, 'The Vampire'

O Splendid and Sterile Dolores
    Our Lady of Pain.
– A.C. Swinburne, 'Dolores'

For the female of the species is more deadly than the
    male.
– Rudyard Kipling, 'The Female of the Species'

She talks just like a woman, yes she does.
She makes love just like a woman, yes she does.
She aches just like a woman
But she breaks just like a little girl.
– Bob Dylan, 'Just Like a Woman'

There are no books like a dame
And nothin' looks like a dame.
There are no drinks like a dame
And nothin' thinks like a dame,
Nothin' acts like a dame
Or attracts like a dame.
There ain't a thing wrong with any man here
That can't be cured by putting him near
A girly, womanly, female, feminine dame!
– Oscar Hammerstein II, 'There's Nothing Like a Dame',
  from the musical *South Pacific*

Oh Charles – a woman needs certain things, She needs to be
loved, wanted, cherished, sought after, cossetted, pampered.
She needs sympathy, affection, devotion, understanding,
tenderness, infatuation, adulation, idolatry – that isn't much to
ask, Charles.
      – Barry Took and Marty Feldman, on *Round the Horne*, BBC
        Radio, 1966

A man without a woman is like a neck without a pain.
      – Graffito

. . . why haven't women got labels on their foreheads saying: 'Danger, government health warning: women can seriously damage your brains, genitals, current account, confidence, razor blades and good standing among your friends.'
– Jeffrey Bernard, in the *Spectator*, 1984

Women: Need for

[The] infantile needs of adult men for women have been sentimentalized and romanticized long enough as 'love'; it is time to recognize them as arrested development . . .
– Adrienne Rich, 'Husband-Right and Father Right'

Women's Liberation

When working toward our liberation
And basic change in civilization
'Lib' is an abbreviation
In which we hear your condemnation.
– Joann Haugerud, in C. Kramarae and P. A. Treichler,
   A Feminist Dictionary

A contradiction in terms.
– Susan Sontag, in *Partisan Review*, 1973

Whether we live with or without a man, communally or in couples or alone, are married or unmarried, live with other women, go for free love, celibacy or lesbianism, or any combination, there are only good and bad things about each bad situation. There is no 'more liberated' way; there are only bad alternatives.
– Carol Hanisch, *Feminist Revolution*

In the penile colony.
> – Erica Jong, title of a group of poems

Not only are women now openly having sex on the tube, but they are even able to admit that they do not always like it. That's liberation. We've come a long way since the days when Lucy Ricardo couldn't say 'pregnant'.
> – The *Daily News* (New York), quoted in Dorothy Uris, *Say It Again*

I'm furious about the Women Liberationists. They keep getting up on soapboxes and proclaiming that women are brighter than men. That's true, but it should be kept very quiet or it ruins the whole racket.
> – Anita Loos, in the *Observer* (London), 30 December 1973

. . . on some days it is hard to figure out how a species that controls 97% of the money and all the pussy can be down-trodden.
> – Larry King (attributed)

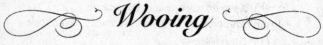

Wooing

Happy is the wooing that is not long a-doing.
> – Author unknown

She whom I love is hard to catch and conquer,
Hard, but O the glory of winning were she won!
> – George Meredith, 'Love in the Valley'

The wooing should be a day after the wedding.
> – John Lyly, *Euphues and His England*

The time I've lost wooing,
In watching and pursuing
    The light that lies
    In woman's eyes
Has been my heart's undoing.
– Thomas Moore, *Irish Melodies*: 'The Time I've Lost'

The sad miscarriage of their wooing.
– William Congreve, *The Old Bachelor*

Men like to pursue an elusive woman, like a cake of wet soap in a bathtub; even men who hate baths.
– Gelett Burgess

A man is like a cat; chase him and he will run . . . Sit still and ignore him and he'll come purring at your feet.
– Helen Rowland

Why, having won her, do I woo?
    Because her spirit's vestal grace
Provokes me always to pursue
    But spirit-like eludes embrace.
– Coventry Patmore, *The Angel in the House*: 'The Married Lover'

                Women are angels wooing:
Things won are done; joy's soul lies in the doing:
That she's belov'd knows nought that knows not this:
Men prize the thing ungained more than it is.
– William Shakespeare, *Troilus and Cressida*

Wrinkles

Beauty is just a flower
Which wrinkles will devour.
– Thomas Nashe, 'Summer's Last Will and Testament'

Age imprints more wrinkles in the mind than it does on the face.
– Michel de Montaigne

Sweet dalliance keepeth away wrinkles.
– Henry Constable, 'Sonnets to Diana'

Hooked for two years now on wrinkle creams creams for
crowsfeet ugliness (if only there were one!)
any perfumed grease which promises youth beauty
not truth but all I need on earth
        I have been studying how women age
                            how
it starts around the eyes so you can tell
a woman of 22 from one of 28 . . .
– Erica Jong, 'Aging: Balm for a 27th Birthday'

If God had to give a woman wrinkles, He might at least have put
them on the soles of her feet.
– Ninon de Lenclos

Please don't retouch my wrinkles. It took me too long to earn
them.
– Anna Magnani, in *Interview* (1978), to the photographer

Women are not forgiven for ageing. Robert Redford's lines of
distinction are my old–age wrinkles.
– Jane Fonda

 *Xantippism*

Woman, wakeful woman's never weary
Above all, when she waits to thump her dreary.
– R.H. Barham, 'The Ghost'

Yes!

Some say Never
Some say Unless
It's stupid and lonely
To rush into Yes
. . .
Some go local
Some go express
Some can't wait
To answer Yes
. . .
Open your eyes
Dream but don't guess
Your biggest surprise
Comes after Yes.
– Muriel Rukeyser, from the musical *Houdini*

You made me love you,
I didn't want to do it.
– Joe McCarthy, 'You Made Me Love You' (music by James
    V. Monaco)

Between a woman's Yes and No, I would not venture to stick a
pin.
– Miguel de Cervantes, *Don Quixote*

My favourite word is YES.
– Lenore Kandell

How long I pleaded I can never guess,
    Nor can I recollect the things we said,
Now after months, you answer yes,
    And you are in my bed.

Yet, though stretched out and naked here you lie
    You close your lips, you turn away; you weep.
Finally you consent . . . And I
    Worn out with coaxing, sleep.
– *The Greek Anthology*

When you arouse the need in me
My heart says yes, indeed, to me
Proceed with what you are leading me to.
– Carolyn Leigh, 'Witchcraft'

When a woman says yes to her avid lover
Should be written in wind and running water.
– Catullus, *Odes*

. . . she receptive but to me,
dances and sings around me
'Yes and no and maybe so
and everywhere all over.'
– Alan Dugan, 'On Rape Unattempted'

. . . and then I asked him with my eyes to ask again yes and then
he asked me would I yes to say yes my mountain flower and first
I put my arms around him yes and drew him down to me so he
could feel my breasts all perfume yes and his heart was going
like mad and yes I said yes I will Yes.
    – James Joyce, *Ulysses*

⊷ *Young and Old* ⊶

There goes a saying, and 'twas shrewdly said,
Old fish at the table, but young flesh in bed.
– Alexander Pope, 'January and May'

In your amours you should prefer old women to young ones. They are so grateful.

    – Benjamin Franklin, letter, 25 June 1745

Quite a few women told me, one way or another, that they thought it was sex, not youth, that's wasted on the young . . .

    – Janet Harris, *In Praise of Ms America*

Young Love

I loathe that I did love
In youth that I thought sweet.

    – Thomas Vaux, 'The Aged Lover Renounceth Love'

Youth

When I was a school boy, I thought a fair woman a pure goddess; my mind was a soft nest in which some one of them slept, though she knew it not.

    – John Keats, letter, 18 July 1818

Burning youth.

    – Michel de Montaigne, *Essays*

Unbridled youth.

    – John Lyly, *Euphues and His England*

How long does youth last?
So long as we are loved.

    – *The Golden Book of Countess Diana*

The daughters of Albion
. . .
comb their dark blonde hair in suburban bedrooms
powder their delicate nipples
wondering if tonight will be the night
their bodies pressed into dresses or sweaters
– Adrian Henri, 'Mrs Albion You've Got a Lovely Daughter'

Early marriage, long love.
– German proverb

Fifteen-year old nymphs, dawn of womanhood
Who will enter the palace of my soul?
– Jules Laforgue, *Les Complaintes*

But in the Lower Sixth we all got religion or Communism – it goes with acne you know. Vanishes as soon as you have proper sexual intercourse.
– Kyril Bonfiglioli, *Don't Point That Thing At Me*

They try to tell us we're too young to love
Too young to be really be in love.
– Sylvia Dee, 'Too Young to Love' (music by Sid Lippman)

Young I am, and yet unskill'd
How to make a Lover yield:
How to keep and how to gain,
When to love; and when to feign.
– John Dryden, *Love Triumphant*: 'Song for a Girl'

From best sellers to comic books, any child who hasn't acquired an extensive sex education by the age of 12 belongs in remedial reading.
– Will Stanton, in *Reader's Digest*, March 1971

I was a child and she was a child,
    In this kingdom by the sea;
But we loved with a love which was more than love –
    I and my Annabel Lee;
With a love that the winged seraphs in heaven
    Coveted her and me.
– Edgar Allan Poe, 'Annabel Lee'

If youth knew; if age could.
    – Henri Estienne, *Les Prémices*

Teenage boys, goaded by their surfing hormones . . . run in packs. They have only a brief season of exhilarating liberty between control by their mothers and control by their wives.
    – Camille Paglia, *Sex, Art, and American Culture*

I would there be no age between ten and three-and-twenty, or that youth would sleep out the rest; for there is nothing in the between but getting wenches with child, wronging the ancientry, stealing, fighting.
    – William Shakespeare, *The Winter's Tale*

INDEX